Economics: Marxian versus Neoclassical

Economics:
Marxian versus Neoclassical

Richard D. Wolff
and
Stephen A. Resnick

The Johns Hopkins University Press
Baltimore / London

© 1987 The Johns Hopkins University Press
All rights reserved
Printed in the United States of America on acid-free paper

Originally published, hardcover and paperback, 1987
05 04 03 02 01 00 99 98 97 96   7 6 5 4 3

The Johns Hopkins University Press
2715 North Charles Street
Baltimore, Maryland 21218-4319
The Johns Hopkins Press Ltd., London

Library of Congress Cataloging-in-Publication Data

Wolff, Richard D.
  Economics: Marxian versus neoclassical.

  Bibliography: p.
  Includes index.
  1. Comparative economics.   2. Economics.   3. Marxian economics.
4. Neoclassical school of economics.   I. Resnick, Stephen A.   II. Title.
HB90.W65   1987   330.1   87-4131
ISBN 0-8018-3479-1 (alk. paper)
ISBN 0-8018-3480-5 (pbk.)

A catalog record for this book is available from the British Library.

Contents

Detailed Table
of Contents

To Our Readers

We wrote this book to accomplish two broad goals. First, we wanted to produce an introduction to Marxian economics that would incorporate several major analytical breakthroughs achieved in Marxism in the last twenty-five years. Second, we wanted to define and develop that introduction in relation to the dominant economic theory taught explicitly in the United States and prevalent implicitly within most readers' minds. From many years of teaching introductory courses, we have learned that discussing Marxian theory in the context of a sustained comparison with neoclassical theory is the most effective method of presentation. Unfortunately, no currently available book presents Marxian economics within such a framework of comparative theory.

Certain presumptions underlie this book's organization and style. The core introduction to Marxian theory in chapter 3 assumes little or no familiarity with the subject. It proceeds from first principles through basic analytics to various applications. Every effort has been made to integrate the changes in Marxian theory over especially the last twenty-five years into a systematic exposition. Since Marxian economics includes several distinct theories, we identify the particular theory we have found most convincing and which we therefore present here. Similarly, the overview of neoclassical economics in chapter 2 offers a basic grounding in neoclassical micro- and macroeconomics.

Thus, this book is directed especially to the reader who is interested in mastering the basics of neoclassical micro- and macroeconomics and in learning what Marxian economics is and how it compares to neoclassical theory. For college and university teaching purposes, the book serves both introductory and more advanced courses. As a supplementary reading, it is a useful accompaniment at all levels of economics— including introductory courses—where instructors wish to introduce students to alternative approaches or merely to sharpen students' knowledge of neoclassical theory by comparing it with Marxian theory. Finally, for courses across the social sciences generally, this book introduces economics as a field struggling with its own disagreements and alternative visions like all the other disciplines. The book clearly dissents from any notion of economics as a technical or mechanical profession.

Throughout the volume, but especially in the first and fourth chapters, important philosophical issues are addressed as they pertain to a comparison of economic theories. Issues of epistemology are raised to acquaint readers with our method for comparing economic theories. We discuss verification and validity to address the important question necessarily posed by any such comparative endeavor—namely, How can we assess and decide between the competing claims and analyses offered by different economic theories? Consistent with the method of the book throughout, we explain that theoretical differences in economics are matched by theoretical differences within philosophy, including the epistemological issue of how to decide between alternative theories.

We believe that the particular method used in this book to compare and contrast different economic theories may also serve as a useful analytical tool to compare still other forms of thinking. What we describe here as a particular theory's entry-point concepts, logic, produced objects, and social consequences may be considered as so many indices of difference among theories. Readers are presented with a concrete examination of a particular theory in terms of how it differs from alternative theories.

This book offers, then, two interdependent formulations that are not, to our knowledge, available elsewhere. First, economics as a discipline is presented in a format of sustained comparison of alternative theories. Modern principles of discourse analysis are applied to the confrontation between Marxian and neoclassical economic theories. The distinguishing features of these theories are examined in juxtaposition as a method of teaching economics. Second, a Marxian theory is developed systematically and rigorously from its first principles and assumptions through its formal economics to some illustrative applications to social analysis.

Acknowledgments

We wish to thank Professor Donald Katzner, one of our respected colleagues who specializes in neoclassical economics, for his careful reading, comments, and criticisms of both the neoclassical and the Marxian parts of this book. We also wish to express our appreciation to the many teaching assistants who have worked with us over the years and to the countless students in our introductory courses whose reactions to the ideas contained in this book helped to shape it.

Economics: Marxian versus Neoclassical

1   Two Different Theories

A. This Book and Theories of Economics

This book contrasts two very different and clashing kinds of economics. One is usually called neoclassical economics and the other Marxism. Each is a distinct way of understanding how economies work and how they interact with societies as a whole. In other words, these are two different *theories* about the economic part of society. This book invites you to confront the two major economic theories that compete for our attention in the modern world.

We wrote this book because students need to know that there is more to economics than just the currently dominant neoclassical theory. We also think students deserve to know how these two theories differ. Most important, we want to show how understandings based on one theory versus the other will lead individuals, families, governments, and societies in very different directions.

A.1. Theories: Economic and Otherwise

Attempts to understand how economies work—economic theories—exist in our minds alongside theories about how everything else in life is organized and connected. All of our theories, whether we are aware of them or not, play major roles in shaping all of our experiences.

Some examples can make this point clear. The particular theory of love and feeling that we hold will influence our intimate relationships all through life. The person whose theory of love holds it to be identical with sex will probably have very different experiences in life than a person who thinks that sex and love are related but distinct. Theories of spirituality and religion affect many aspects of daily living. A government founded on a theory of society which holds that the Bible or the Koran is the absolute source of law will often behave very differently from a government committed to a theory of the necessary separation of religion from politics. The different theories of what is beautiful among people produce correspondingly different choices about how cities construct their streets and parks, how architects design homes and other buildings, and how individuals style their hair, clothing, personal manners, and so on.

Natural scientists debate contesting theories of biology, chemistry, and physics. Their differing theories lead them to make different experiments and different discoveries. Technological change varies from community to community depending in part on which theories are believed and acted upon by community members in general and by the scientists among them in particular.

Similarly, different economic theories have different impacts on society. How an individual makes economic decisions (about careers, personal expenditures, investments, and business opportunities) depends in part on how he or she thinks about the economy. Likewise, the economic policies preferred by political leaders depend on their understandings—their preferred theories—of the economy. Which political candidate gets your vote is influenced by how you understand the candidates' economic thinking and proposals.

We all form judgments about the causes of and cures for poverty, inflation, recession, and unemployment. Whether casual and superficial or carefully researched and sophisticated, our views about economic issues affect our behavior. What do economic trends suggest to you about your personal career choices? Do you favor a welfare system to assist poor people? Is technology the key to Japan's recent economic growth? Is it better to lower taxes or raise government spending in order to build prosperity in America? Is private enterprise the problem or the solution in terms of our economic future? To think through answers to such questions is to engage in economic theorizing. The particular economic theory we use shapes the answers we find convincing, answers that in turn will shape our actions throughout life.

Do you think that capitalist enterprises would carry the U.S. economy to great new heights if only they were freed from irrational government regulations? If you do, your political loyalties and activities differ sharply from someone whose theory suggests rather that only government action has kept the U.S. economy from depression. If your theory connects poverty and unemployment to the basic class structure of the United States, your commitment to overcoming such problems implies that you favor changes in that class structure. A different economic theory sees social problems as the result of bad individual choices that should be remedied by education and laws, not by changes in the class structure.

Suppose that your particular theory of economic development viewed future prosperity as dependent on the formation of mammoth corporate giants through the merging of U.S. companies into multiproduct, multinational conglomerates. With that understanding, it would make little sense for you to support government policies favoring small business and little sense for you to seek a career in small business. A different theory of economic development might focus instead on small businesses as the chief generator of jobs, new products, and new technologies. People who believed that theory would favor the opposite government policies and would tend toward the opposite personal career choices.

Different personal decisions and different social policies grow out of such different beliefs. Each of these beliefs or understandings of the economy grows out of a distinct economic theory. Partly as a result of the basic differences that exist among current economic theories people arrive at different conclusions and quite literally see different economic and social realities. Different theories have different impacts on each of us, on our society, and on the future of both.

A.2. Economic Theories in Disagreement

This book might not have been necessary if everyone agreed about how economies work. If one economic theory had won universal assent, we would probably teach it in the manner that algebra, grammar, and auto mechanics are usually taught. In that case, regular textbooks would suffice to educate each generation about economics. However, profound disagreement rather than agreement characterizes economics.

In America and around the world, very different theories produce intense debates over how economies work, how they develop, and how they ought to be changed. Neoclassical and Marxian economic theories contradict each other in basic ways. Their proponents contest for people's allegiance. (At the same time, to complicate matters, advocates of different versions of neoclassical and Marxian theory fight among themselves. In this book, we will concentrate on the two major kinds of economic theory, and only secondarily consider their differing versions.) Since we all have to live with the consequences of the struggle between the two great economic theories, we all need to compare and evaluate them. This book aims to help you do that.

Deeply felt thoughts and convictions are woven into the economic theories people believe in and use. How we think about the economy is influenced by how we think about nature, politics, religion, and so on. We do not easily change our allegiance to economic theories, precisely because these theories are closely connected to our understanding of the world and of ourselves. In short, different basic philosophies are involved in different economic theories. We aim to show how much is at stake in the current debates and conflicts among economic theories. Whatever your preferences might be, among these theories, you will likely benefit from a clarification of just what distinguishes one theory from another.

A.3. Are We All Economic Theorists?

Economic theorizing is something absolutely everyone does. We all make some sort of sense of the production and distribution of goods and services. But it is possible to be unaware of the particular economic theory used by your mind. Every time you decide to produce or buy or borrow or invest or save something, your mind is at work. That is, you weigh various factors in reaching your decision. You take some account of various aspects, implications, and possible consequences of your decision. Which factors you weigh and which aspects you take into account depend on your theory of how the economy works.

Now you obviously cannot think about and consider everything in reaching your decision. So you consider only *some* things, weigh only *some* factors, focus on only *some* aspects. In a word, you select certain things to consider and you consider them in the particular way you think is appropriate. The things you select and how you consider them are matters that depend on your theory of how economies work. Your conclusions about economic issues in your life likewise depend on that theory.

You may not be self-conscious about the theory you use to reach each economic decision you make. Nevertheless, the decisions you make and the actions you take are influenced by economic theory. Therefore, whether or not you take formal courses in economics, you necessarily use some economic theory throughout your life.

Every time a person explains why some people are wealthy and others are poor, he or she uses one or another economic theory to produce that explanation. The same applies to explanations of why some people are employed while others go jobless, why some nations rank high or low in levels of income, and why some careers look promising while others do not. The explanations we generate with our theories then lead us to take certain actions—actions that will differ according to which theory we use.

For example, suppose that the theory we use holds that individuals' incomes are rewards for what they contribute to production. What they get to spend on goods and services equals what they have contributed to producing them. Workers give their labor, landlords their land, and capitalists their money and equipment (machines, offices, factories, etc.). In this theory, wages and salaries are labor's reward while rents compensate the contributors of land. Finally, interest and profit are the rewards that capitalists obtain for contributing their capital. From the standpoint of this theory, individuals' incomes may well seem to be fair: your earnings match your contributions. Rich people contribute much while the poor offer little or nothing. A believer in this theory might oppose government programs that shift incomes from rich to poor as unfair and absurd: unfair because they punish those who contribute to production and indulge those who do not; and absurd because such punishment will discourage contributions to production and so will diminish the total output of goods and services available in our society.

Now suppose instead that we use a different theory. We believe that some people receive incomes without contributing anything, while others contribute more than they get back in income. In this theory, a portion of the goods and services produced by some becomes the income of other people who made no contribution to production. The rich may then be understood to be those in a social position to get their hands on what other people produce. A believer in this theory might well be outraged at what he or she sees as a kind of theft and would then look favorably upon government actions that take income from certain people and shift it to others. Precisely such actions would seem to be fair and appropriate.

Two people who thought about the world by means of these two theories would likely favor different government policies (on taxes, welfare, and much else), support different political parties, and show very different attitudes toward wealth and poverty. In short, these two people would act very differently just as they think very differently.

A.4. Theories and Society

So far we have been stressing how economic theories matter, how alternative theories lead people to different conclusions, different experiences, and different actions in society. However, the relation between theories and society is a two-way street. Not only do theories shape society but society shapes theories. Precisely because different theories lead individuals and communities in different directions, we have to ask the question, Why are there different theories?

This question has provoked various answers—and whole philosophic systems—across human history. We think that social conditions impact upon individuals in such a way that they come to invent and to endorse alternative theories. In different environments, people experience life differently and think about its meaning (theorize) differently as well. For example, rural and urban people do not typically think about nature in the same way. Teen-agers and the aged often conceptualize life quite distinctly. Women and men display sharply contrasting notions about sex and child-rearing in many societies. Wealthy suburban executives may well theorize about the pleasures of life in a fishing village in a manner that is utterly incomprehensible to the villagers, who think about fishing in a radically different way.

Modern psychology has taught us that the members of one family will often experience and understand family relations in radically different ways. A wife's theory about marriage, when verbalized, often stuns and amazes her husband, who "sees" it all very differently. Parents and children often generate sharply divergent theories of the family's problems. Such divergent theories can and often do lead family members to expectations of and resentments toward each other which threaten the ability of individuals to remain in the family. Different experiences in the world, from one culture to another and from one family member to another, generate different theories about—different ways of making sense of—that world.

Sometimes the different theories are quite similar and compatible. Then people have a feeling of "being in agreement," sharing a vision of how their world works. At other times, the different theories stand in contradiction to one another. Then people may feel a certain tension about how to understand and cope with the disagreements that keep intruding upon their conversations and interactions.

Along these lines, we find it reasonable to suppose that people may well understand economics differently, literally "see" different things when they survey the economic scenery around them. What they see and what they think are different because their life situations and experiences are different. We expect alternative theories of economics to emerge for the same reasons that alternative theories of love, politics, or religion have emerged in history. The complex diversities of our lives provoke ways of seeing our surroundings and ways of thinking about them that add up to being alternative theories of how the economy works alongside our alternative theories about everything else.

Sometimes the different economic theories have seemed close to one another and not the occasion for profound tension about the causes and consequences of their differences. That has not been the case since Marxism arose to challenge classical political economic theory during the nineteenth century. It is not the case now. Neoclassical and Marxian economics not only clash as profoundly different theories. They are also linked in most people's minds to many other theoretical and social conflicts that engage the passions of our time.

Today, social conditions around the world shape and propel the theoretical confrontation of neoclassical and Marxian economics. At the same time, the theoretical clash between these alternative economic theories affects and will continue to affect the development of modern society. Thus we have a perfect example of the two-way mutual conditioning of society and economic theories: society as a whole determines the nature of and conflict among economic theories and is itself shaped by them.

By understanding the nature and implications of the differences among economic theories, we can better appreciate the interconnections between them and contemporary social issues. No matter which theory you find more convincing, your grasp of economics will benefit from exploring their confrontation.

B. Theoretical Differences

In what ways do economic theories differ? The simplest answer is to say that they focus on different aspects of the economy and interpret them in different ways. They result in different understandings of economics. It is rather like two schools of painters, one emphasizing landscapes presented in an impressionistic style, the other concentrating on geometrically abstract portraits. The collection of works assembled by each school will reveal quite different feelings about life, different artistic visions.

With two kinds of economic theory, much the same process occurs. Neoclassical economics emphasizes individual behavior, which, it argues, is motivated by rational self-interest. The economy, as neoclassical economists theorize it, is the aggregate end product of individuals maximizing their own material self-interest. Marxian theory emphasizes social structure more than individual behavior. It centers attention on what it terms "class exploitation," which, it claims, is interwoven with every other aspect of society in complex and contradictory ways. The economy, Marxists theorize, is the place in society where exploitation occurs and exerts its powerful influence over the rest of social life. It is no surprise, then, that neoclassical and Marxian economists produce different analyses of economic issues, different visions of the economy they aim to understand.

B.1. Neoclassical Theory

Neoclassical theory attaches basic importance to three economic acts that are attributed to all individuals: owning, buying, and selling. It assumes that all goods and services are privately owned by individuals and that all individuals seek to maximize their satisfaction from consuming goods and services. Neoclassical economists proceed to analyze what such rationally motivated individuals will do with their property as they maximize their satisfaction. Will they sell their own goods and services for money to buy the goods and services of others which they prefer? Will they sell the service that is called their labor to an individual who will use it to produce other goods and services? Or will they buy the labor of others and the machines of others, and so on, in order to carry on production themselves?

Notice right away that neoclassical theory is based on presumptions about individual human nature. Notice also that the arena in which individuals are presumed to act economically is the market: literally the place where things are bought and sold. At the center of attention are individual private property owners who are free to sell or not sell what they own in the markets around them. Finally, notice that the theory divides goods and services into two broad groups: (1) those that are destined for individual consumption; and (2) those that are destined to be used up in producing other goods and services. The market is understood as a place where individuals come with their property to sell and/ or to buy as they wish for the purpose of maximizing their satisfaction.

Neoclassical theory does not just analyze markets, it celebrates them. Markets are praised as the best possible institution in which to accommodate the diverse goals of diverse individuals with diverse property holdings. All actions in markets are thought to be voluntary; you buy or sell only when you want to. You advance your interests by selling something only if and when you can find in the market someone whose own interests are advanced by buying what you wish to sell. Every transaction is mutually beneficial or else it will not occur. Thus neoclassical economists reach the concepts of efficiency and optimality. Free markets are seen as the most efficient and best way to ensure that economic affairs benefit everyone, consumers and producers alike. Free markets bring genuine social justice to the economic interactions of individuals. A philosophic notion of justice is closely intertwined with neoclassical economic theory.

Markets are not necessarily free. Individuals may get together outside the market to manipulate it to their advantage and to the disadvantage of others. Governments may impose regulations on the market behaviors of some or all individuals. Unfree markets will not have the efficiency or the optimality of free markets. They will be less just. Confronted by possibilities of this sort, neoclassical theory displays a strong bias toward laws and traditions that aim to block all such interferences in free markets.

Neoclassical theory's analysis of the desirability of free markets amounts to a conclusion of major importance. It continues to have very important political consequences in our lives as leaders influenced by neoclassical theory strive to remove governmental and other interferences from markets worldwide. Social changes and political (and even military) conflicts crucial to global survival may unfold as governments devoted to free markets encounter governments that view markets differently. Such governments may well be influenced by economic theories that do not equate economic justice with markets and that assess their economic problems and solutions altogether differently. As we have said, economic theories matter.

B.2. Marxian Theory

By contrast, Marxian economic theory proceeds by focusing first and foremost on class exploitation. It defines "class" as a process whereby some people in society produce goods and services for others without obtaining anything in exchange. Marxian theory begins not with presumptions about human nature but rather with presumptions about social relationships, which shape and change what human beings are and think and do. Individuals are understood to be born into social arrangements they did not create nor choose to live with.

[margin note: whole social picture]

In Marxian theory, the logic runs from an analysis of social relationships to the resulting patterns of individual behavior. The emphasis is on class as one economic relationship within the broader society. This reflects Marxism's view that the class division of society into exploiters versus exploited—those who obtain goods and services produced by others versus those who must produce for others—is unjust and has an undesirable influence upon every aspect of that broader society. Marxian economic theory also is intertwined with a philosophic position: that the individualism and free markets favored by the neoclassicals serve to hide and perpetuate class injustice.

[margin note: gender? race?]

Marxian economic theory approaches the economy as a complex set of relationships, and includes class exploitation alongside the buying and selling and owning emphasized by neoclassical theory. Indeed, a major purpose of Marx's original critique of classical economics was to remedy what he saw as its fear and loss of theoretical nerve in the face of class exploitation. Thus Marxian economic theory persists to this day in its insistence on the role of class in economic analysis. Starting from its presumption of class exploitation, Marxian theory proceeds to explore how other aspects of an economy and of the broader society interact with that society's specific class structure (its specific division of citizens into antagonistic class groupings).

Marxian theory is no less biased than neoclassical theory. Both theories have their biases, but the biases, like the theories, are different. Marxian theory concludes that class divisions—particularly those labeled as "capitalist"—damage modern societies in countless ways and impose suffering that could be avoided. The point is that stopping the suffering and undoing the damage would require changing the class structure. Those who obtained the fruits of others' labor without providing anything in return would have to give up that position; the social division between capitalists and workers would have to be abolished.

Governments influenced by Marxian theory may well aim to alter the class structures of their societies in specific ways. Justice for them is not a matter of free markets, but rather of far-reaching (revolutionary) class transformations. Social progress for them requires such transformations. As they strive to accomplish class transformations, they encounter governments that equate progress with free markets and that resist government-led class changes as unacceptable interferences in those markets. Here again major political confrontations loom as clashing economic theories inform alternative strategies.

B.3. Theoretical Differences Today

The differences between the two economic theories are not minor. They amount to profound disagreements about how economies work and ought to be changed. Each reflects and helps develop very different visions of social life. Different personal and policy decisions are made by the adherents of each theory. The history of our time bears the imprint of both theories and of their critical reactions to each other.

Neoclassical theory, whose first systematic contributor was Adam Smith at the end of the eighteenth century, is the prevalent economic theory in the United States today. Most professional U.S. economists subscribe to one or another version of it. Most Americans use the basic arguments of neoclassical theory when making sense of the economic issues in their lives.

Marxian theory, whose foundation was presented by Karl Marx in the second half of the nineteenth century, has attracted many economists in the hundred years since Marx's death. Relatively few professional economists in the United States work within the Marxist theoretical tradition, although their number has grown rapidly over the last fifteen years. Elsewhere in the world, many professional economists look favorably upon Marxist theory in one or another of its versions. Similarly, Marxist theory enjoys far greater general public support in most countries of the world than in the United States.

There are other economic theories as well. Only limitations of space prevent us from giving them the serious attention they deserve. We chose to aim this book at a critical assessment of neoclassical and Marxian economics because they are the two major contesting theories in the world today. But the kind of analysis presented here could and we hope will be extended to the other economic theories alive in our world.

C. Comparing Different Economic Theories

Comparing two different economic theories is a tricky business. Comparisons of different things always are. We can fortunately ease our task by making good use of much recent work concerned precisely with the problem of comparing theories (see the recommended readings at the end of this chapter).

In this book we will compare neoclassical and Marxian theories as two different kinds of something we will call "theory in general." This procedure is rather like distinguishing apples from cherries by showing how they are different kinds of fruit, or differentiating igloos from split-levels by showing how they are different kinds of housing.

C.1. Comparing Theories in General

A theory in general amounts to a set of sentences. Sometimes the words "concepts" and "ideas" are used as synonyms for what we mean by sentences. The groups of sentences or concepts of which every theory is composed display some basic similarities. The sentences of any theory focus on particular things—usually called "objects" of the theory. No one can think about everything imaginable, so all people necessarily narrow their mental energy to focus on some among the infinity of possible objects. Every theory is a means of making sense of some particular objects. The selection of the objects for attention—for theorization—is explained historically in terms of the events and problems that have provoked human beings to think about particular objects in particular ways.

To illustrate this discussion of theory in general, let us briefly compare three specific kinds of theories. Relations among moons and stars have long fascinated people and have been the major objects of theories in the fields we call physics and astronomy. Intimate interpersonal relations provoked interest in new ways of studying the human psyche about a hundred years ago and became characteristic objects of what we now call psychological theories. In economics, the emergence of capitalism from European feudalism in the seventeenth and eighteenth centuries provoked thinking about some particular objects: the production and distribution of goods and services. Modern economic theories evolved from that thinking.

All theories share one characteristic: the sentences or concepts making up a theory do not merely contain objects; they also tell us specific things about those objects. They define their objects. Astronomical theories contain sentences that define what planets and stars are, what precise qualities entitle them to be understood and analyzed as such. Psychological theories define their objects as well. A major originator of modern psychological theory, Sigmund Freud, wrote sentences asserting that the human mind contains something he called "the unconscious," and he proceeded to define this object of psychological theory

as thoroughly as he could. Many psychologists since have extended and
elaborated Freud's theory into a large collection of sentences about the
unconscious and its linkages to all parts of modern life.

Economic theories likewise do not merely contain such objects as
goods and services and production and distribution. These theories'
sentences offer definitions of these objects, thereby attaching particular
senses or meanings to them. Indeed, the content of economic theories is
the set of sentences that attaches specific meaning to the objects deemed
suitable for attention.

All theories are alike insofar as none ever stands still. As people live,
they not only use their theories to cope with the world around them but
they also change them continually. As new experiences occur, people
feel the need to extend their theories to try to take account of those experiences. They then define some new objects and link them somehow to
the previous objects of their theory. In this way theories grow and develop explanations of more and more objects. However, new experiences may also provoke people to question some aspect of their theory
which, in light of the new experiences, looks doubtful. It is then that the
growth of theory goes hand in hand with changes in the theory.

When astronomers find a new body in space, they may not only extend their theory to take account of it. They may also feel the need to
revise certain of their sentences about (concepts of) gravity or the trajec-
tory of light or other specific objects of astronomy. Astronomical theories then grow and change together. Similarly, psychological theories
grow and change depending on how people extend the theories, where
they direct the attention of their theories, and what alterations they feel
impelled to make in them as a result. The same is true of economic
theories. New experiences with recession or inflation or foreign trade
problems may provoke not only extensions of the sentences of the theory
to explain these experiences but also changes that the theory appears to
need.

It is also common for developments outside of a theory to change it.
For example, new developments in theories of chemistry may lead astronomers to alter one of their theories. New developments in the study
of brain anatomy may likewise induce psychologists to change their sentences about, say, schizophrenia. Often in the history of economics,
changes in mathematics have helped transform economic theories. Basically, changes in theories can result from all kinds of influences, from
developments inside the theories themselves as well as from all other
parts of the society in which the theories exist.

C.2. The Logics of Different Theories

All theories are also similar in that they establish and follow rules about how they will connect the objects of their theorizing. There is a systematic quality—or "logic"—to the way every theory links up the parts of reality it is concerned to understand. Theories can and do differ about which particular logic to use in linking their respective objects, but all theories use some logic.

A theory's logic concerns its particular notion of cause and effect. Many theories assign the role of cause to some of their objects and the role of effect to others. Astronomers might explain the shape of one planet's orbit by the size of a certain star: the object "star" would then be the cause, while the object "planetary orbit" would be the effect. In psychology, childhood abuse might be the cause, and adult neurosis the effect. In economics, the object "recession" might be theorized as the effect of another object, "interest rates."

It is also possible that a theory might link its objects in a different kind of cause-and-effect relationship. Every object of a theory might be understood as necessarily always both cause and effect, in which case it would never be possible to isolate one from the other. The objects of such a theory would necessarily be linked to one another in a logic of mutual causation rather than in a logic that separates causes from effects.

C.3. How Theoretical Differences Matter

The three basic properties of all theories—the ability to select objects to theorize about, to define those objects, and to establish logical linkages among the objects—provide us with a convenient basis for drawing key distinctions between different astronomical or psychological or economic theories. Thus, neoclassical theory and Marxian theory will be shown to be different collections of sentences about different objects that are linked in different ways. Neoclassical theory and Marxian theory are alternative sets of sentences with which people can and do make sense of the world. In more formal language, the two different sets of sentences constitute alternative knowledges or alternative sciences of economics.

Our comparison of neoclassical and Marxist economic theories will have to show clearly how their respective objects are defined and linked differently to produce their alternative understandings of the economy. We will note that even when both theories use the same words—for example, "value," "price," "commodity," "wage," and "profit,"—they define such objects differently. They literally mean different things by those words. Indeed, the same holds in all other kinds of theory. Freudian and non-Freudian psychologists attach different meanings to words like "libido," "ego," and "unconscious." Different theories in astronomy offer different definitions for terms like "universe" and "black holes in space." Indeed, when talking with each other, two students will often use the same words—for instance, "love," "work," and "fun"—but will turn out to have quite different meanings for each of them.

Finally, our comparison will lead us to ask whether it matters much that people using different theories arrive at different understandings of things like the economy. Is it all some sort of random chance that makes you theorize in one way and me in another? Can we all just compare and marvel at the different theories we each find appropriate in our daily lives? Or is this a more serious issue, since persons who think about the world in a certain way will likely also act in certain ways to cope with the world? If your theory of economics leads you to strive to change the U.S. economy in ways that my theory holds to be damaging to the nation's future, we have something beyond a disagreement in theory to deal with. Theories are one way by which people arrive at their decisions about how to act, and if such actions bother us, we will likely want to challenge the theories that lie behind them.

Thus, we will end this book with an effort to come to terms with the problem of how theories matter in our society. Knowing what social consequences flow from using one economic theory versus another will help each of you sort out your feelings about both theories.

D. An Overview of Two Theories

Because our goal is to understand the current confrontation and debate between the world's two major economic theories, we will begin with a general overview of each theory. This basic outline will stress the contours of each theory in such a way as to alert us to significant points of difference between them. It will also serve as a guide to the detailed examination of both theories to which chapters 2 and 3 are devoted.

D.1. The Objects and Logic of Neoclassical Theory

Neoclassical economic theory directs the bulk of its attention to some distinctive objects. Individuals, markets, commodities, technologies, and prices figure most prominently, followed by money, income, savings, and investments. In making sense of (theorizing about) these objects, neoclassical economic theory defines and attends to a long list of other objects. Chief among these are individual preferences, utility, supply, demand, production, distribution, labor, capital, growth, GNP, interest rates, and uncertainty.

These and the other particular objects that play central roles in neoclassical economic theory form part of a general image of how society works. For neoclassical economists, society is the collection of individuals in it. Individual wants, thoughts, and deeds combine to make society what it is. To understand an economy is then to make sense of the aggregate effects of individual wants and acts. Neoclassical theory does this by demonstrating how individuals maximize their material self-interests by utilizing their owned resources and the available technology in market transactions. What happens in an economy is always explained as the result of individuals acting in this way (with more or less allowance being made for possible external interference with individual market freedoms).

As we will show, neoclassical economic theory also distinguishes itself by the particular cause-and-effect concepts it uses to connect its particular set of objects. Its notion of causality usually has a few objects combining to cause some other object. It expresses this relationship by attaching the description "dependent variables" to objects it views as effects and "independent variables" to objects it holds to be causes.

This particular notion of causality has been called "essentialism," or sometimes "determinism," among philosophers for many years. In recent years, the term "reductionism" has become popular. In this book, we will use these three terms as synonyms. What do they mean?

They refer to the presumption that any event can be shown to have certain causes or determinants that are essential to its occurrence. Essentialist (or determinist or reductionist) reasoning proceeds as follows: (1) when event A occurs in society, we know that an infinite number of other events are occurring simultaneously and that an infinite number of other events have occurred previously; (2) we presume that a few of this vast number of other events were the key, chief, "determinant," or "essential" causes of A; and (3) we therefore define theoretical work as separating the essential (determinant) from the inessential (nondeterminant) causes. The result is an "explanation" of A: the cause of A has been *reduced* to its final determinants. Hence the term "reductionism" refers to theories that reduce the explanation of events in the world to a few essential causes.

For example, suppose that event A was an increase in the price of coffee during August 1986. A quick survey of economic news that month would show that many other events happened then as well: interest rates fell, oil prices fell, the price of tea rose, the value of the dollar rose, unemployment worsened, and so on. Further research would indicate that millions of other economic and noneconomic aspects of our world changed during and before August, 1986: rainfall increased, tax rates were cut, President Reagan's health became an issue, military conflict in Central America spread, and so on. Faced with this overwhelming mass of data on simultaneous and prior occurrences, all of which probably had some impact on the price of coffee, what do neo-classical economists do?

Believing that they can determine which of the many influences on the price of coffee were "the most important," they group these influences—typically such things as individual income, the cost of producing coffee, weather, taxes, and a few other preferred influences—under the heading "supply and demand." Thus they affirm the basic logic of neoclassical theory: they presume that the change in the price of coffee (dependent object or "variable") resulted from changes in the supply of and demand for coffee (independent objects or "variables"). Neoclassical economists then investigate exactly how some or all of what they believe to be the final causal determinants produced the effect in question. That is why the term "determinism" describes this particular causal method so accurately.

Reductionists or determinists explain the events they deem to be important by centering on the essential causes of those events. This presumption—that it makes sense to think that events have some particular, fundamental causes that can be isolated—runs deep in the consciousness of many people. It appears in many theories, not only in neoclassical theory.

Neoclassical theory is reductionist across the entire range of its analytical claims. At the most general level, economic development can be reduced to an ultimately determining cause: individuals pursuing their self-interest. More narrowly, market prices are presumed to have an ultimate cause—for example supply and demand. Profit rates are thought to have an ultimate cause—for example, the marginal contribution of capital to the production of output. Interest rates are thought to be determined by savings, investments, monetary conditions, and perhaps a few other selected factors.

Neoclassical economists do often argue among themselves over which precise causes are the essential determinants of the objects of their theory. Their arguments vary from issue to issue and usually turn on the debaters' different preferences among a small group of generally favored essential causes. What we want to stress here, however, is that they do not question or dispute the reductionism common to them all. They presume, as if it were natural, that an essence—an ultimately determining cause—of every event exists and needs only to be found via proper theoretical work. Each event can be explained by (reduced to) that essence. Indeed, a subfield of growing importance in recent decades—econometrics—develops and applies mathematical tests to determine which essentialist hypotheses of economic theory best fit the facts that are collected by neoclassical economists.

D.2. The Objects of Marxian Theory

Marxian theory has its distinctive objects too, those aspects of the economy that it deems to be most worthy of attention. First among these is class, which it defines as the relationship among people in which some individuals work for others while obtaining nothing in return. To explain class, Marxian theory requires the notion of surplus. Some people in society produce a quantity of goods and services that is greater than what they get to keep. This surplus is delivered to people who did not assist in its production. Class relations exist when this kind of surplus production and deliverance occurs in society. Beyond class and surplus, Marxian theory focuses on such objects as capital, labor, labor power, commodities, values, production and distribution, accumulation of capital, crises, and imperialism.

Further, Marxian theory attaches distinctive qualities and qualifications to its objects of theoretical attention. For example, there are different kinds of relationships in which surplus gets produced by some and delivered to others. Indeed, these different qualities of class relationships are used in Marxian theory to divide human history into distinct epochs: capitalist, feudal, slave, communist, and some other kinds as well. Marxian theory also distinctively qualifies certain of its objects—labor and capital—with the adjectives "productive" and "unproductive," and another of its objects—surplus value—with the adjectives "absolute" and "relative."

This partial and preliminary listing underscores a remarkable difference in the neoclassical and Marxian theories. Notwithstanding the considerable overlap in the words and phrases that appear in both theories, basic objects in one theory exist as secondary objects or are altogether absent in the other. Self-interest-maximizing individuals are as scarce in Marxian theory as surplus labor is in neoclassical theory. Qualifications that are central to Marxian theory—productive, unproductive, relative and absolute—do not figure significantly, if at all, in neoclassical theory. Likewise, the adjectives "dependent" versus "independent," which neoclassical theory attaches to its objects, do not exist in Marxian theory.

D.3. A Digression: Theories and Their Objects

Recognizing such sharp differences in the two theories' basic objects suggests that we can and should amplify a general point made earlier about different theories. We have been saying that theories differ if they focus on different objects. Now we see that objects in and for one theory may literally not exist in another. Class exploitation is a key object for Marxian theory, while most neoclassicals would deny its existence; likewise, the self-interest-maximizing individual as specified in neoclassical theory would be rejected as an imaginary creation by most Marxists. This tells us something important about the objects of any and all theories.

Objects of theories do *not* exist out there in the world just waiting for theories to observe and explain them. Our view of the world—the objects we find in it—is itself shaped by the theories we use to analyze the world that we see. It is important that we not get caught in a philosophical version of the old question, Which came first, the chicken or the egg? It is not the case that first came objects in the world which everyone can and does observe; and then came theories that selected various sets of these objects and explained them. Nor is it true that we first have theories in our heads which then determine both the particular objects we see and how we understand them.

Rather, human beings are always observing *and* thinking at the same time. What we see is shaped by how we think just as much as how we think is shaped by what we see. Marxists observe class and theorize about it; their theory plays a role in influencing what they see just as their observations shape their theorizing. Neoclassicals observe individual-maximizing behavior and theorize about it; their theory plays a role in influencing what they see just as their observations shape their theorizing.

Of course, what each of us observes is determined by more than the theories we find convincing. Theories we reject may also be important enough in our communities to force us to consider their objects and find some sort of place for them in our theories, or to adjust them to fit into our theories. Some neoclassical economists do admit that class exists, but typically they define it quite differently from Marxists. Similarly, some Marxists have come to agree that self-interest-maximizing individuals are factors in any economy's development, although they discuss them in ways most neoclassicals would oppose.

What this discussion teaches us is to realize that all theories not only explain the world differently but also influence us to see a different world to explain. Part of the difficulties faced by people with different theories when they try to communicate their understandings to one another is that the world they see is not the same for each of them. For successful communication to occur, both sides need to grasp that they differ not only on how to explain the world but also on what they perceive that world to be.

This is not cause for alarm about the chances for humans to talk and interact positively. Communication among us is not made impossible because we see and think about the world differently. On the contrary, communication can be richer and more productive precisely because of our differences as long as we are committed to honestly facing them and learning from them.

The diversity of human life which enriches and stimulates all cultures extends not only to different ways of dressing, praying, cooking, dancing, and the like. People are also diverse in their thinking and observing—in how their minds work and how their senses interact with (see, hear, taste, touch, and smell) their environments. Trying to understand all such differences is the mark of an advanced civilization eager to learn from all the cultural diversity within it. Communication is necessary and enriching among people precisely because of their differences.

As civilizations have learned slowly that there is no one right way to eat or dress or pray or love or vote, we need to remember also that there is no one right way to see our surroundings or to think about what they mean. How people theorize about their world and how they observe the world are different. Neoclassical and Marxian theories thus involve more than different ways of analyzing the economy. Their objects of analysis—the "observed realities" they aim at—are also and correspondingly different. A chief purpose of this book is to confront their differences.

D.4. The Logic of Marxian Theory

In addition to its concept of class exploitation, what is often most striking about Marxian theory is its distinctive notion of causality, of how its objects connect to one another as causes and effects. As chapter 3 will explain, the Marxian theory presented here rejects any presumption that economic (or, for that matter, noneconomic) events have essential causes. Such presumptions are referred to as "economic determinism" when there is thought to be an essential economic determinant of the event, or as "cultural" or "political" determinism when an essential cultural or political determinant is thought ultimately to cause the event.

In contrast to these determinisms (essentialisms), the Marxian theory of chapter 3 will presume that any event occurs as the result—the effect—of *everything else* going on around that event and preceding that event. If we suppose that the world comprises an infinite number of events, then the occurrence of any one of them depends on the influence of *all* the others, not some "essential few." This means that since all events add their unique effectivity or influence to producing the occurrence of any one happening, no single event can ever be considered to occur by itself, independent of the existence of the others. Events thus always occur together, in relationships with one another. It follows that Marxian theory cannot use the independent-versus-dependent variable or cause-and-effect terminology of neoclassical economics. It cannot do so because each event is always understood to be simultaneously a cause (it adds its own influence to the creation of all others) *and* an effect (its own existence results from the combined influence of all others on it).

In the Marxian tradition, this kind of logic was often referred to as "dialectical" reasoning. Dialectics has become the Marxian way of understanding how events exist (are caused). However, despite its place within the Marxian tradition, we will not use the term "dialectics" in this book. We will use instead the newer and, we think, more exact term "overdetermination" to refer to this Marxian notion of causation. "Dialectics" is a term with a long history in both Marxian and non-Marxian philosophic discourses. It is overloaded with diverse meanings deriving from often bitter debates, especially among Marxists. One important reason for preferring "overdetermination" is to distance its meaning from many of the meanings that have been attached to "dialectics." "Overdetermination" gives us a more precise definition of a specifically Marxian notion of causality without burdening that definition with the complex intellectual history of dialectics.

To illustrate this Marxian notion of overdetermination, consider the occurrence of an economic recession. It is not presumed to follow from high interest rates or government spending or foreign trade or any restricted group of such factors. Rather, in this Marxian view, a recession is "caused" not only by these but also by all other factors that exist in our world. Natural changes in climate and soil chemistry, political changes in voting and legal patterns, cultural changes in religious and sexual preferences—these and many other factors like them play roles in shaping—in influencing—the occurrence of a recession. For Marxian theory, none of these factors can be ruled out as causes—each in its particular way—of the recession. Indeed, the prefix "over-" in the term "overdetermination" is a way of signaling the reader that this event, a recession, is (over)determined by the influences emanating from *all* of these factors. If we decide to focus our attention on only some of the causes, that is no problem so long as we are aware of and explicit about the necessarily partial and incomplete analysis that results.

Such a notion of causality sometimes startles people. They rightly wonder whether we can ever explain anything if we are required to investigate everything in order to do so. If the world is infinitely complex, if everything is caused by everything else, we can hardly examine an infinity each time we propose to understand or explain some event. How do Marxists respond to this dilemma?

Marxists answer that no explanation, no matter what theory is used to produce it, is ever complete, total or finished. Human beings can no more fully explain an event than they can fully appreciate a work of art, fully understand another person, or fully control their environment. Instead, we all do these things partially, utilizing our thoughts and feelings as best we can to produce some appreciation of a painting, some understanding of a friend, and some control over our environment. So it is with any theory. It uses its particular apparatus—its objects, qualifications, and notions of causality—to produce its particular (and inevitably partial) explanation of an event.

Marxists thus insist that they, like everyone else, are producing their distinctively partial explanations. The point is simply that the Marxian explanation is different from the non-Marxian one; both are partial. Indeed, what differentiates Marxists is their view that theories and explanations are all partial, their own included, while neoclassical theorists presume that final causes of events exist and that their theory can and will disclose them in a finished and completed explanation. Once discovered, these final causes by definition cannot be reduced to anything else. That is why such theorists believe that they have obtained a complete explanation.

By contrast, Marxists cannot talk of independent and dependent— or essential and nonessential—variables among the objects of their theory. Each aspect of society, for them, is dependent on all the other aspects. No event or aspect of a society is independent; nothing determines other things without itself being determined by them. Marxists do not look for the ultimate causes of events, because they presume that such final explanations do not exist. Neoclassical theorists do look for and claim to have found such essences among the objects of their theory. Hence they order aspects of society into dependent and independent variables.

So Marxian theorists produce their partial explanations of social development and contrast them with the partial explanations produced via alternative theories. Marxian explanations focus on the class aspects, class causes, and class consequences of social life. Marxists do not claim that they focus on class because class is the essential, ultimate cause of social structures and changes. Such a claim would violate their own commitment to overdetermination, their rejection of the presumption of and the search for essential causes of any kind. Marxian theory is antiessentialist and antireductionist. Its analyses proceed in terms of the mutual cause-and-effect relationships (overdetermination) between class and nonclass aspects of any economy and society chosen for examination and explanation. Class exploitation is no more a cause of historical development than any of the other nonclass and noneconomic components of a society.

Marxists justify their antiessentialist focus on class on two grounds: (1) class as an aspect of social life has been neglected; and (2) the neglect of class has prevented people from constructing the kind of societies which Marxists would like to see. A theory of social structures and historical changes which emphasizes class, the Marxists argue, can help remedy the neglect—especially by neoclassical theory—of class exploitation. Marxists want to direct attention to class because they see it as a part of social life that will have to be changed if social justice is to be achieved. Marxists clearly feel that their theory will stimulate the needed attention. Notice that their justification of the focus on class is not a claim that it is some final and ultimate determinant of historical change, but rather a judgment about how analytical thought can and should be oriented to achieve social goals.

D.5. Communication between Neoclassical and Marxian Economists

Much separates neoclassical from Marxian economic theory. People in both camps try to make sense of the world they both live in, but they do this differently and so produce different explanations of that world. It is almost as if each kind of theorist lived in a different world. As we will see, they produce different understandings of capitalism, profits, wages, and prices. Yet they do inhabit the same world and they do definitely communicate with each other. Marxian and neoclassical economists read each other's books and articles, debate with each other at conferences, and talk together in countless settings. Noneconomists convinced by one or the other theory likewise communicate with each other in all kinds of situations inside families, workplaces, and social gatherings of all sorts.

An interesting question thus arises: What happens when people committed to different theories communicate? The answers vary. Sometimes one side gives way to the other; a "meeting of minds" occurs as people who think one way decide to change their minds and think the other way. Basic disagreement gives way to unanimity. This is one kind and result of communication among people. Sometimes, after each side has presented its knowledge and the theory it used to produce that knowledge, neither side abandons its positions. Both reflect on and react (in their own ways) to the differences between them. This is another kind and result of communication.

Sometimes, people holding one particular theory about how the world works reach the conclusion that some other theory has dangerous social consequences in the sense that people who believe it tend to act in dangerous ways. Then discussion changes into verbal and/or physical battle as people holding these two theories seek to control, constrain, and sometimes even eliminate one another. This too is a kind of communication.

How neoclassicals and Marxists communicate—in mutually instructive exchanges of analyses, in discussions that result in a "meeting of minds," or in tense hostilities that spill over into conflict—depends on all the social conditions that overdetermine that communication. Neoclassicals and Marxists have experienced all three kinds of communication over the past hundred years. Too often, communications in the United States have been laced with hostility and suspicion, so much so *U.S. hostility to Marxism* that little has been learned. Since Marxists have frequently been blocked from university or other positions that would allow their theory more exposure and general discussion, most Americans have had little opportunity to encounter Marxian theory or to communicate with Marxian theorists. This has had negative consequences for the majority neoclassicals and the minority Marxists. We hope that this book will improve matters by enhancing the likelihood for better, mutually instructive communication between the two theoretical traditions.

E. The History of Two Theories

Before moving to in-depth analyses of both major economic theories, we will sketch their histories. Theories, like individuals or groups, are better understood when we know where they came from and how they evolved to the present. The history of each theory also illustrates again how societies shape the theories that arise within them, and how those theories in turn influence the history of those societies.

E.1. Transition from Feudalism to Capitalism in Europe

The transformation of Europe from a feudal to a capitalist region of the world altered radically the way life was lived on that continent. Across the seventeenth and eighteenth centuries, everything changed: how people cultivated the soil, reared their children, understood God, designed their monuments, and organized their economies, to name only a few examples. Not surprisingly, such vast changes provoked people to think in new ways about their lives. New theories arose, clashed with, and cross-fertilized one another. Gradually a few caught the popular imagination and became the broadly accepted ways of making sense of a changed world.

The old theories, born and developed within feudal society, struck Europeans as no longer adequate or acceptable. New social conditions not only provoked, they also required, new theories to understand them. People sought some sense of control over the often traumatic flow of events, and new theories seemed important as contributions toward such control.

The theories were expected to aid in coping with social change and even in directing the path of change. New theories were to be practical guides to social action. Thus, the new theories, once widely adopted, did exert great influence on how capitalism actually developed. The new theoretical commitments shaped social development not only in Europe but also globally as European capitalism expanded through successive waves of colonial acquisitions.

Many theories inherited from feudalism underwent great changes during the centuries of transition to capitalism. For example, the religious theories of God changed sufficiently to induce major conflicts, including protracted military actions, among Europeans. A whole new theory and institution arose, Protestantism, which differed from the formerly predominant Roman Catholic tradition. A key part of the new kind of Christianity emphasized the individual and his or her personal capacity to communicate directly with God and without a specially appointed religious hierarchy acting as an intermediary. Nor did Roman Catholicism pass untouched through the transition to capitalism. The ability of the Roman Catholic tradition to survive into the present attests to its ability to adjust to a profoundly changed world.

Theories of natural science changed drastically too. Newton, Galileo, Copernicus, and many others invented new theories of how the universe and nature worked. The Bible appeared to be no longer adequate as a theoretical guide to coping with life. Scientific investigations of all sorts challenged biblical formulations, or at least modified them.

Instead of answering questions about life's mysteries by invoking God as *the* cause, science sought *the* cause elsewhere, usually in some aspect of physical nature or human nature. Instead of invoking God as the essential cause of all phenomena, the new scientific attitude found essential causes in nature and individuals (the discovered "laws" of physics, biology, politics, economics, etc.). The result was not only new theories of how nature worked (and how it might be controlled by people), but a new sense of the power, possibilities, and rights of the individual. As the poet Alexander Pope later put it, "The proper study of mankind is man."

The powerful ascent of science combined with the changes and divisions within religion to generate a broad new theoretical attitude. The mysteries of nature and society, previously ascribed to the will and workings of God, became instead riddles the human mind was thought able to solve. Science, viewed as the close investigation of how nature and society work, could and would unravel the mysteries. Not Divine Will but gravity, or thermodynamics, or centrifugal force, or the cellular structure of living organisms, would explain events in nature. Not Divine Will but markets, the accumulation of wealth, and individual thirst for political power would explain events in society.

The complex and interconnected changes in ways of thought that occurred amid the transition from feudalism to capitalism gave rise to some basic themes in most of the new theories. Human individuals, not God, occupied center stage. The new theories exalted the individual as the center of attention: individuals could comprehend the universe, individuals could make the world go round, the individual was the proper foundation for social life.

Is this the enlightenment?

Perhaps most striking of all the changes in thought was the rediscovery and reinterpretation by Europeans of ancient Greek notions of political life. The idea of democracy attracted and inspired growing numbers of Europeans. As they understood it, individuals shaped society by agreeing to the limits a social form of existence imposes on each individual's freedom. Thus the only acceptable and ultimately durable form of government in any society was one that derived its power and legitimacy from, in Thomas Jefferson's phrase, the "consent of the governed." This differed greatly from the feudal notion that government represented part of God's plan, a plan that hardly needed the consent of individuals. In feudal times, kings and nobles claimed that their power to govern derived from divine rights (granted by God); as capitalism displaced feudalism, not only divine rights but the kings and nobles themselves generally disappeared.

replaced by corp. exes?

"Humanism" was the name often given to the broad change in theoretical attitude that accompanied the emergence of capitalism. It summarized the new focus on the individual as the source and object of life and thought. Humanism placed the individual at the center of the universe, rather in the manner that previous religious thought had accorded that place to God. A human essentialism displaced the earlier divine essentialism. As the German philosopher Ludwig Feuerbach put it, "God did not create man; it was the other way round."

the white man

E.2. The New Economic Theories

The transitional changes in European society stimulated not only transformations in existing theories but also altogether new theories. Economic theories were such new theories. The idea of thinking about the economy as a distinct aspect of society, of separating it out from other parts (such as family life or morality or religious practice), was new. So too was the idea that the economy was a system of particular relationships within a society. The idea that the production and distribution of goods and services were subject to systematic "laws," rather like nature and the universe, was a striking proposition.

The growth of theories that designated "the economy" as their object had a powerful impact on Europe. As these theories elaborated their sentences—their concepts and arguments—about the economy, people paid increasing attention to the basic notion that there existed a special part of society called "the economy." They eventually came to believe that societies as a whole depended in important ways on an internal economic system. It therefore made sense for individuals to study the economy and to design government policies aimed at specific economic results. Individuals and governments used one or another of the various economic theories then available to reach decisions that affected the course of social developments throughout Europe.

The seventeenth and eighteenth centuries produced many bits and pieces of economic theory as people struggled to understand the newly emerging capitalist world. Pamphlets were written about the new systems of production that were developing in the rapidly growing towns. There, employer-employee relationships that involved wage payments were replacing the previous landlord-peasant-rent system of feudalism. The production of goods and services for sale in market exchanges instead of for local consumption made people eager to think through how markets worked. They were most intently concerned to understand why market prices rose and fell as they did.

Writings on that subject poured forth wherever commodity trade developed and shook societies that had not previously accomplished their production and distribution of goods and services through market transactions. These were societies, largely feudal, in which religious and customary rules governed most of the decisions about who produced what and how the products were to be divided among the population. Such societies had little need to worry about market price movements, for they did not rely so much, or at all, on market exchanges. When market transactions grew—a nearly universal accompaniment of the transition to capitalism—the worrying increased and turned into the formation of theories to explain price movements.

Money, which had been present before, took on new importance as it became the universal medium for buying and selling in markets. It became the means to act successfully in market-oriented economies, to gain one's livelihood. Pamphleteers wrote much about the mysteries and power of money: why it was so valuable and what determined its precise value. The problems of governments occupied their attention as well. How should governmental policies—on taxes, on regulations governing wages, prices, rents, and interest rates, on building canals, harbors and roads, on foreign trade, and so on—be designed and effectively implemented?

Many valuable contributions to economic analysis were made in the pamphlets, journals, and other writings that appeared in those years. Passionately committed arguments were provoked amid a growing group of active writers. This was especially true in Western Europe and above all in England, where the transition from feudalism to capitalism had deepened more rapidly than elsewhere. In the late eighteenth century, general interest and an abundance of writings made it possible to organize the somewhat fragmented thinking of two centuries into a general theory of how the new capitalist economy worked.

E.3. Classical Political Economy

Not surprisingly, the new general theory was deeply humanist in structure and tone. The cause and motor energy of the economy was the individual. The growth of wealth depended on individual initiative, ingenuity, and self-interest. Problems and crises afflicting an economy were to be understood as consequences of particular individual actions taken in response to the specific social conditions that constrained those individuals. In short, the first modern, general economic theory also served as the foundation of the neoclassical theory we treat in this book.

Adam Smith's *Wealth of Nations* (1776) introduced this general theory. A second English writer, David Ricardo, revised and condensed Smith's somewhat rambling work into a more formal, textbook-style exposition of basic economic theory, *The Principles of Political Economy and Taxation* (1817). The general economic theory provided by Smith and Ricardo came to be known widely as "classical political economy" and sometimes as "political economy." With many additions and changes, it dominated European thought about economics from 1780 to 1880. Karl Marx read the works of Smith and Ricardo very closely and devoted voluminous critical commentaries to them. His *Capital,* volume 1 (1867), offered a basic alternative economic theory to that of Smith and Ricardo. Marx gave *Capital* the subtitle *A Critique of Political Economy.*

Over the last hundred years, both classical economics and the Marxian alternative have undergone changes and additions. Both classical and Marxian theorists have extended their theories to areas not included in the original formulations. Theorists in each camp have debated and argued among themselves as well as with members of the opposing camp. As a result, significant changes continue to be made in both theories.

E.4. The History of Neoclassical Economics

The classical school of economics shifted its focus quite dramatically after the 1870s. From its concern with macroeconomic issues—the capitalist economy as a whole, and especially its growth over time—classical economics turned to detailed studies of the decision-making processes of individuals and individual enterprises—what we now call microeconomic issues. Terms like "individual preferences" and "marginal utilities," "production functions" and "marginal costs," which had rarely figured in classical economics, now took center stage.

Of course, not all classical economists became microeconomists. Since major macroeconomic problems (inflation, depression, stagnant growth, etc.) beset all the capitalist economies periodically, some economists maintained their macroeconomic orientation. However, the broad shift toward a microeconomic theoretical foundation was clear, especially in the tendency to view macroeconomic problems strictly as the results of decisions reached by individuals and firms. This shift was broad and deep enough to warrant a new name for classical economics: neoclassical economics. The period from 1870 to 1930 saw most of the basic propositions of neoclassical economics established and woven mathematically into an impressive economic theory.

The events of the 1930s, however, shook neoclassical economics to its roots. A destructive and lasting depression staggered nearly all of the West European and North American capitalist economies. The massive unemployment, bankruptcies, and attendant social disruptions that ensued forced a back-to-the-drawing-boards anxiety among neoclassical economists. Their theories, in both the original classical and the post-1870 neoclassical form, had prepared no one for such a depression. Neoclassical economists had few explanations to offer, and fewer still that seemed adequate to the vast human tragedy that spread everywhere in the 1930s. Most serious of all was their failure to offer clear and effective proposals for remedying the situation. The policies they suggested to the governments of the depressed economies met with little success prior to the onset of World War II in 1939–1940.

However, an innovative economist in England who was able to cast a critical eye on neoclassical theory from within, John Maynard Keynes, did produce a theoretically important reaction to the Great Depression. In his *General Theory of Employment, Interest, and Money* (1936), Keynes tried to persuade neoclassical economists—he dubbed them "orthodox" in the book's preface—"to re-examine critically certain of their basic assumptions." Keynes's reaction to the worldwide depression of capitalism took the form of a critical reassessment of neoclassical theory.

Keynes shifted the tradition back toward macroeconomics from its focus (excessive and flawed in Keynes's view) on microeconomics. His reformulation of neoclassical theory also emphasized certain obstacles in the structure of capitalist economies which prevented them from realizing the predictions often contained in neoclassical analyses: full employment, smooth operation, and regular growth. Keynes endorsed ac-

major to change this C of P. century

tive government intervention in and regulation of the capitalist economy as indispensable to delivery of the economic well-being that people would and should demand.

Keynes's work provoked the entire body of neoclassical economists. It has deeply affected public discussion of economic problems and policies throughout the world since its publication. Some neoclassical economists were outraged by Keynes's critical reformulation. They have labored ever since to show that he misunderstood neoclassical theory and vastly overrated some occasional, temporary "market imperfections" that can afflict capitalism. Contrary to Keynes, these neoclassical economists argue that the capitalist market itself cures whatever market imperfections may temporarily occur. *ultra conservative* Other neoclassical economists were inspired to continue and develop Keynes's beginnings. Their premise has been that Keynes properly identified the problems that government could and should deal with directly. Their analyses have favored government intervention in the economy to avoid depression, overcome intractable market imperfections, and so generate economic growth and social stability. *→environment, civil rights?*

The intense debate among neoclassical economists over the legacy of Keynes has probably been the central issue agitating this theory for the last fifty years. Sometimes the debate has centered on microeconomics versus macroeconomics. Sometimes the two sides have accused each other of abandoning the neoclassical tradition altogether. Sometimes the debaters on one side have even accused the other side of disloyalty to capitalism itself. (It is worth remembering that various socialist critiques of capitalism were heard increasingly during these decades.)

Politicians and political controversies also got caught up in the debate. Republican Presidents Eisenhower, Nixon, Ford, and Reagan often couched their speeches in anti-Keynesian terms. The Democrats Roosevelt, Truman, Kennedy, and Carter frequently chose Keynesian language. Each side both framed and publicly justified their administrations' economic policies by relying on pro- or anti-Keynesian variations of neoclassical economic theory. Indeed, liberals and conservatives in the United States still often distinguish one another according to their attitudes toward the Keynesian innovations in neoclassical theory.

Thus the administrations that were influenced chiefly by Keynesian economists tended toward major interventions in the economy: enhanced government monitoring of the private sector's economic performance, greater regulation, more economically motivated spending and tax change initiatives, and the like. The administrations that listened rather to the anti-Keynesians tended toward deregulation, less government oversight of the private economy, lower spending rates, and so on. Of course, practical politics has rarely permitted any administration to be all pro or all con in relation to Keynesian theory; mixtures of both approaches are usual, but with the emphasis tilting one way or the other.

At all times, U.S. citizens have felt direct and indirect consequences as government economic policies have changed in part because of the debate among neoclassical economists. Again we can see how society and theory continually shape each other or, as explained earlier, overdetermine each other. Social change (a depression) impacts on a theory (neoclassical economics), and the resulting theoretical changes and debate influence the development of a society.

In chapter 2 we will explore and analyze neoclassical theory in light of this debate, which has greatly influenced neoclassical theory's current interpretations of the capitalist economies. However, our purpose there will also be to capture the enduring, basic qualities of neoclassical theory, those which both Keynesian and "orthodox" economists have neither questioned nor rejected.

E.5. The History of Marxian Economics

Karl Marx's work focused overwhelmingly on the capitalist economic system. That is why, to understand it, he spent so much time on the writings of Smith, Ricardo, and the other classical and even preclassical economists. He gained much from their work and often acknowledged his debt to their theorizing. However, the theory that took shape in Marx's mind broke away from the classical theory. For him the transition from feudalism to capitalism stimulated a different way of seeing the modern world and a different way of theorizing about its meaning.

Whereas the classical economists welcomed and celebrated capitalism's emergence from feudalism, Marx saw the transition as a very mixed blessing. Whereas the classicals justified capitalism on the grounds of its technical dynamism, productive efficiencies, and rapid rate of overall economic growth, Marx was struck as well by the massive human costs of capitalism. He reacted to the suffering of the workers in capitalist factories and offices, to the drudgery and powerlessness of their lives. For Marx the liberation of productive capacities accomplished in the transition from feudalism to capitalism was not accompanied by the liberation of the masses of people from oppressive living conditions.

Marx never denied what he termed the "historically positive contributions of capitalism": above all its technical and productive breakthroughs. He rather aimed to explain why, despite those breakthroughs, the transformation of most people from feudal peasants to capitalist wage laborers occasioned so much suffering and so little human liberation. In his view, the masses of people continued to be denied the enjoyment of the goods and services their labor made possible. They still lacked the freedoms that for so long had been limited to a tiny proportion of the populations of the world, those who lived off the surplus produced by others.

Marx's reaction to capitalism clearly differed from the reactions of the leading classical economists. Marx's theoretical training also differed quite sharply. Whereas the classical economic authors, chiefly British, developed their ways of thinking in the particular atmosphere of eighteenth-century English philosophy, Marx studied in the German philosophical tradition that culminated in G. W. F. Hegel. Marx's personal history likewise departed from the middle-class stability that characterized most classical political economists. While he began life in circumstances similar to theirs—Marx was the university student son of an educated state bureaucrat—his radical leanings changed his life. When political influences blocked his career as a university professor, he turned to active political involvements.

Revolutionary upheavals in a Germany wracked by the tensions of transition from feudalism to capitalism provided Marx with ample opportunities to learn about capitalism's darker sides and to speak out against them. Consequently, in the 1840s the German authorities exiled Marx, as did the authorities in France and Belgium when he sought asylum there. He finally settled in London, where he lived the rest of his life under endlessly difficult and financially insecure conditions of the sort that beset most political refugees.

All of the mature works of economic analysis for which Marx is famous were written in England. Cut off from his native Germany and from the immediate scenes of social upheaval, Marx understandably shifted his emphasis from polemical writings and daily activism to systematic reading, study, and theorizing (although political activism was always an important part of his life). By contrast, Adam Smith spent his life as a university professor in Glasgow, Scotland, while David Ricardo lived the life of a rich banker in London.

These different conditions help explain how and why Marx and the classical economists produced different theories of capitalism's structure and development. Whereas the classical economists focused on the individual as the beginning point of their analyses, Marx began his theory with an emphasis on class as a common feature of both the fading feudalism and the rising capitalism. By "class" he meant one particular process in a society. In this class process, some members of the society—the workers—perform "surplus labor." Marx defined this as labor beyond that needed to produce the goods and services the workers themselves consumed. The fruits of this surplus labor, in Marx's view of both feudalism and capitalism, passed immediately to persons other than the workers who produced the surplus. Marx carefully defined this situation as "exploitation": the production of surplus by one group and its receipt by another.

In the case of feudalism, individuals called "lords" obtained this surplus through regular deliveries from their peasants and serfs. What capitalism accomplished was a change in the form of this surplus labor arrangement, but not the abolition of a class structure that divided people into the surplus-producers and the surplus-receivers. Under capitalism the masses of people were still workers, still surplus producers whose surplus passed to other people. All that changed, in terms of class, were the details and the particulars and the names. New people called "capitalists" replaced feudal lords; but both were receivers of other peoples' surplus. New producers of surplus called "wage laborers" or "proletarians" replaced the feudal peasants and serfs. Exploitation continued; only its particular form changed, and with it the name given to the surplus, from feudal "rent" to capitalist "profit."

Much of Marx's theory spelled out the important economic and social consequences of this historic change in the form of the class process from feudal to capitalist. His became a class theory of society in the sense that it emphasized an understanding of both the changes and the underlying continuity in the class processes of feudalism and capitalism. Marx's focus on class as against the neoclassicals' different emphasis on the individual reflected and also influenced the two different agendas for social change. Marx clearly identified with those people who wanted further social transitions beyond capitalism: not merely another change in the form of exploitation, but rather the abolition of exploitation. Marx envisioned a society in which the people who produced the surplus would also receive it and decide how to utilize it: a workers' society to which he attached the name "communism." No longer would people be set against one another as surplus-producers versus surplus-receivers.

Whereas the classical economists celebrated capitalism as the fulfillment of human aspirations, Marx and Marxists after him strove for further social transitions toward communism. Indeed, they labeled transitional periods, when capitalism would be replaced by communism, as "socialism." Politically they defined themselves as socialists committed to establishing such transitional periods. Marx believed that his theory, with its class analysis of capitalism, was an indispensable contribution to the political project of establishing socialism and, beyond that, communism.

Marx reasoned that in order for capitalist society to be changed into communist society, people would have to understand the class structure of capitalism. Before they could establish and maintain a new communist class structure, people would have to understand how class processes interacted with (overdetermined and were overdetermined by) all the other processes of social life. Because he found such an understanding lacking in the available social theories of his time, Marx worked to produce a new theory that would address the issues of class in ways needed by socialists.

Marx's theory is a class theory—one focused on the class aspects of societies—not because class is a more important social force than music or religion or climate, for example. It is a class theory because class was and largely remains the overlooked and untheorized component of modern capitalist society. Those who seek to change that society, especially in socialist directions, must understand class if they are to have any hope of making that change. Hence Marx's theory focuses on class.

Most Marxists generally believe that classical and neoclassical economics together constitute an impressively complex and subtle theory. They also find this theory to be uniquely comforting to those who wish history to stop at capitalism rather than, say, continue to socialism. Marxists typically feel that their alternative theory gives comfort to those who seek instead a socialist transition out of capitalism.

While intense disputes attend all their discussions about capitalism, communism, and how the socialist transition between them is to be achieved, Marxists usually agree that Marx did make a crucial contribution. He taught his readers that any socialist agenda for basic changes to produce a better world must contend with class as an issue, that this better world could not be erected unless its partisans understood the issue of class as well as the other social and personal issues that motivated their commitments.

Marx wrote little about what the proposed communist society might look like. He preferred to analyze the present rather than speculate on the future. His few remarks on communism reflect his life-long focus on class. His vision of a communist society's class structure centered on the idea that in it, all working people would both produce surplus labor and also receive it. That is, the social division between workers and capitalists would be abolished. Everyone who labored would by rights also have an equal say in how much surplus was produced, who was to get it, and what was to be done with it.

The Marxists who came after Marx took up the task of going beyond these sketchy suggestions. At the same time, they extended Marxian theory to topics Marx had written little or nothing about. For example, the intense European expansion into Asia, Africa, and Latin America during the nineteenth and twentieth centuries led Marxists to new theories about foreign trade, colonialism, and international finance. Similarly, the growth of large enterprises (often linking manufacturers and bankers in close cooperation) generated new Marxian theories about monopoly and economic stagnation in advanced capitalist economies. Of course, when any theory is extended to new topics, it undergoes all sorts of changes that occasion all kinds of debates among its practitioners; Marxian theory has been no exception. Marxists have entered new fields and tried to generate Marxian approaches to such diverse topics as literary criticism, psychoanalysis, anthropology, and biology. In many of these fields, Marxian theories have emerged, as in economics, as the basic alternative to the prevalent theory.

The development of Marxian economics, like that of Marxian theories in other disciplines, has been influenced by debates among the Marxists themselves. Intensity and passion have ruled these debates as much as they did the neoclassical debates over Keynes. A central issue in the Marxian debates since 1917 has been the Soviet Union. Have the policies of that country—under V. I. Lenin, then under Josef Stalin, and since 1953 under a succession of leaderships—constituted a confirmation of, a challenge to, or a refutation of, Marx's theories and hopes? Different answers to this question and the related issue of one's attitude toward communist movements around the world have agitated all writers in Marxian economics from 1917 to the present. A similar debate stirred Marxists after the 1949 revolutionary victory of the Chinese Communist Party in China. How have the policies and evolution of that country under Mao Tse-tung and the leadership since his death affected Marxian theories? Despite these debates, we have yet to see detailed Marxian examinations of the class processes (forms of the production and distribution of surplus labor) that exist in these two countries.

Another major provocation of debates among Marxists has been the successful development of large, mass-based socialist and communist parties in West European noncommunist countries in the twentieth century. Marxists in these countries have sought to connect their theoretical work to the practical political struggles waged by these parties in parliament and other public arenas. Marxian theories have been influenced by the twists and turns of party politics. Thus, Marxian notions of "Eurocommunism" have emerged; they focus on how socialist transitions might be accomplished without the class violence that characterized the transition from feudalism to capitalism or the anticommunist violence many expected from a threatened capitalist establishment. Marxists have also produced new theories about ideology and mass psychology as large socialist parties have struggled against conservative parties over the political loyalties of masses of European voters.

Still another major development since Marx's time has provoked debates among those interested in Marxian economics: the rise of powerful trade unions in most capitalist societies. Such organizations gather workers around the proposition that collective action and bargaining can best improve their position in conflicts with their capitalist employers. Trade unions have thus quite naturally attracted Marxists' interest. In theoretical terms, Marxian economists have worked to extend their theory to cover issues of concern to trade unionists. To take some examples, Marxian theorists have sought to explain when and how capitalists will obtain the help of state power in their confrontations with workers over wages, salaries, and working conditions. Marxian economists have also tried to explain trends in the investment plans of major corporations and to relate them to union organizing strategies. Marxian economists have also analyzed the relationships among modern, multinational corporations, their employees in the advanced capitalist countries, and workers in the so-called less developed economies of Asia, Africa, and Latin America.

In the decades since 1945, Marxian theory has undergone some of its most intense challenges and changes. In the advanced capitalist societies today, Marxian theory is in a period of intense self-examination and reformulation. Marxists are arguing over whether class analysis is to remain the central contribution by Marxism to the complex movements toward socialism and communism. They disagree on whether to accept and absorb portions of neoclassical theory, and, if so, exactly which portions. In many parts of Asia, Africa, and Latin America, Marxian theorists are debating the applicability of the current state of the theory to the specific development problems that face these societies. In the communist countries, economic growth across the period and the emergence of deep divisions among these countries have likewise prompted much rethinking of Marxism.

In this introductory book, we cannot give all these developments their due. Our emphasis must be on the basic contours of Marxian theory as an alternative to neoclassical theory. However, in the case of Marxian theory, as in our discussion of neoclassical theory, we must take account of some of the debates and rethinking since they so profoundly agitate and influence Marxian theory today.

F. Conclusion

One major objective of this book is to acquaint readers with the central differences of the two dominant economic theories in the world today. Another equally important objective is to aid readers in reaching their own conclusions about the context and consequences of these theories. Depending on which one you find convincing, your understanding of economics will be influenced in one direction or another. In turn, how you understand economics will necessarily influence your general beliefs about the world and your actions in the world. In short, your theory matters tangibly in terms of your conversations and other actions day by day.

Our concluding chapter will therefore seek to present some of the different consequences—in terms of people's general beliefs and actions—that flow from one theory as opposed to those that emanate from the other. Our premise is that you will be concerned to know how the differences in theory explained in this book make a difference in daily life. We can assure you at this point that they make significant differences indeed.

G. Suggested Readings

Althusser, Louis. *Reading "Capital."* London: New Left Books, 1975.

A leading modern Marxian theorist examines the specific originality and social implications of Marx's theory.

Dobb, Maurice. *Studies in the Development of Capitalism.* New York: International Publishers, 1947.

An examination, using Marxian theory, of the transition from feudalism to capitalism in Europe. Suggests linkages between social changes and developments in the way people theorized about those changes.

Foucault, Michel. *The Archaeology of Knowledge.* New York: Harper and Row, 1976.

A modern non-Marxian philosopher examines the basic ways in which theories differ from and contradict one another.

Godelier, Maurice. *Rationality and Irrationality in Economics.* New York: Monthly Review Press, 1972.

An original attempt to think through the basic differences among economic systems and to connect them to the basic differences among economic theories.

Hilton, Rodney, ed. *The Transition from Feudalism to Capitalism.* London: Verso, 1978.

A collection of famous essays by economists and historians examining the transition in Europe, its causes and its social effects.

Kuhn, Thomas S. *The Structure of Scientific Revolutions.* Chicago: University of Chicago Press, 1962.

To date, the most famous and influential American study of what scientific theories are and how they change and clash across history.

McCloskey, Donald N. *The Rhetoric of Economics.* Madison: University of Wisconsin Press, 1985.

A contemporary demonstration, by an American neoclassical economist, of the ways in which economic theories are complex efforts to persuade people and shape the course of social change.

Rorty, Richard. *Philosophy and the Mirror of Nature.* Princeton: Princeton University Press, 1979.

A modern non-Marxian American philosopher's demonstration that all theories are alternative ways of seeing and understanding the world, rather than more or less adequate "mirrors" of reality.

2 Neoclassical Theory

A. The Neoclassical Tradition

What is neoclassical theory? The purpose of this chapter is to provide an answer to this question. We intend to present the logical structure of neoclassical theory in terms of the three indices discussed in chapter 1. We will proceed in a parallel fashion for Marxian theory in chapter 3. This chapter begins by specifying neoclassical theory's conceptual point of entry—namely, the unique concepts it recognizes as the focus and starting point of its analysis of society. Next, it discusses neoclassical theory's logic, the reductionist method it deploys to link its entry-point concepts to all the other ideas contained within its theoretical structure. Finally, it examines what that theory produces, its unique analysis of the objects with which it is concerned.

In presenting the overall structure of neoclassical theory, we have assumed that our readers are basically familiar with the theory's specific parts, typically those covered in an introductory economics text. Our intention in this chapter is not to teach or even review the components of neoclassical theory—the analytics and derivation of supply and demand, the income determination model, and so forth. Rather, it is to discuss the overall structure and logic of the theory.

This task is often neglected in introductory neoclassical textbooks. Too often the writers of such texts proceed like a sophisticated French chef who assembles all the specific ingredients of a rich meal, but then fails to combine them into a fully cooked dinner. We have assumed that our readers are familiar with the appropriate ingredients of neoclassical theory, but that no one has yet carried out the last, crucial step of combining. We expect, as in any prepared meal, that the fully cooked outcome will be very different from its uncooked individual parts. We aim to present a prepared meal, neoclassical theory, and then to compare it to a very differently prepared dinner, Marxian theory. We will then have established one of the key conditions for discussing, in the final chapter of this book, the interesting question of how and why one theory may taste better than the other.

A.1. Neoclassical Theory's Contributions

The originality of neoclassical theory lies in its notion that innate human nature determines economic outcomes. According to this notion, human beings possess within their own given natures the inherent rational and productive abilities to produce the maximum wealth possible in a society. What is required is a set of societal institutions that will permit this inner human essence to work itself out to the greatest happiness of the greatest number. Capitalism is thought to be the one type of society which provides these institutions. It best conforms to human nature; it is the proper societal reflection of private rationality and technology.

The writings of both the early classical and the later neoclassical economists focused on and underscored this key idea. For the readers of Adam Smith, the new spokesman for and advocate of capitalism in 1776, it was a revolutionary idea, for capitalism was still struggling against a declining but powerful noncapitalist set of social institutions and ways of thinking. Smith's notion that maximum wealth for the society corresponded to the maximum freedom given to each individual to pursue his or her own economic self-interest was, to say the least, startling. Indeed, over two hundred years later, it still seems to be a shocking and radical idea.

Classical economists explored and pushed this idea. On the one hand, the long transition from feudalism to capitalism in England had created new social conditions that demanded a new theory to explain them. New ideas were needed to explain what determined the value of the wealth that was being turned out in ever-increasing quantities by the growing industrial factories. New ideas were required to explain the distribution of wealth among those who were thought to be responsible for its production. Ideas had to be created to explain how such a productive economic system could be reproduced and extended. And ideas were needed to explain and deal in one way or another with the seemingly continual and increasingly dangerous cycles exhibited by this new wage-labor, profit-seeking society. The early classical writers responded to the pressures of the times. They addressed the issues of their day, which, for them, demanded not only these new explanations but also new policies: Why was free trade better than restricted trade between nations? Why were the monopolies granted by governments to merchant companies destructive to growth? Why should guild restrictions on craft production give way to individuals' producing and selling whatever the market would bear?

On the other hand, these new ideas helped introduce and shape the complex ways in which the newly emerging industrial capitalists and wage laborers understood and related to one another. They acted in part to shape the way the state related to enterprises and households in society. In other words, these ideas of the classical writers helped create, but also changed, the very capitalist society to which they were responding.

A principal aim of first the classical and then the neoclassical analysis of society was to demonstrate how capitalism could reach its potential only if all economic and noneconomic barriers to private wealth maximization were removed. Even for some of classical and neoclassical theory's severest critics, such as John Maynard Keynes (1883–1946), the goal remained the removal of obstacles (in Keynes's case the obstacle was a lack of effective demand) that prevented and distorted this maximizing behavior. It took a very different kind of critic—Marx—and a very different kind of theory—Marxism—to fundamentally challenge the classical and neoclassical economists' common essentialization of the human subject and the institutions understood to be created by human subjects.

A.2. Neoclassical Theory since Adam Smith

When Adam Smith died in 1790, no country in the world had yet become a fully capitalist society. England, however, was well on the road to capitalism and would be followed after the 1850s by the countries of Western Europe, by the United States, and by Japan. Neoclassical political economy grew rapidly in all these countries, extending its theory to groups and issues the two most famous classical economists, Adam Smith (1723–1790) and David Ricardo (1772–1823), had barely mentioned. Neoclassical analysis of consumer choice, the behavior of firms, income distribution, business cycles, market structures, general equilibrium, foreign trade, growth, and development led to lively debates. In time, of course, such analysis and debates changed neoclassical theory. Indeed, classical political economy gave way to neoclassical theory as it extended its ideas to explain how human choice (preferences) is an essential determinant of the value and distribution of commodities in a capitalist society. And, in fact, neoclassical theory eventually gave way to different kinds of neoclassical theories.

The depression of the 1930s dealt a major blow to neoclassical theory. For perhaps the first time, neoclassical economists were not confident that the theory that had developed over the previous one hundred fifty years adequately explained current economic behavior in the capitalist economies. They feared that the only solution this by now well-developed theory could offer to the depression was to allow the markets to self-correct themselves. Moreover, it seemed that the market solution, even if it was viable, would come too late to save capitalism. The immediate danger was that of a social revolution by the unemployed, the poverty stricken, and the generally disillusioned individuals in society. Into these dangerous times for capitalism and neoclassical theory stepped John Maynard Keynes, who was an important neoclassical economist in his own right.

Keynes attempted two things: to extend neoclassical theory to explain why the operation of markets alone would not end the depression, and, most important, to offer a way to end it without destroying capitalism in the process. However, extending the theory in this way also altered it, as Keynes himself well recognized. Therefore, the changes introduced into the theory divided neoclassical economics into two more or less distinct parts: a microeconomic part often referred to as that branch of economic theory developed in the spirit of Smith, Ricardo, Leon Walras (1834-1910), and Alfred Marshall (1842-1924), and a macroeconomic part typically called, after the economist who did the most to develop it, Keynesian economics.

A.3. Which Economic Theory Shall We Present?

To present an economic theory that somehow encompassed all variations within the neoclassical and Keynesian traditions would be an overwhelming task. Yet to present only one approach from each would be to invite the criticism that we have ignored viable alternatives.

Nonetheless, we have chosen to follow the latter course. Only one version of neoclassical theory and one of Keynesian theory will be presented. They are the approaches with which we feel most comfortable because we have found them to be the most persuasive and coherent, especially as alternatives to Marxian theory. They are also fairly representative of the approaches that have been taught in most micro- and macroeconomics textbooks in the last twenty years or so. And this last consideration is of some importance to us since we intend for this chapter on neoclassical theory to serve as an overall view of the theory our readers have already encountered in an introductory course on neoclassical economics.

B. Market Values: The Analytics of Supply and Demand

Let us begin where most introductory economics courses start after the usual initial lectures preparing the students for what is to come. The first set of questions—and these are not minor questions—often asked by neoclassical economists concern the value of produced things and resources in society. More specifically, What determines the values, the prices, of goods and services produced by human beings? What determines the values of the owned resources that are necessary to produce these goods and services?

The economist asks for an explanation of why we must part with money to acquire produced things and resources and why some of these things and resources require us to part with more money than do others. Why does an apple cost money, and, typically, why does it cost less than an automobile? Why does the performance of work command a wage? Why is the reward for work different from that for savings? What explains the origin of profit in society?

Parallel to all questions asked by individuals about their social and natural environments, these economic questions require some kind of a theory in order to be answered. As we pointed out in chapter 1, to answer any question about the world—in this case the economic world—is to deploy some theory. To answer these particular value questions, we need a theory of value or price.

Neoclassicals provide one theory: the neoclassical theory of value, which produces its unique answers. In contrast, Marxists provide their contending Marxian theory of value, which produces its particular answers. These are two radically different theories of value and thus produce different answers to the same economic question asked about society.

Typically, the neoclassical answer to these value questions and, indeed, to almost all neoclassical questions involves the specification and use of what might be called market analysis. Markets are considered to be locations or sites in society where values are determined. As you likely already know from your neoclassical text, one of the first and most important devices of neoclassical market analysis is the graph depicting supply-and-demand schedules. These schedules are taken to reflect the behavior of individual buyers (agents of demand) and individual sellers (agents of supply) who interact with one another in and through these markets. The interactions of these buyers and sellers determine the market prices of whatever they buy and sell.

Figure 2.1 depicts the demand behavior of all buyers as Σd (where Σ signifies the summation of all the individual demands, d) and the supply behavior of all sellers as Σs (where Σ signifies the summation of all the individual sellers, s). The interaction of buyers and sellers determines the price of the commodity, $\hat{p}$. We may say, then, that $\hat{p}$ is the neoclassical economists' answer to the question of what will be the specific price for this commodity. We now know how much this commodity is worth, according to this particular theory of price.

This is as good a place as any to explain our use of mathematical graphs and equations to present neoclassical theory. There is certainly no necessity to use mathematics. Everything argued by neoclassical

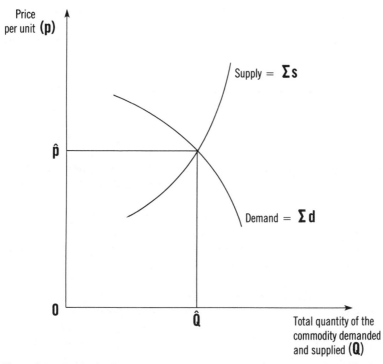

Figure 2.1.   Determination of price by market actions of demanders and suppliers.

economists could be explained just as clearly and logically without it. However, mathematics has become the preferred language of modern neoclassical economics, and therefore it seems appropriate to use some of its language to convey its structure.

Beginning with a few essential ideas about human nature, and on the basis of a few simple rules of mathematics, neoclassical theorists have been able to construct a deductive knowledge of some complexity and power. Their basic mathematical reasoning involves what is typically called the "constrained-maximization problem": it is assumed to be in the nature of each human being to maximize his or her pleasure, subject to some societal constraint. The language of geometry is used repeatedly to express this idea throughout the different parts of the theory. Once its key location within the logic of that theory is understood, the use of math is less of a problem for students of economics, and the basic message of neoclassical theory becomes more apparent.

It is interesting, of course, to consider why neoclassical economists prefer and emphasize mathematical formulations. Part of the answer lies no doubt in the deductive logic deployed in the theory. The language of mathematics, especially the use of geometry in the neoclassical argument, lends itself to this form of reasoning. Another part of the answer has to do with the desire of neoclassicals to bestow on economics the aura of Science and Truth. Moreover, we think a similar motivation also exists for many modern Marxists: like the neoclassicals, they too make much use of mathematics, and they too desire the status of Science and Truth for their economics.

Since the "hard" natural sciences link precision and accuracy to mathematics and they are the most respected disciplines in this century, neoclassical and to a degree Marxian economics have always sought to be like them. An equally important part of the answer, therefore, is the neoclassical and Marxian economists' aim to establish their respective theory as more than just one of several alternatives appealing to the public. Neoclassicals and Marxists have used mathematics to suggest that their theory has the force of mathematical necessity. They have presented their propositions mathematically to suggest that their truth is incontrovertible, rather like the claim that $2 + 2 = 4$. They have then extended this idea to suggest that support of any other theory is a matter of gross error, rather like claiming that $2 + 2 \neq 4$. In any case, we use mathematics in this and the next chapter in recognition of its basic place in neoclassical economics and its increasingly important place in Marxian economics, not to endorse the claims that it is the absolutely necessary Truth about economics.

To neoclassical economists, the mathematical analysis of markets focuses on the behavior of those agents who relate to one another by offering to sell and/or buy privately owned goods, services, and resources. The neoclassical answers to our earlier questions now follow directly. The prices of all produced things and resources are determined by the market supply of and demand for them. In turn, this market behavior emanates from the agents of supply (sellers or producers) and demand (buyers). Indeed, market values and the amount of goods, services, and resources produced and sold are understood by neoclassical economists only in relation to this supply-and-demand analysis and thus to the underlying behavior of these individual agents. We may conclude, therefore, that the geometrical analytics of supply and demand is really a kind of shorthand way of discussing a rather complex relationship that exists in society between human beings who at any given moment may confront one another as potential buyers (agents of demand) or sellers (agents of supply).

Apples cost money, then, because of the peculiar interaction of the demand for and supply of apples. Automobiles cost a different amount of money than do apples because of the specifically different supply-and-demand interactions that determine their value.

Laborers receive wages because of the unique demand for and supply of that which they produce and sell, their ability to work. Savers obtain interest or profit from supplying their savings because of the unique demands for and supplies of such savings. Finally, laborers receive a different amount of money than do savers because of the different supply-and-demand configurations that characterize each of these resource markets.

We now have a partial definition of the neoclassical theory of value: a neoclassical theory of value is a neoclassical theory of supply-and-demand behavior. The definition is incomplete, however, because neoclassical theory then asks what exactly causes that behavior. What determines the supply-and-demand behavior of individual human agents?

B.1. The Determinants of Supply and Demand

To answer this question, neoclassical theory goes one step further: it focuses attention on what it believes to be the underlying forces that ultimately shape the behavior of market agents. Its most important hypothesis is that observed market prices are really the outcome of a less obvious, but far more fundamental, interaction between the wants and productive abilities of these human agents. One of its major tasks becomes the demonstration of precisely how the basic underlying wants and productive abilities of human beings ultimately govern, via supply and demand, the determination of market prices. Simply stated, the neoclassical hypothesis holds that the value of all goods, services, and resources is caused by the interaction between human beings' wants and productive abilities.

Put this way, the reductionist logic of neoclassical theory becomes evident in its explanation (i.e., theory) of value. In the first instance, value is caused or determined by the agents of demand and supply. The theory then "looks" behind these agents' market schedules (i.e., their market behavior) to discover the forces that ultimately cause their behavior. A neoclassical theory of value becomes, then, in the last instance, a theory of these forces: the wants and productive abilities of human beings, the individuals who act out their market roles as demanders and suppliers of goods, services, and resources. The logic runs as follows: price is first reduced to individuals' supply-and-demand behavior; then this behavior is reduced to individuals' wants and productive abilities.

Is there a next step? In other words, are there additional forces that determine these wants and abilities? The neoclassicals' answer is no. These wants and abilities are assumed to be the final causal determinants of supply-and-demand behavior and thus of value. One might think of them as the ultimate building blocks of economic behavior. What the neoclassical economist has discovered in these forces are essences. They are the source of effects on other variables (market prices, quantities of goods produced and sold, etc.), but are not themselves affected by these other variables. Individual wants and productive abilities exist as the essential or absolute forces that generate all other economic events, such as demands, supplies, and prices.

Of course, the tastes and productive abilities of human beings may change. Neoclassical theory assumes, however, that such changes are caused by noneconomic factors: factors exogenous to whatever economic variables neoclassical theory focuses on. So, for example, a change in prices or incomes cannot cause a change in tastes or productive abilities. Neoclassical causality runs in only one direction: from individual wants and productive abilities to the rest of the economy. This unidirectional causality is precisely what makes those wants and abilities the essences of economic life for neoclassical theory.

We are now in a position to give a preliminary description of the overall structure and logic of neoclassical theory. Its starting point involves our specifying concepts of human tastes and productive abilities. The notion of tastes or wants is equivalent to what the theory calls the "preferences" or "choices" of human beings. The notion of productive abilities is further discussed in terms of two other related concepts: the production function (the technology of production), and the productive resources (land, labor, machinery, etc.) available to individuals in a society. These three concepts taken together—individual tastes (preferences), the production function, and individual resource endowments— form neoclassical theory's conceptual point of entry. However, they form more than just a way to begin theorizing about the economy. They are also understood in this theory to characterize essential attributes of human beings. The entry point of neoclassical theory is an essentialized one. In stark contrast, the contending Marxian theory will pose not only a completely different point of entry but a nonessentialist one at that.

Neoclassical theory's essentialism means that the three concepts of human tastes, productive technology, and resource endowments generate all the other economic concepts—supply, demand, and price—to which the theory addresses itself. The logic and goal of the theory is to deduce these secondary concepts—supply, demand, price—from those ideas which are taken to be the most fundamental of all—namely, human tastes and productive abilities. Deduction, or what in this book we call "reductionism," is the logic of neoclassical theory. As we will see, this kind of logic is very different from that of Marxian theory.

We can now say that although neoclassical theory does give a special analytical location to markets, it is never satisfied with merely a supply-

and-demand answer to price determination. It cannot be, because market behavior is not understood to be the ultimate cause of price. In other words, supply and demand are not independent and self-reproducing wholes. Their actions are determined by something outside of them. That is why a further reduction of supply and demand becomes necessary, so that the theory can get at that "something." When neoclassical theory finally arrives at individuals' tastes and productive abilities, it has reached the most basic analytical level possible: microeconomics. By definition, it cannot reduce these concepts to anything else. Hence, it has its final and complete answer to the question of price determination.

B.2. Markets, Private Property, Conservatives, and Liberals

Before we begin to discuss exactly how human wants and productive abilities act together to determine prices, we need to comment on one additional feature of the role of markets within neoclassical theory's overall structure. We can get at this best by asking a simple question of the theory: Why do markets play such an important role within the theory? After all, one could easily argue that the history of human beings has witnessed, and still does witness, many societies in which markets do not exist to any significant extent. Some of these so-called nonmarket societies may even have existed for a longer period than market societies. It is therefore likely that the importance of markets to neoclassical theory has little to do with their quantitative importance in the long history of societies. Rather, their special place within that theory has more to do with a quite remarkable insight of one of the founders and most important contributors to what would eventually become neoclassical theory.

Some two hundred years ago, Adam Smith theorized that if a society allowed its citizens the freedom to compete in all markets, then that society would make more wealth available to its citizens than if it did not permit such behavior. If wealth became the measure of the economic progress of a society's citizens and if maximum wealth became the objective of the society, then achieving that objective would necessarily require the establishment of competitive markets. Thus the idea of competitive markets became a key concept first in Smith's classical theory of political economy and later in neoclassical economic theory.

According to neoclassical economic theory, capitalist societies are societies that establish and protect two key institutions. The first is private property: each citizen has the power freely to own, buy, or sell his or her resources and produced goods. The second is a system of fully competitive markets: no citizen has any power to control prices, and all buyers and sellers take market prices as facts on which to base their decisions. When both institutions exist, a society has what is typically called a "private enterprise market economy." Following Smith's insight, that society also has in place the conditions for something more: the achievement of maximum wealth. In other words, capitalism allows and encourages the citizens of a society to reach their maximum production and consumption potential. Thus, given these citizens' tastes and productive abilities, markets and private property offer citizens the optimum opportunity to gain the maximum wealth possible.

This conclusion of neoclassical theory is so powerful and provocative that economists have been arguing for many years about its precise meaning and consequences. For example, there is a group of economists—likely a minority group—who have been unhappy with some of the social effects of private property. This particular institution is understood by them to produce unequal distributions of wealth and power among the citizenry. For that reason, they sometimes advocate keeping the institution of competitive markets (which is still thought to permit the achievement of maximum wealth) while abolishing private property (which causes the unequal distribution of that wealth). Such a changed society may be called "noncapitalist," "mixed," or perhaps even "socialist," because it has lost one of the definitive characteristics of capitalism—namely, private property.

A different group, encompassing the vast majority of neoclassical economists, defends and argues for both institutions. These neoclassicals often insist that private property and competitive markets are mutually supportive of one another. Thus, to eliminate the institution of private property—in the hope of achieving a more equitable distribution of wealth in society—is, in their view, also to jeopardize the competitive market structure that allowed the maximum wealth to be achieved in the first place.

Despite their differences, both groups of economists affirm the importance of markets as vehicles that allow and facilitate the citizens' achievement of maximum wealth. In other words, when markets perform properly, a society is efficient: it produces as much as possible with its limited resources. It follows that imperfections in markets, whatever their source, may prevent a society from achieving its maximum wealth production and consumption. Neoclassical theory recognizes a major economic problem in the existence of market imperfections in modern societies.

Neoclassical theory also proposes solutions to this problem. At one extreme are the economists we will call "neoclassical conservatives." They think the best solution is to protect the institution of private property from those who would reform, regulate, or destroy it, and to do this by leaving competitive markets alone. They argue that most market imperfections are caused by the quite visible interference of human beings and bureaucracies in the workings of supply and demand. In their view, efforts to reform or modify private property and competitive markets are inherently wrong, since they create the very barriers to maximum wealth—the market imperfections—that are the problem in the first place. Leave buyers and sellers alone, they insist; let them pursue their own self-interest in free markets and work out individually their desires, wishes, and abilities to produce. Then all citizens will be better off. These economists warrant the label "conservative" because they want to conserve from change those institutions which define a society as "capitalist" and which encourage maximum wealth for its citizens.

At the other extreme of neoclassical theory are the economists we will call "neoclassical liberals." They believe that the best solution to the problem of market imperfections is for some individuals and institutions to intervene in these imperfect markets to get them to work properly. Market imperfections are understood to flow partly from the very nature of buyers and sellers themselves. The only way to compensate for this imperfection in human nature is to intervene so as to get the market to work properly. To leave the market alone, as the conservatives would have it, is to allow this imperfection to continue and thus to prevent society from reaching its maximum point of efficiency in generating wealth.

The minority of economists mentioned earlier who criticize the role of private property in society would certainly belong to this liberal camp. They might advocate not only the nationalization of property but also the planning of markets by some state body. Such economists would form a kind of left wing within this liberal camp. Most other neoclassical liberal economists would rarely embrace these proposals, but they would argue for some kind of state intervention in society to eliminate or at least lessen the impact of imperfections that block the proper workings of markets.

It would not be surprising to find most economists holding first one position along this spectrum and then, at a different moment, another. Indeed, most neoclassical economists often hold the conservative and liberal positions simultaneously: the conservative one in regard to what are called microissues and the liberal one with respect to macroissues. In fact, this seemingly contradictory position has in part stimulated still other neoclassical economists to try to reconcile the conservative and liberal positions into some kind of neoclassical synthesis.

What is rarely challenged by either conservative or liberal economists, however, is the place and importance given to markets within their theory. The schedules of supply and demand are either considered to be working properly, thereby providing the proper incentives to individuals, or are thought not to be working smoothly, thus creating barriers to individuals' decision-making. In either case, neoclassical discussion and debate always focus on the proper operation of markets, of supply and demand, as *the* way for citizens of any society to achieve the maximum wealth possible with any given technology.

B.3. Preferences: Determining the Demand for Commodities

Forming neoclassical theory's starting and organizing point of entry are the concepts of human preferences (tastes or wants) and of the productive abilities and resources that constrain those preferences. In the following sections, we intend to show how these concepts separately and together act to determine supply-and-demand behavior and thus the value of all wealth in society, including the value of its resources. We will begin with human preferences.

Neoclassical theorists recognize in society one particular aspect of human nature which they take to be one of the essential determinants of economic actions. They assume that it is part of the nature of human beings to be able to make rational choices or decisions in regard to all economic opportunities. For our purposes here, we will be concerned only with individuals' decisions in regard to their final demand for goods and services, and their supply of resources to the production process. In both cases, we will see the essentialistic role played by preferences in helping to cause these particular demand-and-supply behaviors.

Given the importance of a point of entry to any theory, it is not surprising that neoclassical theorists have made vast efforts over the years to refine their understanding of human preferences. That understanding is founded on some basic assumptions. We will not here attempt a full explanation of them, but we will describe in a general way what assumptions are involved in this particular part of neoclassical theory's point of entry.

We would first remind our readers that any theory is merely a series of assumptions (including, obviously, the initial ones, which produce a theory's conceptual entry point) linked together by some assumed logic. As we will see in chapter 3, Marxian theory's entry-point concept involves a different set of initial assumptions compared to those presented here. The difference in initial assumptions will help us distinguish one theory from another. That is why gaining a general understanding of first the neoclassical entry-point assumptions and then the Marxian ones is an important part of analyzing theoretical differences.

The first assumption made by neoclassical theorists concerns the inherent ability of each and every individual in society to rank order in a consistent way all conceivable combinations of goods and services with which they may be confronted, whether now or in the future. In other words, it is taken to be part of our human nature that we are able to express some form of preference or ordering between, say, any two bundles of goods, and that the expressed ordering is made in a consistent way. Each and every individual is assumed to be able to express a preference for one basket of goods over another or to be indifferent between them. Moreover, this expression of choice is assumed to be transitive in nature, which means simply that if an individual chooses basket A over B, and B over C, then he or she will also choose A over C.

Another key initial assumption about human nature is that everyone always wants or prefers more rather than less of any good or service. This is sometimes referred to as the assumption of nonsatiation. Still other assumptions are perhaps less easy to understand, but they are just as crucial to the neoclassical conception of a rational, choice-making individual. One such assumption concerns how individuals will substitute one good for another while maintaining the same total level of satisfaction from consuming both. The assertion here is that as an individual gives up successive units of one of the goods, he or she must increase the quantity of the other good consumed in order to maintain the same total level of satisfaction. This assumption is often referred to in the neoclassical literature as the "diminishing marginal rate of substitution" between two goods. It asserts that the psychological ability or willingness of a human being to give up a unit of one good for another falls as more units are given up. As the good being given up becomes relatively more important, its loss is offset only by an ever-increasing number of units of the good that is being gained. There are other, more technical assumptions, such as that of continuity, which need not concern us here.

We may think of all these assumptions as both defining and revealing to neoclassical observers one particular aspect of human nature— namely, its rationality. Another part of our rationality is the drive to take maximum advantage of our opportunities. Each person, regardless of circumstance, is assumed to conform to this neoclassical view of rationality: we are all rationally motivated, choice-making machines.

What determines this rationality of human nature? The neoclassicals answer this question by dismissing it as pointless. Rationality is understood to be among the most basic components of human nature. Of course, rational preferences may change—just as human nature may change—but they do not change because of some change in the economy. In other words, preferences are understood to be the origin of economic changes, not vice versa. Changes in prices or incomes in a market economy do not cause changes in preferences; they are caused by them. If and when preferences change, they do so for non- or extraeconomic reasons—for example, as a result of biological or cultural changes.

From these few but powerful assumptions about human nature, neoclassical theorists derive an analytical device and use it to examine and even to predict economic choice in society. This device is a set of preference or indifference curves that represent for each and every individual in society his or her tastes or wants for all conceivable commodities. Figure 2.2 illustrates such curves. Advanced economics texts demonstrate how the existence and specific properties of these curves follow directly from assumptions about human nature by making the following basic arguments: (1) that this map of human rationality exists once we assume the inherent ability of all individuals to rank order all conceivable bundles of commodities; (2) that movements in a northeasterly direction, to higher preference curves, represent an individual's attainment of higher levels of satisfaction (derived from the assumption of

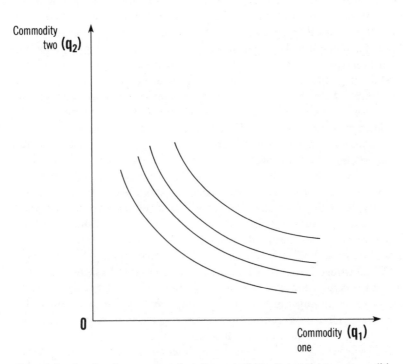

Figure 2.2.   Set of preference curves depicting an individual's taste for two commodities, q_1 and q_2.

nonsatiation); (3) that all curves are negatively sloped (also derived from the assumption of nonsatiation); (4) that there are no sharp jumps or gaps in the curves (following from the technical assumption of continuity); (5) that the curves do not touch or intersect (derived from the assumption of consistent behavior); and (6) that all curves are convex to the point of origin (following from the assumption of a diminishing marginal rate of substitution).

Preference curves are used within neoclassical theory to help explain almost all of the economic choices we make as individuals, including the demand for and supply of all commodities and resources in the economy. The powerful explanatory role of these curves should not be surprising, given the essentialist logic of neoclassical theory. It is precisely the nature of a theoretical essence that it ultimately governs the actions of all other entities treated in the theory.

Neoclassical theory now adds some additional information (i.e., assumptions). Suppose that in a society each individual's income is known, and, in addition, suppose that each individual accepts the prices of commodities as given. In other words, each person has a given sum of money and faces desired commodities over whose prices he or she has no influence. The latter assumption is equivalent to assuming perfectly competitive markets: no single individual in society has any power over price because all individuals, acting together via the market, determine price. We will return to the subject of competitive markets later in this chapter.

With this added information about incomes and prices, neoclassical theory can construct one of its most important diagrams to explain the demand behavior of individuals. Figure 2.3 poses a fundamental neoclassical problem: Individuals' wants are assumed to be *unlimited* (the assumption of nonsatiation as captured by the infinite set of indifference curves labeled, I, II, . . . , in the figure); however, the money incomes of individuals are assumed to be *limited* (as indicated by the only straight line, AB, drawn in the diagram).[1] How, then, do we as individ-

---

1. An individual's money income, y, may be spent on goods and services, $p_1 \cdot q_1 + p_2 \cdot q_2$, where p_1 and p_2 represent, respectively, the prices of the two different commodities, and q_1 and q_2 are the respective quantities of the two goods demanded. The income equation for the straight line AB in figure 2.3 becomes

$$q_2 = \frac{y}{p_2} - \frac{p_1}{p_2} \cdot q_1$$

where p_1/p_2 represents the slope of this line, or

$$\frac{\Delta q_2}{\Delta q_1} = -\frac{p_1}{p_2}.$$

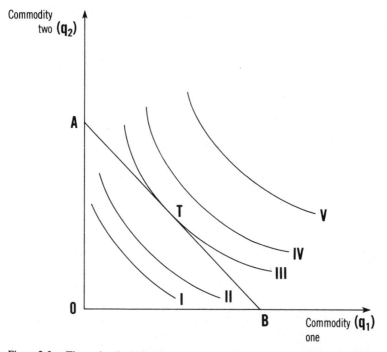

Figure 2.3.   The optimal solution for the consumer is at point T, where the highest preference curve has been reached (III) subject to the income constraint (AB). The optimal point is described in the text as $mu_1/mu_2 = p_1/p_2$.

uals solve this problem—namely, how do we bring our own wants, which are unlimited, into harmony with the limiting economic environment that confronts us?

Figure 2.3 also reveals the neoclassical solution to this essential neoclassical problem. Point T represents the best point attainable by any individual. At this point, the individual has reached the highest preference curve achievable (and thus is maximizing his or her wealth satisfaction), given the resource constraint with which that person is confronted. Point T, then, is the produced result of each individual's struggle to make the best of his or her market opportunities in order to reach the highest possible preference (satisfaction) level. This is precisely what is meant in neoclassical theory by maximizing one's opportunities—what every rational person is presumed to do.

Let us examine this solution more carefully. Neoclassical theory's solution implies its view of the fundamental struggle engaged in by all human beings. We strive to being our *private* ability to choose rationally, as dictated by our own personal nature, into harmony with our *social* ability to substitute, as dictated by the impersonal market. This struggle is necessitated by the constraint the impersonal market, the social environment we face, places on fulfilling our desires. On the one hand, the social ability to substitute is measured by the price ratio between the two commodities: p_1/p_2.[2] It is obviously the market rate, given to the individual by competition, at which one good may be exchanged for the other. On the other hand, the private ability to choose rationally is measured by the marginal rate of substitution between the two goods. It is given to the individual by his or her human nature. The ultimate objective for each individual in society is to bring these two measures into harmony with each other.

Clearly, the ability to choose rationally among commodities is understood in terms of an individual's preferences; indeed, the concept of individual preference governs human choice in neoclassical theory. Let us present the neoclassical measure of this private ability in terms of these preferences in more detail. Consider figure 2.4, where we have labeled two points A and B along the same preference curve. Relative to point A, point B indicates more q_1 and less q_2. A problem arises: How are we to compare this loss of one good with a gain in the other? Is there a unit of measure, some property, that is common to both goods which would allow us to compare this loss and gain?

Neoclassical theory's answer is yes. All commodities are conceived to be sources of satisfaction; hence our preferences for them. A typical phrase in neoclassical theory refers to commodities as sources of "utility." Utility becomes, then, a property that is assumed to be common to all commodities and that may therefore serve as a standard of comparison among them. As we will see in chapter 3, when a parallel question is asked of Marxian theory—How are we to compare the loss of one commodity with the gain of another?—a completely different answer is produced. There the common property will be something called "abstract labor time," not "utility." Each theory will thus produce its own unique standard to understand the substitution of one commodity for another.

According to the definition of a preference curve, any individual will be indifferent to different bundles of commodities along his or her curve. Thus, as seen in figure 2.4, the consumer is understood to receive the same level of satisfaction or utility at point A as at point B. Therefore, if the individual in society is to remain on the same curve, we may think of the loss in satisfaction or utility incurred by giving up some q_2 to be exactly balanced by—that is, to be equal to—the gain in satisfac-

2. This price ratio is precisely the given slope of the income equation presented in footnote 1.

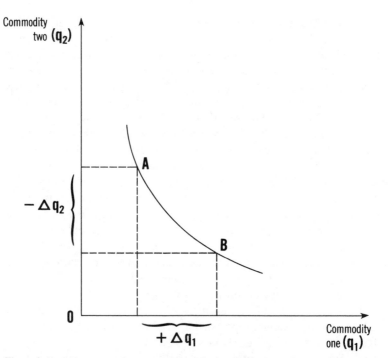

Figure 2.4.   Movements along a preference curve (from *A* to *B*) can be thought of as balancing the loss in utility with the gain in utility:

$$-\Delta q_2 \cdot mu_{q_2} = +\Delta q_1 \cdot mu_{q_1}.$$

$$\underbrace{\phantom{-\Delta q_2 \cdot mu_{q_2}}}_{\text{``loss''}} \qquad \underbrace{\phantom{+\Delta q_1 \cdot mu_{q_1}}}_{\text{``gain''}}$$

tion or utility experienced by gaining more q_1. Figure 2.4 shows the loss in q_2 as $-\Delta q_2$, the minus sign indicating that the consumer has lost some q_2. It shows the gain as $+\Delta q_1$, the plus sign indicating the consumer's additional consumption of q_1.[3] The loss in satisfaction or utility is typically written as $-\Delta q_2 \cdot mu_2$, and the gain as $+\Delta q_1 \cdot mu_1$, where mu_1 and mu_2 represent, respectively, the per unit marginal utilities of the commodities.[4] Along the same preference curve, by definition, these two terms must always equal each other: $-\Delta q_2 \cdot mu_2 = +\Delta q_1 \cdot mu_1$.

3. The notation Δ is a short-hand way of conveying a change in a variable. Thus, $-\Delta q_2$ means a decrease in the amount of q_2 consumed and $+\Delta q_1$ indicates an increase in the amount of q_1 consumed.

4. Recall that neoclassical theory considers the relevant measure of utility to be the marginal (the incremental and not the total) utility experienced by an individual when he or she consumes more or less of a commodity.

Neoclassical theory has used what it assumes to be the common property of both commodities—that they are objects of utility—as its weighting scheme (the respective marginal utilities) to understand the substitution of one commodity for the other.

We now have an exact measure of the private ability to substitute one commodity for another along any given preference curve. Solving the above equation for $\Delta q_2 / \Delta q_1$, we get

$$MRS_{12} = \frac{\Delta q_2}{\Delta q_1} = -\frac{mu_1}{mu_2},$$

where MRS_{12} stands for the marginal rate of substitution of commodity one for commodity two.

Let us recast the aforementioned neoclassical solution in these new terms. The optimal point for the individual (point T in figure 2.3) can now be written as

$$\frac{mu_1}{mu_2} = \frac{p_1}{p_2}.$$

The private ability to choose rationally among commodities, as measured by this ratio of marginal utilities, is equal to the social ability to consume, as measured by the ratio of prices. In reaching this point, the individual has acted in an efficient way in regard to consumption decisions: the best possible consumption result has been achieved given the market constraint faced.

It is but a small step to derive demand curves from figure 2.3. By continually varying the price of one of the commodities, say p_1, we can predict an individual's demand behavior—that is, what amounts of commodity one he or she would like to buy at these different prices. Figure 2.5 illustrates this procedure. In figure 2.5(a) the price of commodity one has been decreased relative to the price of commodity two; the new price lines, denoted in the figure as AC, AD, and AE, indicate the assumed decreases in the price of commodity one. As the constraint faced by the individual changes with each assumed decrease in price, ever-new points of correspondence between the private and social ability to substitute are generated. The logic of the theory that asserts this essential human struggle to achieve the highest possible level of satisfaction guarantees that these new points of correspondence will be reached.

The resulting new points of balance, or what neoclassical economists often refer to as equilibrium points, are indicated in figure 2.5(a) by the letters U, V, and W. Obviously, many such points could be produced. When all of them are connected, a price-consumption locus, denoted in

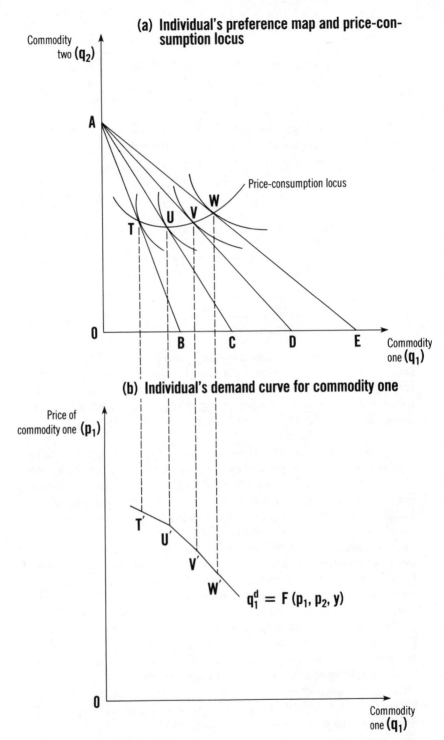

(a) Individual's preference map and price-consumption locus

Commodity two (q_2)

A

Price-consumption locus

W

U V

T

0   B   C   D   E   Commodity one (q_1)

(b) Individual's demand curve for commodity one

Price of commodity one (p_1)

T'

U'

V'

W' $q_1^d = F(p_1, p_2, y)$

0   Commodity one (q_1)

Figure 2.5. Derivation of an individual's demand curve for commodity one (*b*) from the price consumption locus of that individual (*a*).

figure 2.5(a) as TW, is constructed. Each of the equilibrium points of this locus thus represents an equality between the ratio of marginal utilities and the corresponding price ratios.

Figure 2.5(b) shows the derived demand curve for the commodity one depicted in figure 2.5(a). The horizontal axes of both figures are lined up since both measure the demand for q_1. Each point on the price-consumption locus, TW, in figure 2.5(a) is mapped onto the demand surface in figure 2.5(b). Following the dotted lines from figure 2.5(a) to figure 2.5(b), we find the points T', U', V', and W' in figure 2.5(b); these points constitute the demand curve for the commodity q_1. We know that such points must fall in a southeasterly direction because we have previously assumed a continued lower price of p_1 relative to p_2 and an increase in the demand for q_1.[5]

The well-known downward sloping demand curve for any individual is thus logically derived in figure 2.5(b). Using the same procedure, we could derive an individual's demand curve for each commodity: q_1, q_2, q_3, and so forth. By adding up such demand curves across all individuals, we could derive the aggregate demand curve for each commodity in the society (as shown in figure 2.1).

Each of these curves would be constructed from individuals' preferences and incomes and from the prices these individuals faced. The logic of the diagrams illustrates this construction: figure 2.5(b) is derived from figure 2.5(a), and figure 2.5(a) is derived from figure 2.3. In the interaction of preferences, incomes, and prices, therefore, we have a partial answer to our initial question of what determines individuals' demand for commodities. Let us examine this conclusion more closely.

For any particular individual, the prices of commodities are determined, as previously noted, by the market. Preferences are also assumed to be given, in this case by the individual's human nature. What, however, determines the individual's income?

The income of any one individual may be thought of as the wage rate earned per hour times the number of hours worked. If we let w stand for

---

5. Advanced texts in neoclassical theory show how a change in demand for any commodity can be broken down into two distinct parts: a so-called substitution effect, in which the level of utility is kept constant and a consumer is shown to move along the same preference curve in figure 2.5(a), substituting the cheapened commodity (q_1) for the other (q_2); and a so-called income effect, in which initial prices are kept constant and a consumer moves to a higher preference curve because of changed income. Neoclassical theory combines these two effects into what it typically calls the Slutsky equation. Named after the person who first published this result in 1915, the Slutsky equation is considered a fundamental rendering of the neoclassical theory of value, for its purpose is to specifically relate individuals' changed demands for commodities to their underlying preferences for those commodities.

this wage rate and h stand for the hours worked per individual, we have $y = w \cdot h$, where y represents the income earned. The total income for all individuals would then be $Y = w \cdot h \cdot L$, where L stands for the given total number of workers and Y for their aggregate wage income. To keep our focus on the core of neoclassical theory, we will make the simplifying assumption throughout that the total number of laborers is fixed while the number of labor hours they offer varies.

We may now ask what determines w and hL for workers. The answer is the aggregate demand for and the aggregate supply of labor—that is, the labor market, which is depicted in figure 2.6. Figure 2.6 demonstrates that the intersection of the total demand for and supply of labor hours determines simultaneously the wage rate for each individual (w) and the total quantity of labor hours supplied and demanded (hL). Once again recalling the logic of neoclassical theory, we may ask, What determines these particular supply-and-demand schedules and thus the income of individuals?

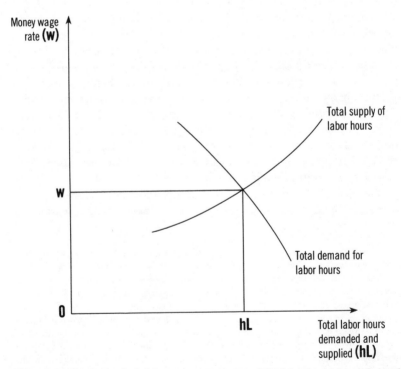

Figure 2.6. Determination of the money wage rate and the labor hours demanded and supplied in the labor market.

B.4. Preferences: Determining the Supply of Labor

According to neoclassical theory, the supply of labor hours by individuals depends on their preferences and on the given real wage rate. Neoclassicals assume that individuals spend income on commodities and that that income is derived from work—that is, from the quantity of hours allocated to work by each individual. The person who offers more hours in the labor market receives more income and can then purchase more commodities. Income provides the individual with satisfaction or utility since it is used to purchase objects of utility—that is, commodities. However, the more hours an individual offers in the labor market, the fewer hours he or she has available for leisure. Neoclassicals assume that leisure has utility for individuals just as purchased commodities do. Therefore, each individual must choose between the consumption of commodities (via offered hours of work) and the consumption of leisure.

Figure 2.7 depicts the choice between real income (the collection of commodities purchased) and leisure. Since we are endowed with only so many hours per day, we must choose between the two items of pleasure. Parallel to our previous map of preference curves, we have drawn in this

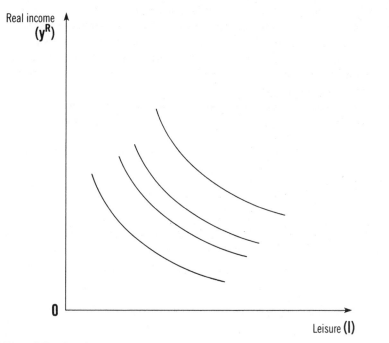

Figure 2.7.   Set of preference curves depicting an individual's taste for real income (y^R) and leisure (l).

diagram a set of curves showing the trade-off between real income and leisure. It is worth underscoring the point that all of our previous statements concerning the derivation of preference curves apply here as well. They are, as always, dictated by our human nature.

Along any given preference curve, we may calculate the individual's private substitution—that is, choice between real income and leisure. To differentiate this marginal rate of substitution from our previous one, we will use the subscripts l for leisure and y^R for real income:

$$MRS_{ly^R} = -\frac{mu_l}{mu_{y^R}},$$

where mu_l stands for the marginal utility of leisure and mu_{y^R} for the marginal utility of real income.[6]

Let us now introduce the real wage rate faced by each individual. It is determined, like all prices, by the impersonal workings of the competitive market. In this case, the question is, How many hours of labor will any individual offer, given this real wage rate and his or her preferences for leisure and real income? To discover the answer, we employ the same procedure that we used in the previous analysis of an individual's choice between any two commodities. The same theme repeats itself in a slightly different form: each individual struggles to achieve the highest preference curve possible, subject to whatever constraints are given. In this example, the goal of the individual is to maximize the satisfaction received from consuming real income and leisure, given the economic constraint of a real wage rate, which is the price of that leisure in terms of the real income forgone.

Figure 2.8 shows a real wage rate line, AX, which has been derived in the following way. Suppose that $0X$ is the total quantity of hours available for both leisure and work. It may be considered the endowment of time available to any individual. Assume, for the moment, that an individual works XX' hours (measured from X) and thus chooses $0X'$

6. This marginal rate of substitution is calculated in the same way we calculated our previous rate. Recall that along any preference curve between real income and leisure we have $-\Delta y^R \cdot mu_{y^R} = +\Delta l \cdot mu_l$, where we assume that a utility loss in real income is exactly offset by a utility gain in leisure. Solving the equation for $\Delta y^R / \Delta l$ yields

$$\frac{\Delta y^R}{\Delta l} = -\frac{mu_l}{mu_{y^R}},$$

which is our MRS_{ly^R}.

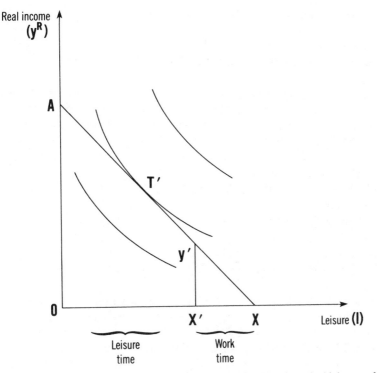

Figure 2.8. The optimal solution for a laborer is at point T', where the highest preference curve has been reached subject to the real-wage constraint. The optimal point may be described as $mu_l/\, mu_{y^R} = w^R$.

hours of leisure (measured from 0). If the individual receives a total real income of $X'y'$ dollars, then the real hourly wage rate is

$$\frac{X'y'}{X'X} = \frac{\text{real income}}{\text{number of hours worked}} = w^R,$$

where w^R stands for the real hourly wage rate.

Introduce, now, the set of preference curves from figure 2.7 into figure 2.8. Using the logic we employed in the previous section when we discovered the most efficient consumption point for the individual (point T in figure 2.3), we can write the optimal point in figure 2.8 as T'. Here the individual laborer has once again brought into harmony the private ability to choose among objects (MRS_{lyR}) with the social ability (w^R) to do so. We may write this new equilibrium situation as

$$\frac{mu_l}{mu_{y^R}} = w^R.$$

To derive the supply of labor hours from this preference map, let us first vary the real wage rate in figure 2.9(a). Suppose the real wage is increased, as indicated by the new lines *XB*, *XC*, and *XD*. New points of equilibrium are reached by the individual indicated in the diagram by the points *B*, *C*, and *D*, where once again the $MRS_{ly,R}$ is brought into equality with each new real wage rate. Connecting these equilibrium points, neoclassicals derive an individual's offer curve of labor hours (indicated in the diagram as *T'BCD*). The supply curve is derived directly from this offer curve.

Figure 2.9(b) lines up its horizontal axis with that of figure 2.9(a) such that the hours of work offered by the individual can be measured in both diagrams (reading from right to left in both). The dotted lines drawn from the offer curve in figure 2.9(a) map out the points *T"*, *B'*, *C'*, and *D'* on the indicated supply curve of labor hours in figure 2.9(b). As the real wage rate increases, the supply of labor hours rises. Simply adding up each individual's supply of labor hours at different real wage rates will generate the aggregate supply curve of labor hours in the labor market.

We have, then, the neoclassical answer to what determines the supply of the labor resource for any individual: choice between real income and leisure; the given real wage; and the given initial endowment of hours. The individual's endowment of hours (24) is as much given by nature as is the choice between income and leisure; as before, the real wage is given by the competitive market. Thus we may conclude that for any given real wage and endowment, the supply of labor is determined by human nature—an individual's preference to acquire real income via work rather than to choose leisure and no income.

B.5. Preferences and Scarcity: Determining the Demand for Labor

We now turn to neoclassical theory's explanation of the demand for this labor and, therefore, to its explanation of wage determination. Any producer's decision about how much labor to hire depends on how that labor will affect the producer's profits. For example, if additional labor adds to profits, then a decision will be made to employ more. If, however, additional labor reduces profits, then the opposite decision will be made.

For any given cost of that labor—that is, wage rate—neoclassical theory recognizes two factors that affect the decision to hire and the impact of that decision on profits. Those factors are the marginal productivity of the additional hired labor (the extra commodity output it will produce), and the price of the extra commodities. If the dollar value of the marginal product is greater than its cost (in terms of the wages

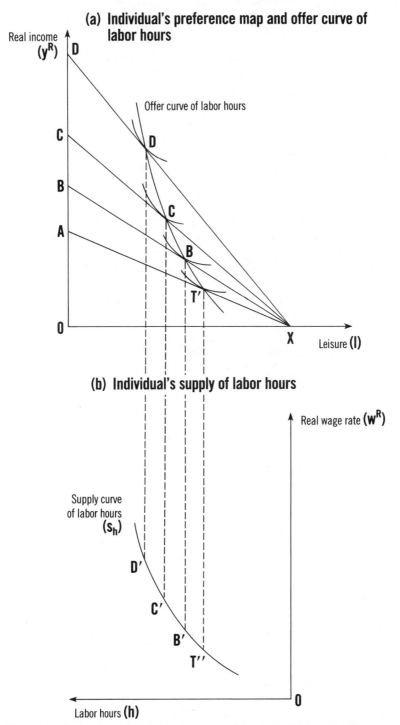

Figure 2.9. Derivation of an individual's supply of labor hours (*b*) from the offer curve of that individual (*a*).

that have to be paid to acquire it), then the labor will be employed. If the dollar value is less, the labor will not be hired. The demand for labor, then, depends on the marginal productivity of labor and the price of the output produced by that labor.

We may state the same proposition in a more formal way. Let us write for a producing firm a profit equation in which we assume for the moment that the only input and thus cost of production is labor. That profit equation would read

$$\Pi = p \cdot q - w \cdot h \cdot L,$$

where Π stands for the firm's profits, p for the price of the commodity being produced and sold, q for the quantity of the commodity produced, and w for the money wage, and where L and h have already been defined. The equation states simply that profits equal total revenues ($p \cdot q$) minus total wage costs ($w \cdot h \cdot L$).

Now let us see what would happen to this profit equation if the quantity of labor hours changed. Before we write down a new equation, however, we need to recall that each producer is assumed to have no power over commodity prices or wage rates. The competitive market gives all output and input prices to each producer. Therefore, in the above profit equation, p and w will not change when the producer produces and sells more output resulting from the assumed purchase of more labor input. Keeping this in mind, the new profit equation becomes

$$\Delta\Pi = \bar{p} \cdot \Delta q - \bar{w} \cdot \Delta h \cdot L,$$

where Δ indicates a change in the appropriate variable and the overbar in $\bar{p}$ and $\bar{w}$ indicates that these variables do not change because of any producer's decision to hire more labor.

To derive the final impact of the changed labor hours on the firm's profits, divide both sides of the profit equation by ΔhL:

$$\frac{\Delta\Pi}{\Delta hL} = \bar{p} \cdot \frac{\Delta q}{\Delta hL} - \bar{w}.$$

If $\Delta\Pi/\Delta hL$ is positive, then clearly an increase in the demand for labor will add to profits. In this case, the dollar value of the marginal product ($\bar{p} \cdot \Delta q/\Delta hL$) is greater than its cost ($\bar{w}$). If, however, $\Delta\Pi/\Delta hL$ is negative, then the additional labor will not be hired. The dollar value of the marginal product is less than the money wage. Only when the given money wage rate ($\bar{w}$) is equal to $\bar{p} \cdot \Delta q/\Delta hL$ will the firm neither gain nor lose profits by expanding or contracting its demand for labor. At that point, it will have maximized its assumed objective—namely its profits.

Clearly, the above profit equation demonstrates that the output price (p) and the marginal productivity of labor ($\Delta q/\Delta hL$) together determine the demand for labor. For this reason neoclassical economists often refer to the *derived* demand for labor, the demand derived from these two variables. The next logical question then becomes, What governs the price and the marginal productivity from which the labor demand is derived?

Let us begin with price. As we have already noted, price is derived from market competition and given to each producer. This means that the amount of a commodity that each producer sells depends only on the demand of consumers for that commodity. The more consumers demand, the more each producer can sell. Consequently, a rise in consumer demand will have a positive effect on a producer's demand for labor.

Recall that for any given wage income and price, the preferences of each individual determine the demand for commodities. Therefore, the demand for labor is, in part, ultimately derived from consumer preferences for the commodity produced by that labor. Once again this particular neoclassical essence makes its powerful presence felt, this time in the labor market.

The number of labor hours hired also depends on the productive abilities of that labor. In turn, the latter depends on whatever skills labor is endowed with and on the availability of other resources and technologies with which that labor can be combined. Typically, a greater amount of other resources per worker produces a higher marginal productivity of workers and thus a demand-for-labor curve that is further from the origin (in a northeasterly direction) shown in figure 2.6. The demand for labor is also affected by the degree to which other resources can be easily substituted for the labor resource. If, for example, other resources are a good substitute for labor, then the demand-for-labor curve in figure 2.6 will be relatively more elastic than it would be if they were not. Thus, both the position and the shape of the demand-for-labor curve depend on available resource endowments, including the technology that is available to produce output, and on the given ability of these producing units to combine together the available resources to produce outputs.

The latter ability of individuals is captured in what neoclassical theorists call a "production function." For any given technology, the production function is the relationship between the quantity of input resources and the maximum quantity of outputs obtainable with those inputs. Its theoretical location within neoclassical theory is as important as the already discussed preference function relating quantities of consumption-inputs to the output-pleasure produced. Both functions act as powerful essences within the theory and both are equally necessary to explain the ultimate determination of values in society.

The production function is sometimes referred to as a "neoclassical production function" if it satisfies certain assumed conditions. Quite parallel to the neoclassical preference function, these conditions permit this production function to exist and have certain properties that are deemed useful by neoclassical theorists. These production conditions are taken to be as natural a part of society as the conditions associated with the preference function. They are taken to be either an inherent attribute of human beings or a part of the physical nature with which we interact.

For the sake of convenience, we will assume only two inputs, labor and something called "capital." The latter will stand for the machines, tools, and other materials used in the production process. Briefly, there are several key production conditions. Both inputs, capital and labor, must be positive for output to be positive, and the more capital and labor the society has available to it, the greater the potential output will be. The marginal product of each input is positive, but this product will fall in magnitude for each input as the quantity of one increases while that of the other is held constant (texts usually refer to this property as the "natural law of diminishing marginal returns"). Thus, the marginal product of capital (labor) will approach zero as the capital (labor) resource is increased while the labor (capital) resource is held constant, and the marginal product of capital (labor) will become infinitely large as the amount of labor (capital) increases while that of capital (labor) remains constant.

Figure 2.10 depicts such a production function. It shows the relationship between real output and a variable amount of labor input when we assume a fixed input of capital.[7] The latter is denoted by $\bar{K}$ in the equation for the production function shown in the figure. The greater the number of labor hours available to produce output, the larger that output will be. However, because of neoclassical theory's "law of diminishing marginal returns," the rate of increase of output tends to fall as more labor is used. In other words, the measure of this "law," the marginal productivity of labor, falls in magnitude when labor is increased while capital is held constant. Finally, the marginal product of labor approaches zero (after point $(hL)_1$ in the figure) as we continuously expand only the labor input.

Figure 2.11 depicts the derived marginal product of the labor curve.

---

7. A similar diagram can be constructed to relate output to a variable amount of capital input with an assumed fixed input of labor.

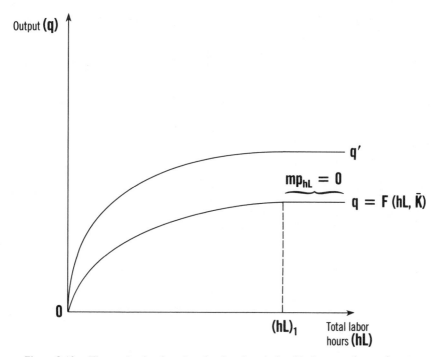

Figure 2.10. The production function showing the relationship between the maximum output (q) obtainable with the available resources: variable inputs of labor (hL) and a fixed input of capital ($\bar{K}$).

Now, an increase in the capital resource will shift both the production function and its associated marginal productivity curve upward as pictured in figures 2.10 and 2.11. An improvement in the initially given technology will do the same. Therefore, the marginal productivity of labor, including its shape and its distance from the origin, depends on both the underlying production function from which it is derived and the availability of the other resource—in this case, capital.

Paralleling our explanation of the origins of human preferences, neoclassical theory takes both this underlying production function (i.e., all of its properties) and the initial resource endowments as given. Once again we encounter the assumption that human beings are endowed not only with some initial quanta of labor and capital resources but also with an inherent technological ability to be productive (expressed metaphorically as their "production function"). We may conclude, therefore, that the marginal productivity of labor (its existence, shape, and position) is governed by these two neoclassical essences: technological and resource (input) endowments.

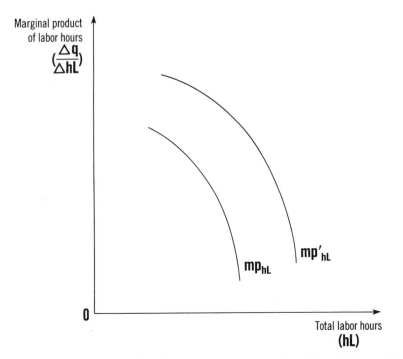

Figure 2.11.   The marginal product of labor hours derived from Figure 2.10. A shift in the curve is due to a change in the capital resource or a change in technology.

B.6. The Determination of Wages and Commodity Demands

The determination of wages follows logically from the supply and demand for labor. First, we add up all the demands for labor hours by each producing unit to derive the aggregate demand in the labor market. Next, we consider the interaction of this aggregate demand with the aggregate supply of labor hours described in the previous section. Figure 2.12 pictures the interaction of these aggregate labor market curves. Initially it might seem that the aggregate supply of and demand for labor by themselves provide the ultimate explanation for what determines wage incomes. However, that would be a superficial analysis. Looking deeper (i.e., looking at the previous figures from which figure 2.12 is derived), we see that the ultimate determinants of the market supply of and demand for labor and thus of wage incomes in society are certain underlying traits of human beings: their preferences, production functions, and resource endowments. This is precisely what has been shown in the last two sections. There is no need to look any further for explana-

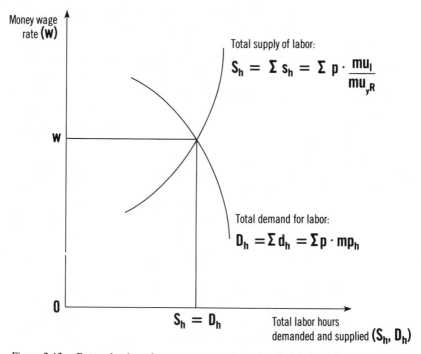

Figure 2.12. Determination of money wages and employment in the labor market as derived from the leisure–real income choice on the supply side and the marginal product of labor on the demand side.

tions, for nothing else in neoclassical theory determines these three essences. As essences in that economic theory they cause economic events but are not caused by them.

A wage income for each consumer and wage costs for each producer in society are determined ultimately by our nature as rational consumers and productive human beings. This conclusion should not be underestimated. It means, for example (barring market imperfections), that the relatively high incomes for some individuals in society can be explained on the basis of those same individuals' preference for work rather than leisure and/or on the basis of the relatively high marginal productivity of their labor. Similarly, the incomes of the poor can be explained on the basis of their choice of leisure time rather than income via work and/or on the basis of their relatively low marginal labor productivity. In either case, ruling out any market imperfections, the wage incomes of individuals in society are explained on the basis of these individuals' own human nature or the technology that is available to them. Indeed, for any given technology (i.e., for any production function and resource endowment), the relatively rich are rich because they choose to be so, while the relatively poor are poor because they choose not to be rich. Simply put, as individuals we are responsible only to ourselves for the wealth we ultimately enjoy in this world. As we will see in the next chapter, this neoclassical conclusion differs dramatically from the Marxian explanation of incomes in a society.

Now that we have considered neoclassical theory's explanation of wage determination, we may return to that theory's analysis of individual demand for different commodities. Remember that we showed how these demands were derived logically from the given preferences and wage incomes of individuals. We have just demonstrated how preferences and productive abilities determine what individuals earn as wage incomes. Therefore, adding this new information to what we already had, we may conclude that the three neoclassical essences (preferences, production functions, and endowments) govern the demand for commodities by each and every person in the society.

B.7. Preferences: Determining the Supply of Capital

In neoclassical theory, labor owners offer their privately owned labor resource to producers in return for a wage. In parallel fashion, owners of capital offer their privately owned resource to producers in return for a price or rental fee. This return, or as we will see, this rate of return, has often been called the "profit rate." It is the percentage return per unit of time earned by the owners of capital. For example, an individual might supply $1,000 worth of owned capital to a producing firm and be paid $100 a year for doing so. The rental price paid would thus be $100 a year for the use of $1,000 of capital; alternatively, the received rate of return on the capital would be 10 percent per year (10% = $100/$1,000). Producing firms must pay this rental price of $100 per year to the owners of capital in order to acquire $1,000 worth of this resource (which is assumed to be necessary for production to take place). In this sense, profits are the return on this invested capital. Profit ($100 per year, or a profit rate of 10% on $1,000 of invested capital) is the income of owners of capital who contribute it to production. From the perspective of firms, such "profits" are considered to be part of their production costs.[8]

To derive the offer curve of an individual's capital resource, we em-

---

8. The difference between the revenues earned by a firm and its total costs is sometimes referred to as short-run producer's profits. These profits will be competed away in the long run. Unless otherwise noted, we will use "profits" to mean the marginal return to capital.

ploy the procedure we used in deriving the offer curve of an individual's labor resource. Suppose that each individual in society could choose between present and future consumption of commodities. In other words, an individual might save some of his or her current income—that is, not consume all of it now—in order to make that saved income available for consumption in the future. Since we assume that both current and future consumption provide utility to individuals, each person must choose between the consumption of commodities now and consumption in the future.

Figure 2.13 depicts this choice: c_t indicates the real amount of current consumption and c_{t+1} signifies the real amount of future consumption. These preference curves satisfy all the properties previously outlined for any object of pleasure. Once again, these properties and these curves follow from neoclassical theory's conception of human nature. Along any such preference curve, we may calculate the private ability of each individual to choose between future and present consumption. To

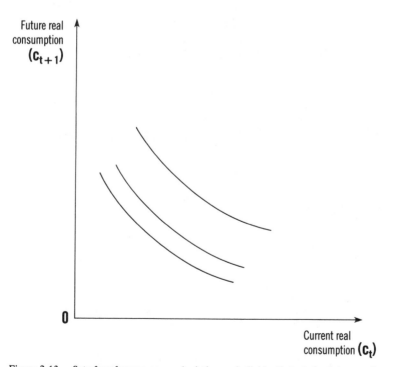

Figure 2.13.   Set of preference curves depicting an individual's taste for future real consumption (c_{t+1}) and current real consumption (c_t).

differentiate this new kind of marginal rate of substitution from previous ones, we have used the subscripts c_t and c_{t+1}. Thus we have

$$MRS_{c_t c_{t+1}} = -\frac{mu_{c_t}}{mu_{c_{t+1}}},$$

where mu_{c_t} stands for the marginal utility of present real consumption and $mu_{c_{t+1}}$ represents the marginal utility of future real consumption.[9] In the neoclassical literature, this measure has sometimes been taken to represent the personal struggle we all go through in attempting to trade off present against future consumption. In a sense, it indicates the degree of our impatience about the future consumption of objects of pleasure.

Figure 2.14 introduces an individual's given current real income as measured by $0A$. At point A, the person spends all that real income on current real consumption items: $y_t^R = c_t$. Suppose, now, that a certain portion of that real income is saved, say, an amount of income equal to AA'. This means that only $0A'$ of that income is being consumed. Let us further assume that this savings takes the form of capital supplied to the production process. We may think of an individual as lending a portion of his or her current real income (savings) to a producing unit. This supplied capital allows the unit, or firm, to produce more goods and services and thus make possible more consumption in the future.

An alternative way to think of the same process is to recall that individuals who do not spend all of their current real income on consumption thereby make possible a diversion of resources from the production of current consumer goods to the production of new capital goods (machines, tools, materials). These new capital goods can then be used to expand consumption possibilities in the future. Therefore, a decrease in current consumption (i.e., savings) makes possible an expansion in future consumption.

Returning to figure 2.14, suppose that AA' of income can be transformed via this process into, say, $A'B$ of future consumption. The slope

---

9. This marginal rate is calculated exactly like the previous rates. Recall that along any preference curve relating present and future consumption we have

$$-\Delta c_{t+1} \cdot mu_{c_{t+1}} = +\Delta c_t \cdot mu_{c_t},$$

where once again we assume that a utility loss in future consumption is exactly offset by a utility gain in present consumption. Solving this equation for $\Delta c_{t+1}/\Delta c_t$, we have

$$\frac{\Delta c_{t+1}}{\Delta c_t} = -\frac{mu_{c_t}}{mu_{c_{t+1}}},$$

which is our $MRS_{c_t c_{t+1}}$.

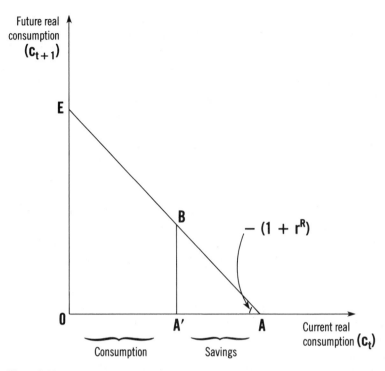

Figure 2.14.   The trade-off between current and future real consumption: the real rate of return on supplied capital.

of a line drawn from point A on the horizontal axis, passing through point B, and ending at point E on the vertical axis measures the amount of future consumption gained relative to the present income given up (i.e., the present income saved rather than consumed). If we let r^R be the real rate of return earned by an individual on the savings of AA', then this slope, measured by $A'B/AA'$, also is equal to $(1 + r^R)$. In other words, the individual's savings of AA' is assumed to have been loaned to producers in the form of capital and earns a rental of r^R per cent per unit of time. The individual thus will have available in the future more consumption than is given up in the present: the earned rental income of $r^R \times AA'$ plus the original principal of AA'. Real consumption in the future may expand by that total amount:

$$A'B = AA'(1 + r^R).\text{[10]}$$

10. Any individual is assumed to be able to choose between consuming all of his or her real income now and saving a portion of it in order to make such savings available for

The borrower of this capital—that is, the producing unit—must be able to earn this real rate of return by using the capital productively in order to pay the lender for the use of this savings. In other words, the reward of r^R to the individual for not consuming now must correspond to the real rate of return earned by the borrower's productive use of this capital. The latter rate is measured by the contribution of capital to output or what is known in neoclassical theory as the marginal product of capital.

In this important sense, the lender gets back a real reward, a real rate of return on savings, exactly equal to what that loaned capital contributes to output. This distribution rule for the reward to capital owners is, of course, perfectly parallel to that used to calculate the correct real reward to the owners of the labor resource. The latter received a real wage exactly equal to what they contributed to output, no more and no less. (Recall from our previous analysis of the demand for and supply of labor that the real wage received by each laborer, w/p, is equal to the marginal product of labor.)

This neoclassical theory of the distribution of output to the owners of resources rules out the possibility that any owner might receive less or more than what his or her resources contributed to producing outputs. After each resource owner is paid its marginal product, there is, according to this logic, nothing left to distribute; the total output made possible by all the resources has been exhausted. As we will see in the next chapter, the Marxian theory of distribution is radically different.

Let us now bring together the set of subjective preference curves and the given rate of real return on capital supplied to producing firms. According to the usual neoclassical assumption, the latter is given to

---

future consumption: $y^R = c_t + SAV$, where SAV stands for current savings out of real income. In our previous notation, c_t represented the individual's current real expenditures on the two commodities, q_1 and q_2. We may write this future consumption in terms of current savings as

$$c_{t+1} = SAV(1 + r^R),$$

where $A'B = c_{t+1}$ and $AA' = SAV$. Any individual's current income may be written, then, in terms of present *and* future consumption:

$$y^R = c_t + \frac{c_{t+1}}{(1 + r^R)},$$

where $c_{t+1}/(1 + r^R)$ tells the consumer what his or her future consumption is currently worth. Solving this equation for c_{t+1} yields $c_{t+1} = (1 + r^R) \cdot y^R - (1 + r^R)c_t$, and $\Delta c_{t+1}/\Delta c_t = -(1 + r^R)$, which is the slope of line AE in figure 2.14. If the individual decides not to save, then $y^R = c_t$; and if he or she decides to save all current income and thus not to consume anything now, then $y^R = c_{t+1}/(1 + r^R)$. In the latter case, we have simply $y^R = SAV$.

each individual by the force of market competition. Figure 2.15(a) demonstrates the optimal point T'' for the individual. At this point, the individual has brought the private ability to choose among objects $(MRS_{c_t c_{t+1}})$ into balance with the social ability to do so $(1 + r^R)$. We may write this new equation as

$$\frac{mu_{c_t}}{mu_{c_{t+1}}} = (1 + r^R).$$

This equality signals that the individual has reached the highest possible level of satisfaction from present and future consumption, given the economic constraint faced. In that sense, the individual is maximizing his or her market opportunities.

So in all three spheres of an individual's economic life—the commodity, labor, and capital markets—the most satisfactory consumption point has been reached. Each individual acting in his or her own self-interest—that is, maximizing his or her own preferences with no regard for anyone else—has been able to achieve the maximum feasible utility in terms of specific commodities purchased, income and leisure, and present and future consumption, given the market conditions (and thus opportunities) faced.

To derive the supply of new capital from this preference map, we may vary the rate-of-return line, as shown in figure 2.15(a), to derive new equilibrium points B', C', D'. Connecting them, neoclassicals derive $T''B'C'D'$ as the individual's offer curve of supplied capital. As the reward to savings rises, the individual is assumed to offer more savings (the indicated movement is from right to left along the horizontal axis: savings increase and current consumption decreases).

Figure 2.15(b) lines up its horizontal axis with that of figure 2.15(a). We may then measure the supply of new capital offered by the individual in both diagrams. The dotted lines drawn from the offer curve in figure 2.15(a) map out points $T'''B''C''D''$ on the curve indicating supply of capital in figure 2.15(b).

We now have the neoclassical answer as to what determines the supply of capital in a society: the choice between present and future consumption, the given real rate of return, and the initial endowment of current real income. Given the last two variables, the supply of new capital is dictated by one's own human nature—the degree of impatience one has in regard to future consumption. And, once more, by adding up each individual's supply of capital, we derive the aggregate supply of capital in a society—in other words, the capital market supply curve.

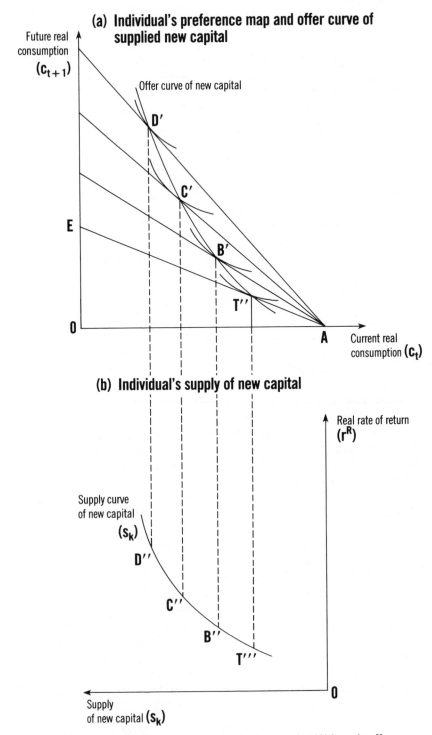

Figure 2.15. Derivation of an individual's supply of new capital (*b*) from the offer curve of that individual (*a*).

B.8. Preferences and Scarcity: Determining the Demand for Capital

Let us now turn to what causes the demand for new capital. The logic parallels completely that used to explain the determination of the demand for labor. Once again, the production and utility functions are the essential determinants of demand.

As usual in neoclassical theory, each producing firm is assumed to attempt to maximize its profits (the difference between total revenues and the costs of production). It does this by equilibrating the dollar value of the marginal product contributed by capital and its cost. This new profit-maximizing position for each may be written as

$$\bar{r} = \frac{\Delta q}{\Delta k} \cdot \bar{p},$$

where $\Delta q / \Delta k \cdot \bar{p}$ is the dollar value of the marginal product of capital, $\Delta q / \Delta k$ is the marginal product of capital itself, and $\bar{p}$ and $\bar{r}$ stand respectively for the given output price and for the given money rental on capital faced by the firm. From the perspective of the firm, it must earn a money rate of return of r on this capital to pay exactly for its cost. Adding up across all producing units, we derive the aggregate demand for capital in the economy.

The price of output ($\bar{p}$) is ultimately determined by consumers' preferences for the commodity. The marginal product of capital is governed by the underlying production function and the assumed given endowment of the other resource—labor. Therefore, the existence, shape, and position of the demand for capital is governed by these three essences: the predetermined preference and production functions and the given resource endowments.

B.9. The Determination of Profits

The rate of return (r) multiplied by the total amount of capital supplied and demanded gives us the total earnings, what is often called "profit income," going to the owners of capital. These earnings refer only to what the owners of capital, like the owners of any resource, have contributed to the production process.[11] Each resource—labor and capital—receives as income from the economy precisely what it contributes to make that income possible. Owners of the labor resource received their reward for not consuming leisure, just as owners of the capital

11. Once again, "profits" is understood here to mean the marginal return to capital and not short-run producer's profits (the difference between revenues and costs), which are competed away in the long run.

resource received theirs for not consuming all of their current income. The private decisions to abstain from leisure and current consumption permit these resources to flow to producing units, where they enjoy a particular (marginal) productivity.

Given neoclassical theory's parallel treatment of returns to productive resources, we could just as easily have referred to the earnings of labor as "profits." In the case of labor, "profits" would then be the name for the rate of return to labor hours (w) multiplied by the total amount of labor hours supplied (Lh). However, we will retain the conventional labeling of wages returned to labor and profits returned to capital in order to make clear the sharp difference between the neoclassical explanation for the source of profits as the return to capital, and the Marxian explanation for the source of profits as exploitation, presented in the next chapter.

Figure 2.16 brings together the derived aggregate supply of and demand for capital to determine simultaneously the money rate of return on capital and the amount of capital demanded and supplied in the economy. We now know, however, that both market curves are grounded in three forces that determine their very existence, shape, and position. These forces explain, therefore, the level of, and whatever change occurs in, the rate of return on capital. They are: the inherent marginal productivity of the capital resource (technology), the initial endowments of labor and capital, and the degree of impatience of individuals for future consumption (preferences).

B.10. The Distribution of Income in Society: Wages and Profits

Neoclassical theory provides a unique explanation for the distribution of income, for what owners of capital and labor respectively receive from society's produced output. The specific preferences of individuals regarding the resources they may supply, the specific production functions available to producing firms, and the initial resource endowments owned by individuals combine to determine the distribution of wage and profit incomes among them. Wages and profits reflect a balance between "scarcity" (captured by the given production function and resource endowments) and "tastes" (captured by the respective utility functions for income versus leisure and present versus future consumption). Each owner of a resource receives a return to that resource which is worked out by this balance.

It follows that the neoclassical explanation for what ultimately determines income and its distribution in society is remarkable both for what it claims and for what it rules out as a possibility. The claim is that each individual gets back from society a quantum of wealth exactly propor-

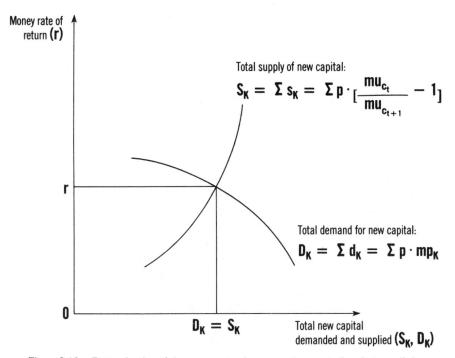

Figure 2.16.   Determination of the money rate of return and amount of capital supplied and demanded in the capital market as derived from current and future consumption choice on the supply side and the marginal product of capital on the demand side.

tional to what each has contributed to society. This theory of distribution is remarkable for its inherent fairness. It is also remarkable for what it rules out: exploitation. Exploitation, in the sense of some individual or set of individuals receiving some produced wealth from society without giving any in return to it, is clearly not possible. Yet, exploitation is precisely what Marxian theory claims does exist in society. What neoclassical theory logically rules out as a possibility is, in fact, the entry point of Marxism. This paradox has both fascinated and provoked economists for the last hundred years.

We want to make one final comment on income distribution. The question of whether an individual is either a wage or a profit receiver (or possibly both) can be answered only by examining that individual's preferences. Some may prefer, for example, to offer labor hours and consume all their income now. Such individuals would receive only wage incomes. Others may prefer to do the opposite; they would receive only profit incomes. Still others may prefer to do both, thereby receiving both wage and profit incomes. The key point is that their decision to occupy one or more of these positions is a function only of their personal preferences, which are grounded in their human nature. The decision of one individual to be a profit-receiver has absolutely nothing to do with the decision of another individual not to be one. This is guaranteed by the initial assumption that the preferences that produce such decisions are essential parts of each person as a unique individual.

How, then, could one fault an individual for receiving, say, a relatively large profit income, since for any given technology, that profit is caused by that same individual's decision to be thrifty, to abstain from being a spendthrift? According to neoclassical theory, profit income is due partly to an individual's personal actions in regard to saving and partly to the productivity of a thing called capital. This explains the source of profits in an economy. Therefore, to criticize an individual for receiving a relatively high profit income is virtually absurd. Are we to cast blame on the inherent productivity of a nonliving thing, capital—which makes about as much sense as criticizing a flower for being too beautiful? Or are we to damn an individual's preferences for savings and future consumption—which makes hardly any more sense?

B.11. Preferences and Scarcity: Determining the Supply of Commodities

We now have sufficient background to discuss the neoclassical determination of the supply of commodities. Recall, first, that each resource was paid the dollar value of its marginal product. This result was derived from the condition that each producing unit maximizes its profits. For the resources of labor and capital, we have the respective input demands from each producer:

$$w = mp_{hL} \cdot p$$

and

$$r = mp_K \cdot p.$$

Let us solve each equation for the price variable faced by each producer:

$$p = \frac{w}{mp_{hL}}$$

$$p = \frac{r}{mp_K}.$$

It follows, then, that for each producer

$$\frac{w}{mp_{hL}} = \frac{r}{mp_K}.$$

Profit maximization implies an equality between the extra cost (w) incurred by a producer per extra output added by labor (mp_{hL}) and the extra cost (r) paid per extra output produced by capital (mp_K). To maximize profits, each producer equates the extra cost per extra output received from each resource input.

Each of these ratios is nothing more than the extra dollar costs incurred by a firm per unit of extra output produced. This expression is what neoclassicals call the "marginal cost" of a producing unit. Therefore, we may rewrite the above equation for each producer as follows:

$$\frac{w}{mp_{hL}} = \frac{r}{mp_K} = mc_q,$$

where mc_q stands for the marginal cost of a firm, or the extra total costs incurred per unit of extra output produced.

Now, let us recall that each producing unit in the economy is assumed to maximize its profits. Let these profits be equal to the difference between total revenue and total costs:

$$\Pi = \bar{p} \cdot q - c,$$

where $\bar{p}$ is given by the competitive market to each producer and c now stands for total costs, the sum of wages ($w \cdot h \cdot L$) and capital ($r \cdot K$) costs. Consider the change in a producer's profits when both revenues and costs change:

$$\Delta\Pi = \bar{p} \cdot \Delta q - \Delta c,$$

where $\bar{p}$ is a constant because each producer is assumed to be a price-taker.

To consider the impact on profits of a change in the quantity supplied by the producer, divide both sides of the equation by Δq to derive

$$\frac{\Delta\Pi}{\Delta q} = \bar{p} - \frac{\Delta c}{\Delta q},$$

where $\Delta c/\Delta q$ stands for the marginal cost of output which we just derived from a firm's input costs and production function (the profit-maximizing equality between w/mp_{hL} and r/mp_K).

If $\bar{p} > mc_q$, the extra dollar profit received by the producer from supplying more output is greater than the extra dollar cost to do so. Clearly, the firm will want to supply more since that particular action raises the level of its profits. If, however, $\bar{p} < mc_q$, then the firm will have absolutely no desire to supply more output. Indeed, it will want to produce less because the extra dollar cost of producing more would be greater than the extra benefit the firm would receive by doing so. Pro-

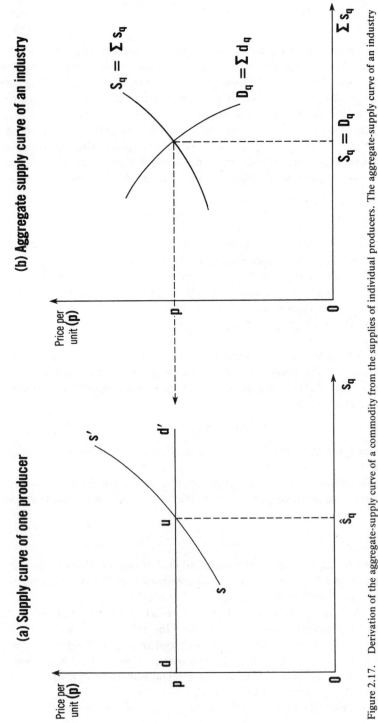

Figure 2.17. Derivation of the aggregate-supply curve of a commodity from the supplies of individual producers. The aggregate-supply curve of an industry (b) is the sum of the supplies of the industry's individual producers, one of which is represented in (a).

ducing more in such a situation would only lower the firm's level of profits. It is only when $\bar{p} = mc_q$ that the producer has maximized profits. At that point, marginal profits are neither rising nor falling.

This equation and the resulting dynamic of a producer are illustrated in figure 2.17(a), where *dd'* represents the demand curve facing a producer, and *ss'* indicates the firm's marginal cost. For the different levels of prices faced by this firm, different quantities will be produced according to the firm's given marginal-cost condition. For example, it could maximize its profits only at the point where the given demand price intersects the firm's marginal cost curve (point *U* in the diagram). Any point to the left of *U* would mean that profits could be expanded if the firm supplied more ($\bar{p} > mc_q$ in the above equation). That would be the firm's signal to expand. Any point to the right of *U* would mean that profits could be expanded if the firm supplied less ($\bar{p} < mc_q$ in the above equation). That would be the firm's signal to contract. Neoclassicals conclude that this marginal-cost curve is the competitive firm's supply curve. By adding up all such curves across all producing units, they derive the aggregate industry supply curve for each commodity in the economy. This is shown in figure 2.17(b).

In neoclassical theory, the supply curve of any commodity is a function of its input costs and the marginal productivities of those inputs. However, as shown in previous sections, those input costs and productivities are derived, in turn, from individuals' preferences, ability to produce, and resource endowments. We may conclude, therefore, that the supply of commodities in a society is also derived ultimately from these same three essences, which form, of course, the entry point of neoclassical theory.

According to this account, firms supplying commodity outputs are purely passive entities. Their producing behavior merely reflects more basic underlying behaviors: those which flow from the preferences of suppliers of resources to firms and from the preferences of consumers of the products produced by them. The producers' behavior likewise reflects the relative scarcity of resources shaped by the available production function (technology) and by the resource endowments given naturally. Given the technology, any firm's behavior reduces to and is therefore explained in terms of the will of those who own and supply its capital and its labor as well as the will of those who demand its commodities in the market. It has no autonomous will of its own.

B.12. Demand and Supply Again: The Determination of Prices

We have now assembled all the parts needed to complete the explanation of the neoclassical theory of value. Figure 2.18, which summarizes

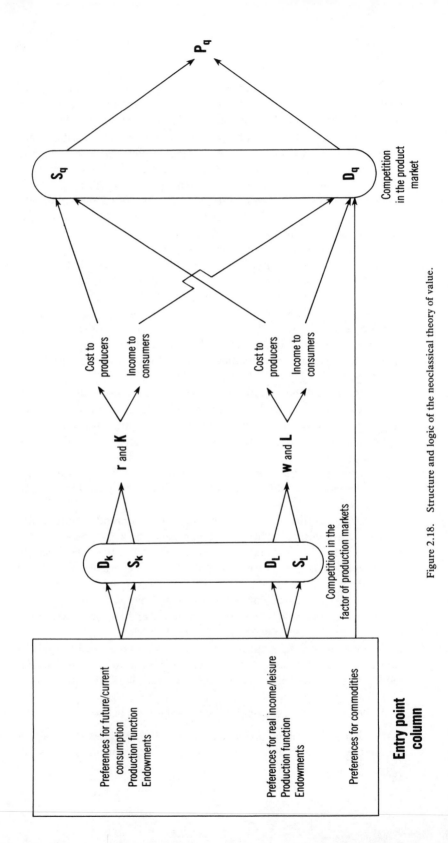

Figure 2.18. Structure and logic of the neoclassical theory of value.

the overall structure and logic of the theory, combines the different pieces of the argument presented in the previous sections. Reading from left to right, we first encounter the theory's three governing essences—preferences, production function, and endowments—in the entry-point column. Following the arrows emanating from this column, we see the influence of preferences on the demand for commodities (along the bottom of the diagram), and the influence of preferences, the production function, and endowments on the supply of commodities (upper part of the diagram). Other arrows trace how preferences and productive abilities determine the different demands for and supplies of the two resources in what are called factor-of-production markets. In turn, the arrows emanating from these competitive resource markets show the influence of incomes on the demand for commodities and of costs on the supply of commodities. Finally, the resulting demand for and supply of commodities act together to cause price, as shown in the last column on the right of the diagram.

In neoclassical theory, the value of things, after all is said and done, depends upon our tastes and productive abilities as human beings. The value of our wealth and well-being may rise or fall depending upon what we ourselves want and what we ourselves are capable of producing. The mystery of value dissolves into the mystery of our own human nature.

One may start anywhere in figure 2.18 and by following the arrows eventually retrace the ultimately determinant influence of human preferences and productive abilities. That is precisely why they are considered to be essences: in one way or another, all other conceived objects owe their existence to them. Whatever the economic objects of neoclassical theory—incomes, prices, supply, or demand—they ultimately rest on the fundamental building blocks of human tastes, technology, and endowments. There is nothing to the left of the entry-point column in figure 2.18 which might explain what caused those fundamental building blocks. If one supposed that tastes and technology were themselves caused by human genes, then a theory of biology would be required to help explain economic behavior. And, indeed, that is the direction in which some economists would take neoclassical theory.

As we claimed initially in this chapter, figure 2.18 demonstrates that reductionism is the overall logic of neoclassical economic theory. Reductionism is likewise the geometric method used in all of the previous diagrams elaborating the theory. The meaning of each diagram ultimately rests on the same three essences. The power of those essences is that they ultimately determine what will be.

C. Efficiency and Markets: Adam Smith's "Invisible Hand"

If each and every individual in a fully competitive society acts rationally in his or her own self-interest—consumers maximizing utility and producers maximizing profits—the result will be an efficient allocation of both consumption outputs and resource inputs. In neoclassical theory, the term "efficient" when applied to a society means that that society has attained the greatest wealth possible given the constraints it faces. An extraordinary conclusion on the part of neoclassicals is that if each citizen in a society acts in a selfish manner, maximizing individual self-interest, then with supply equal to demand in all markets, that society will have the maximum possible wealth available to it. It will have fully realized its potential output.

Of course, the availability of more goods and services to a society does not say anything about how they will be distributed among its citizens. Indeed, assuming different individual resource endowments and tastes, it would not be surprising to discover that some individuals receive more produced wealth than others. Neoclassical theorists have always recognized that possibility. They have also recognized that the produced inequality of rewards could become a political issue that would require some economic action. Consequently, over the years they have devised various schemes to, in effect, redistribute some income from certain citizens to others. However, these redistribution schemes have been designed to disrupt the efficiency of a market economy only minimally.

There is a close connection between this efficient or optimal consumption and production result and the role of competitive markets. To see this connection, first recall that competitive markets require that each individual in the society be a price-taker. Each is assumed to have no power over the determination of price. Also recall that each is assumed to own privately all commodities and resources. Consequently, while each individual has no power over price, each has complete power over the disposal and acquisition of privately held wealth.

This asymmetry of individual power on the one hand bestows complete freedom to the market to determine prices of commodities and resources, and on the other hand provides each person with the complete freedom to decide what wealth and how much of it he or she will supply to and demand from others. The specific decision taken by each in regard to this demand for and supply of privately owned wealth depends, as we have seen, on that person's unique maximizing behavior. In a sense, the condition of private property permits this selfish behavior to take place. Individuals may offer and demand as much as they please of what they privately own and desire whether it be labor, capital, or commodities. Their offers and demands depend on their own personal likes and dislikes. The competitive fact of the market, however, forces them all to be price-takers and thus constrains their offers and demands. We recognized this each time we presented a diagram showing the interaction between an individual's private utility maximization and various socially determined price constraints.

In neoclassical theory, markets are sites of social interaction between existing owners and prospective buyers of wealth. Markets offer each group an opportunity to gain wealth. Individuals may do so by offering to either supply or demand some good or resource. The common goal of each individual is to reach his or her highest possible preference curve. Achieving that goal defines the neoclassical notion of maximizing social wealth. Efficient or competitive markets allow the maximum social wealth to be achieved by these private wealth-seeking sellers and buyers. Neoclassicals often say the same thing in slightly different terms—that is, an efficient market cannot offer opportunities to one person to improve his or her wealth position without also making someone else worse off. In contrast, inefficient markets offer opportunities for gain which individual buyers and/or sellers may take advantage of without making anyone else worse off.

Neoclassical theory combines the private decisions of all pleasure-maximizing individuals to derive the market demands and supplies for all commodities and resources. Thus, the power of each individual to make decisions in his or her own self-interest is competitively aggregated into the markets, which then act to negate any individual's desire for power over prices. The tyranny of the market as a ruler of price is a product of the very freedom individuals have to own and dispose of their privately held wealth as they see fit.

In neoclassical theory, there is a precise and necessary correspondence between a fully competitive private-property economy and an optimally efficient one. The insight of Adam Smith is retained in neoclassical economics: each individual having the power (freedom) to act in his or her own self-interest will be led as if by an "invisible hand" (the fully competitive market) to actions that produce the maximum wealth (efficiency) for a society of individuals.

Recall that when individuals maximize utility subject to given market prices and income, the private marginal rate of substitution between any two consumption goods is brought into equality with the ratio between their market prices. Let us write such an equilibrium equation for each of the many different individuals in a society:

$$MRS_{12}^A = \frac{p_1}{p_2}$$

$$MRS_{12}^B = \frac{p_1}{p_2}$$

$$MRS_{12}^C = \frac{p_1}{p_2}$$

$$\vdots \qquad \vdots$$

$$MRS_{12}^N = \frac{p_1}{p_2}$$

where MRS_{12}^A, MRS_{12}^B, MRS_{12}^C, and so forth, stand for the different marginal rates of substitution between commodities one and two for individuals A, B, C, and so on. Since each one of these individuals is, of course, unique, the marginal rate of substitution between any two commodities is unique to each as well.

Yet these equations point to a striking fact: all of the private, unique marginal rates of substitution are brought into equality with a common price ratio. Utility-maximizing buyers all face the same price ratio when confronting that market. It follows that their private rates of substitution must then be set equal to market price ratios and thus to one another. The competitive market has forced this equality, which may be formulated as follows:

$$MRS_{12}^A = MRS_{12}^B = MRS_{12}^C = \ldots = MRS_{12}^N.$$

Let us then summarize this key neoclassical conclusion. As each individual $(A, B, C, \ldots, N)$ maximizes his or her own selfish interest, there results, as if by some mysterious force, an equality among the private abilities of individuals to substitute one good for another. What is this mysterious force? The answer is clear: it is nothing other than the competitive market. First the competitive market permits each person to make exchanges for the maximum gain possible. Then it brings those gains into balance or harmony with one another. The resulting equality of marginal rates of substitution is neoclassical theory's precise definition of an efficient distribution of consumption commodities among individuals in a society.

This distribution of commodities is considered to be an efficient one first because each and every individual has reached his or her highest feasible preference curve; each has therefore made the most of the market opportunities faced, and in that sense each is best-off. Second, the resulting equality of individuals' different marginal rates of substitution means that it is not possible to improve the welfare position (the consumption gain) of any one individual without simultaneously damaging some other individual's position. Therefore, neoclassical theory has shown that no other possible result could improve upon this particular competitive market solution. In that sense, the achieved distribution of commodities among individuals is optimal.

Let us now turn to the production side of the economy. Recall that each producing unit is also assumed to act in its own self-interest by maximizing profits. Each unit has the complete freedom to produce any quantity it desires. As a result, the quantity chosen by each indicates that this is the point at which its marginal cost of production equals the given market price.

What, then, determines this market price, if individual producers have no power over its determination? The summation of all firms' marginal costs produces the aggregate supply in the industry producing that commodity. The summation of individual demands from all the utility-maximizing consumers produces the aggregate demand for the commodity produced in that industry. Together, the two aggregates determine the price that confronts each individual producer and consumer in an economy as a given (figures 2.17(a) and 2.17(b)).

Let us write the equilibrium conditions for the production of commodities one and two by each of the many—that is, n—producers in that economy:[12]

$$p_1 = mc_1^a \qquad p_2 = mc_2^a$$
$$p_1 = mc_1^b \qquad p_2 = mc_2^b$$
$$\vdots \qquad \vdots \qquad \vdots \qquad \vdots$$
$$p_1 = mc_1^n \qquad p_2 = mc_2^n$$

We may now bring together the two sides of the story told so far. By maximizing his or her own interest (consumption), each consumer produces an efficient consumption result:

12. Summing up all of these individual marginal costs, we derive the aggregate supply in each industry for commodity one and commodity two:

$$S_1 = \Sigma mc_1^i \quad \text{and} \quad S_2 = \Sigma mc_2^i,$$

where Σ stands for summation and i signifies n possible producers. The aggregate demand may then be written as

$$D_1 = \Sigma d_1^j \quad \text{and} \quad D_2 = \Sigma d_2^j,$$

where j signifies that the demand has been summed across N possible consumers. The equilibrium condition in each market is $S_1 = D_1$ and $S_2 = D_2$.

$$MRS^j_{12} = \frac{p_1}{p_2},$$

where $j = A, \ldots, N$ individuals (consumers). By maximizing its own interest (profits), each producer in the two industries produces an efficient production result. For the two commodities produced in the economy, we may write this result as an equality between the ratio of marginal costs for producers and the market price ratio:

$$\frac{mc^i_1}{mc^i_2} = \frac{p_1}{p_2},$$

where $i = a, \ldots, n$ producers.

The marginal rate of substitution for individuals and the ratio of marginal costs for producers are both equated to the same market price ratio. Therefore, they are also equal to each other. Rewriting the marginal rate of substitution in terms of marginal utilities, we have as the optimal result in a competitive economy

$$\frac{mu_1}{mu_2} = \frac{mc_1}{mc_2}.$$

Neoclassical theorists call this equality of "consumption" and "production" a "Pareto optimal point," after the theorist who first discovered it, Wilfredo Pareto (1848–1923). It indicates that the demand (ratio of marginal utilities) and supply (ratio of marginal costs) sides of an economy are in balance with each other.

C.1. Pareto Optimality

The Pareto point is optimal in the sense that it signifies that a society has fully realized its potential output. It is operating at the outer limit of its productive capability, given the technology and resource endowments available to it. To see this, first consider the concept of a society's potential output. This refers to the total quantity of goods it could potentially produce with its given production function and its initial resource endowments. Neoclassical theory uses a geometric diagram to illustrate this concept. As shown in figure 2.19, this diagram is called a production possibilities curve.

The diagram indicates that a society produces its maximum output potential, q_1 and q_2, if it operates at any point along its frontier, PP', but not below it. This frontier is delineated by the PP' curve in figure 2.19. The curve itself is derived from the production functions of the two commodities and their given labor and capital resource endowments. In other words, these two neoclassical essences govern the shape

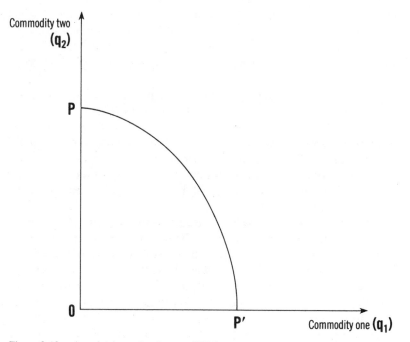

Figure 2.19.   A society's production possibilities curve.

and position of the curve. We may conclude, therefore, that the relative scarcity of commodities in a society follows from the relative scarcity of its resources and from the productive abilities of its producers.

The trade-off between the two commodities along the production possibilities curve is known in neoclassical theory as the "marginal rate of transformation." It shows the decreased production of commodity two that would be needed to increase the production of commodity one. Any point along the curve measures the quantity of commodity two that would have to be decreased in order to release sufficient resources of labor and capital to produce an additional unit of commodity one. Recall that the marginal cost of producing commodity one measured how much an extra unit of that commodity would cost in terms of resources. If the production of commodity one were expanded by a unit, this cost would be MC_1. By the same logic, if the production of commodity two contracted, the marginal cost of resources saved would be MC_2. The ratio of MC_1 to MC_2 relates the extra cost of resources required to produce one more unit of commodity one to the resources released by reducing the total production of commodity two by one unit. This ratio of marginal costs is therefore the same as the marginal rate of transformation, for they both measure the opportunities and costs that a society confronts when it considers producing more of some and less of other commodities—that is, moving along its production possibilities frontier.

We may substitute the marginal rate of transformation for the ratio of marginal costs and write the Pareto optimal point simply as: $MRT_{12} = MRS_{12}$. In a competitive economy in which each individual maximizes his or her own utility and his or her own profits, an equality between this utility-maximizing (MRS) and this profit-maximizing (MRT) behavior will result. At this point, the citizens of the society, the various utility- and profit-seekers, will have available to them the maximum wealth possible.

The fact that $MRS_{12} = MRT_{12}$ means that the allocation of resources throughout the economy is Pareto optimal. However, if these marginal rates were not equal, then it would be possible to increase the welfare possibilities of consumption by means of a reallocation of resources. In other words, an inequality between these two marginal rates would indicate that consumers preferred a different output mix in the economy than the one produced.

For example, suppose the equated marginal rates of substitution of consumers equal one-fifth. This means that individuals in the society are willing to give up five units of commodity one for each unit of commodity two gained. Suppose the marginal rate of transformation at a point on the PP' curve in figure 2.19 is one-third. This means that three units of commodity one must be given up to produce an additional unit of commodity two in the society. In this situation, the producers are making commodity one in excess of what consumers would like. Producers are making an additional unit of commodity two at a marginal cost of three units of commodity one given up, while consumers are willing to give up five units of commodity one to gain an additional unit of commodity two.

Consumers, therefore, can be made better-off by a reallocation of resources in which more of commodity two and less of commodity one is produced. Suppose this happens. The society produces three fewer units of commodity one and gains one unit of commodity two. Suppose that individual A's real consumption falls as a result of these three units of commodity one being given up. More than enough units of commodity two have been produced to compensate individual A for this loss in consumption and still have units of output left over to raise the welfare position of other individuals (B, C, and so on) in society.

To see this, recall that the MRS_{12} of each and every individual, including A, was one-fifth. It follows that reducing A's consumption by the assumed three units of commodity one requires a three-fifths' increase of commodity two to maintain A's same level of satisfaction (utility). Since society gained one unit of commodity two by moving along its PP' curve, three-fifths of this gain may be given to A, with the result that there is no change in A's welfare position. The remaining two-fifths of commodity two may then be divided in a number of different ways among all the other individuals in society ($B, C, \ldots, N$), thereby raising their welfare. This example illustrates that the output mix of an economy in which $MRS_{12} \neq MRT_{12}$ is nonoptimal, since by reallocating resources to alter this mix it is possible to raise the welfare position of at least one individual without hurting the welfare position of anyone else.

In neoclassical theory, the achievement of a correspondence between producers' selfish maximization of their own profits and consumers' selfish maximization of their own preferences is also the achievement of a perfect harmony between physical and human nature, between scarcity and choice. The two parts of our human nature—unlimited wants and the ability to produce and satisfy them—are in balance. At this point the maximization of profits for each and every private producer is the same as the maximization of economic happiness for each and every consumer.

The demonstration that maximum profits are consistent with and indeed necessary for the maximum happiness of individual consumers is surely a radical conclusion for neoclassical theory. It underlies dramatic policy proposals and consequences. Neoclassicals can, and many times do, endorse government policies to enhance profits on the grounds that such policies would thereby benefit everyone. Similarly, they often oppose policies that would reduce profits, claiming that reduced profits would necessarily reduce the happiness of individuals.

For neoclassicals, the equation of profit maximization with the maximization of consumer satisfaction seems to be in complete conformity with our nature as human beings. Yet, as will be shown in chapters 3 and 4 of this book, this conclusion is radically different from the one arrived at by Marxists, who argue that the maximization of profits corresponds to the maximization of exploitation, and thus discord, in society. The social implications of the two theories could not be more different.

C.2. Criticisms of Neoclassical Theory

As with any theory of life, economic or otherwise, neoclassical theory has received its share of criticism over the many years of its development. At one time or another, some have found it wanting for its allegedly inadequate representation of key events and major changes in the real world. One criticism of this kind reproaches the theory for mirroring inadequately, and thus explaining improperly, the real world of giant corporations wielding power in all kinds of markets. Rather than reduce the behavior of firms to passive responses to given technologies and preferences, these critics find firms to be active seekers of power over all kinds of economic activities. A similar criticism is that neoclassical theory omits from its explanation the very visible hand of the state in so many aspects of our lives. According to these critics, the behavior of agents of the state must be understood in all their complex effects if we are to specify properly the workings of supply and demand in the economy. A current criticism by some economists is that neoclassical theory does not adequately treat the role of uncertainty in all human decisions as it affects the operation of markets. A longstanding criticism of the theory focuses on its alleged inability to explain and produce effective policy to prevent the regular recurrence of recession and inflation in capitalist societies.

Such criticisms have different results. Some theorists seek and develop alternative (non-neoclassical) ways of explaining economic events, ways that incorporate the realities they think neoclassicals ignore or misrepresent. Perhaps a more typical reaction is for theorists to develop and change the existing body of neoclassical theory to make it adequate to the economic event(s) and change(s) observed and emphasized by critics. In this regard, neoclassical theorists have introduced over the years a number of new concepts to address such issues as imperfect competition and the theory of the firm, public expenditures, taxes and the theory of the state, uncertainty and the theory of information, and business cycles and the theory of the equilibrating role of markets versus the state. Consequently, neoclassical theory has changed over the years partly as a result of the criticisms leveled against it. Of course, it is always an open question whether such changes actually satisfy critics or perhaps even challenge the theory's basic entry-point concepts and/or logic, thereby producing a tension and perhaps even a crisis within neoclassical theory.

Other kinds of attacks have been made on the structure and logic of neoclassical theory as well. Some individuals, for example, have claimed that they have found serious internal inconsistencies within the body of the theory itself. For them, the explanation of value and distribution presented in the previous pages of this chapter is seriously flawed. It is so, they argue, because of logical errors they have found in how the theory explains the determination of prices of outputs and resources.

According to one of the most famous of these attacks, there is no logical way for neoclassical theory to explain the distribution of income in society because of the inherent difficulty it has in measuring the value of capital. Indeed, the claim has been made that there may not be any unit by which this resource input can be measured independently of the equilibrium prices that are explained partly on the basis of that input. Consequently, these critics argue, one of the entry-point concepts of neoclassical theory, the initial capital endowment, can no longer be considered an essence.[13]

A different criticism, but one that is also directed at the internal consistency of neoclassical theory, questions the exogenous nature of human preferences. The claim here is that since neoclassical theory assumes that individuals are integral parts of society, the preferences of each must be affected by the complex economic and noneconomic actions of all the others. In a sense, that is precisely the basis on which such critics define the term "social": to be a social being is to negate the possibility of having one's choices "autonomously" formed in society.

Somewhat related to this last point is a well-recognized problem in neoclassical theory that has received much attention over the years. First, recall that according to the theory, individuals are assumed to interact with one another only through and in markets. It follows that they will affect one another only by means of the price changes produced in and by those markets. Now, suppose that through their economic actions they affect one another in a number of other ways as well. For example, suppose the consumption pattern of one individual affects the preferences of a different individual (note that this claim is similar to arguing that preferences cannot be assumed to be exogenously determined). Case in point: the consumption of cigarettes by one consumer may produce an adverse effect on the utility of another. Similarly, the effect of the production of one commodity on the production of another can take place outside the realm of market relationships. For example, the production of oil in offshore wells can alter the production of fish by a fishing boat.

In neoclassical theory, such extramarket interactions among consumers and among producers are called consumption and production externalities respectively. They are called "externalities" because, when present, the private decision of each consumer or producer impacts on the decision of a different individual in nonmarket ways. A third type of

13. Actually, this particular criticism of neoclassical theory has a long history and has produced an enormous economics literature. Perhaps one of the most important contributors to it was Piero Sraffa, whose book, *Production of Commodities by Means of Commodities* (Cambridge: Cambridge University Press, 1960), was influential in generating an entire school of thought dedicated to showing the logical inconsistency of neoclassical theory. In fact, the subtitle of Sraffa's classic book is *Prelude to a Critique of Economic Theory*.

externality is thought to emanate from what are called "public goods"—for example, national defense and clean air. In these instances the consumption of any public good provided by a state body cannot be privatized—that is, cannot be bought or sold by individuals—as can the consumption of other commodities. Each citizen in the society consumes, as it were, the same amount of the public good whether that citizen wants it or not.

In the case of externalities, markets fail to operate in an efficient manner, and thus the Pareto optimality point cannot be achieved. Indeed, a common theme in most of the criticisms directed at neoclassical theory is the failure of markets to work properly. Market imperfections do not allow a society to achieve an efficiency of production or consumption. The sources of such imperfections vary; they include the market power wielded by giant corporations, state interference in the operation of markets, the inability of human beings to foresee the future, and production and consumption externalities. They all interfere with the God- or gene-given ability of human beings to make the rational market choices that result in a Pareto-type optimality of production and consumption. Because of these market imperfections, societies enjoy less wealth than they should; they suffer the effects of unemployed resources; and they face increased political tensions among their citizens.

These criticisms have been articulated by both neoclassical theorists and analysts committed to other theories. Indeed, over the years some of the most telling criticisms have been made by practitioners of neoclassical theory. Of course, criticisms of neoclassical theory by contending Marxian theorists have not been lacking. Marx himself often ridiculed what he considered to be some of the more outrageous assumptions of classical economics that had been carried over intact into neoclassical theory. For example, he thought it absurd to attribute a profit reward to capital, a thing, when for him the relationship between laborers and capitalists was the source of profit. As we will see, Marx was confronting the neoclassical entry-point concept of marginal productivity with his own entry point, that of class. Marx's criticisms were not an attack on the logical consistency of neoclassical theory; rather, they were part of a different theory of how economic realities are organized and how they function.

These and still other criticisms, whether they challenge the internal consistency of neoclassical theory or confront it with a completely different theory (as many Marxists do), stimulate many responses by neoclassical economists. Such criticisms are among the conditions that produce changes in the theory by helping set in motion these intellectual responses. The criticisms push neoclassicals to ask new kinds of questions of their theory, questions that have not been asked previously; they provoke neoclassicals to correct discovered "errors" or contradictions within the theory; and they stimulate some creative individuals to invent new concepts to deal with the criticisms. Paradoxically, the richness, power, and uniqueness of neoclassical theory are due in part to the attacks of its harshest critics. At this point, we want to examine in some detail one of the most famous criticisms levied at neoclassical theory. We also want to discuss the kind of reactions it produced—and still produces—within that school of thought.

D. The Challenge of Keynes

Ever since 1936, when John Maynard Keynes (1883-1946) published *The General Theory of Employment, Interest, and Money,* there has been controversy over the meaning of this work and its specific implications for neoclassical theory. To date, it has more or less split neoclassical economic theory into two branches: microeconomics and macroeconomics. The former deals with the formal structure of neoclassical theory; the latter typically deals with the Keynesian contribution. Generally speaking, neoclassical economic theory is taught today in terms of this split, which began with a text written over fifty years ago.

As might be expected, many neoclassical economists are extremely uncomfortable with this dichotomy. They have labored over the years to synthesize the two parts. Indeed, for some the term "neoclassical" is taken to mean an attempt to shape the traditional classical and the Keynesian contributions into a new form of economic reasoning. This effort began almost as soon as the ink was dry on Keynes's book. In 1937, John Hicks produced a famous article in which he attempted to explain the contribution of Keynes and its relationship to the then dominant economic theory. The article was aptly called "Mr. Keynes and the 'Classics': A Suggested Interpretation."[14] Since then economists of every political persuasion have continued the effort. In fact, the argument and analysis produced in Hicks's article have become almost as famous as the Keynesian text on which they were based.

Over the years some economists have argued that the Keynesian theory provides a devastating critique of neoclassical theory. For them, it is as much an alternative to neoclassical theory as we argue that Marxian theory is. In sharp contrast to this position, other economists insist that the Keynesian contribution is at best overblown and at worst logically flawed. For them, its major contribution is only to suggest some important but overall minor changes that need to be made in the basic and still quite adequate neoclassical theory. Between these two extremes we

---

14. *Econometrica* 5 (1937): 147-59.

find a middle position: it is possible to incorporate the Keynesian contribution into neoclassical theory, thereby modifying the latter somewhat but enriching and strengthening it as well.

This middle position has dominated the thinking of most neoclassical economists since World War II. However, in recent years a sharp defense of the integrity of neoclassical theory against the influence of Keynesian thinking has reemerged in the writings of many leading economists. They both attack Keynesian theory and reaffirm the neoclassical body of thought, more or less as we have presented it so far in this chapter. Of course, changes have been made in that theory in response to the Keynesian challenge, but the basic structure of the theory in terms of entry-point concepts and logic remains much as Keynes originally found it.

Let us examine in more detail the content and implications of the Keynesian critique. First, Keynes introduced into neoclassical theory not only new concepts (in itself not terribly surprising) but also the possibility of an entirely new and different entry point. That, we believe, has been a source of major problems for neoclassical economists these last fifty years. An additional and distinct source of controversy has been Keynes's rejection of a significant portion of neoclassical theory's traditional entry-point concepts. It is precisely this addition of some new and rejection of some old neoclassical entry-point concepts that has produced such difficulties and controversy for neoclassical theorists.

On the one hand, Keynes accepted the essentialized concepts of given initial endowments of resources and their inherent marginal productivity as posed by traditional neoclassical theory. In this regard, he seemed to accept the scarcity side of the neoclassical theory of value. Such acceptance might give some comfort to those who worry about the integrity of neoclassical theory. On the other hand, Keynes profoundly questioned, if he did not reject outright, the usefulness of given human preferences for explaining economic behavior, especially in regard to the supply of savings and labor. Here he seemed to reject the utility side of the neoclassical theory of value. In place of utility, he offered the concepts of mass psychology and habit to explain the supply of savings, and the concepts of power, institutions, and again mass psychology to determine the supply of labor hours.

Keynes's criticisms of neoclassical theory and the changes he introduced led logically to different explanations of the determination of price, income, and employment. Furthermore, Keynes also shifted the overall focus of economic thinking by treating the new concepts of psychology, habit, and power in terms of the behavior of masses of people rather than of individual decision-makers (whose actions are aggregated to explain mass behavior). In other words, Keynes's focus of analysis became the economy as a totality from which he deduced specific individual behaviors. In contrast, neoclassical theory stresses the essential determining role of the individual producer and consumer. This shift in focus may account in part for the very different views of the state that distinguish Keynes from other neoclassicals.

Why did Keynes challenge neoclassical theory in these ways? Why did he question the utility-based determination of the supply of labor hours and consequently its explanation of wage rates and employment in the labor market? Why did he question the utility-based determination of the supply of savings and thus its determination of rental rates and capital investment in the capital market? Why did he accept and not question neoclassical theory's assumed given resource and production constraint on the economy? Our answers to these questions must begin with the times in which Keynes taught and wrote.

After World War I in Europe, the world economy experienced generally some twelve years of uneven but nonetheless continuous expansion. This growth ended dramatically with the depression of the 1930s, which ushered in a period of economic decline. The capitalist economies experienced falling prices, incomes, and wealth and rising unemployment. The resulting social effects provoked many to question the institutions that made capitalism and thus this economic misery possible. The times imperiled the continuation of capitalism: it was at risk because of the crisis it was thought to have caused. Moreover, there was, of course, the challenge of the contending Marxian theory, which was advocated by many around the world. Marxism not only explained capitalism as the source of its own crisis but also offered an alternative set of social institutions that promised to abolish capitalist crises permanently.

Like economists throughout history, Keynes was provoked in part by the events of the day. We add the words "in part" because some of Keynes's theory was developed before the Great Depression. Nonetheless, it is fair to say that Keynes developed much of his own theory and his criticism of neoclassical thought partly in response to the threat the depression presented to capitalism. In the broadest sense, his goal was to save capitalist society from the dangers posed by rising unemployment and falling wealth. It was for these reasons that he offered explanations for what was happening in the labor and the savings and investment markets that differed from those presented either by the dominant neoclassical theorists or by the ever-dangerous Marxists. And it was for these reasons that he was not terribly concerned with questions of scarcity: in times of less than full utilization of resources, a rise in such resources will compound rather than solve an unemployment problem.

Perhaps most important of all, he offered a way to rid the society of the depression while reforming but not destroying the crucial institutions that made capitalism possible in the first place.

D.1. The Neoclassical Answer to Capitalist Recessions

To better understand the Keynesian alternative and solution, let us return for a moment to neoclassical theory and ask how it explained the depression of the 1930s and what policies it proposed for overcoming and preventing depressions. First, neoclassical theory recognized that recessions (in its sense of downward deviations of prices, wages, and profit rates from their equilibrium levels) are always a possibility. Their causes could include: (1) changes in physical nature, such as a poor harvest due to lack of rain; (2) changes in human nature, such as a fall in investment spending because humans foresee the future imperfectly; (3) changes in technology altering commodity-production functions; and (4) changes in institutions such as individuals acquiring monopoly power in markets or a change in the state's supply of money.

Examining such reasons carefully, we learn that economic decline can be explained in terms of either physical or human nature. For example, a temporary imbalance between the demand for and supply of labor may result from some development in physical nature which causes changes in that market: improved rainfall produces an increase in the food supply, which lowers the death rate and thereby shifts the supply curve of labor to the right, putting downward pressure on wages. Alternatively, downward pressure on wages may follow a shift in the demand for labor to the left because firms expect difficulty in selling their products. The problem here is human nature. Individuals cannot foresee the future, and thus they make decisions with uncertainty, worrying about what the outcome of those decisions will be. Since human beings are naturally endowed with uncertainty, their supply-and-demand behavior is quite shiftable. The existence of a temporary disequilibrium in any market is thus always a distinct possibility.

Neoclassical theory treats changes in technology the same way it treats changes in physical nature: it considers both to be exogenous to human beings. For example, it treats a new way of combining capital and labor together to produce output the way it would treat "improved rainfall": as a gift of nature. The result of such a gift may be a change in the shape of the demand curve for labor (which becomes more inelastic as capital and labor become poorer substitutes for each other) or a dampening of the shift of the labor-demand curve to the right following capital accumulation because of the introduction of a labor-saving innovation in society. In either case, employment will grow less rapidly than it would otherwise.

The neoclassicals treat the problems caused by imperfections in markets, on the other hand, like those arising from uncertainty. The effects of imperfections and uncertainty on the labor market can be traced ultimately to our nature as human beings. For example, unemployment may exist in the labor market because individuals have joined together to form a union to use its collective power to enforce a wage that is higher than the market equilibrium. What is the source of this market imperfection, this barrier to full employment? It is found in our aggressive genes: we are endowed with a will for power. Individuals often attempt to control markets in order to gain special advantages for themselves at the expense of others.

All such neoclassical explanations for deviations in the wage rate from the full employment wage can be expressed in terms of and ultimately reduced to either human or physical nature. This is hardly surprising, since as we have already noted, these are the essences to which neoclassical theory reduces all its arguments. It follows that these deviations are not endogenous to the capitalist system itself, for their cause is found outside of that system—in the essential determinants of economic life.

What, then, is the neoclassical solution to these deviations from a full employment equilibrium? Basically it is that the society of individuals should do absolutely nothing, except in the case of market imperfections caused by individuals who have gained control over prices. The latter problem is special; it requires state intervention to rid the society of barriers to its achievement of both full employment and maximum wealth for its citizens. It follows that the state, in one way or another, must tame the individual will for power. It must do this to enable competitive markets to fulfill their destined role in capitalist society. Indeed, if the state did more than maintain competitive markets (and private property), it might well become a contributing factor to a depression. Why is this so?

Recall that, given private property and competitive markets, markets inherently tend to equilibrate when each and every individual is left alone to maximize his or her own interest. That equilibrium is defined as one in which supply equals demand in all markets. In a word, the society has achieved its Pareto optimal point. Assuming that the state performs its proper minimal role of securing the existence of private property and competitive markets, those markets will permit and encourage the society of private-property owners and maximizers to achieve and reproduce a full-employment equilibrium.

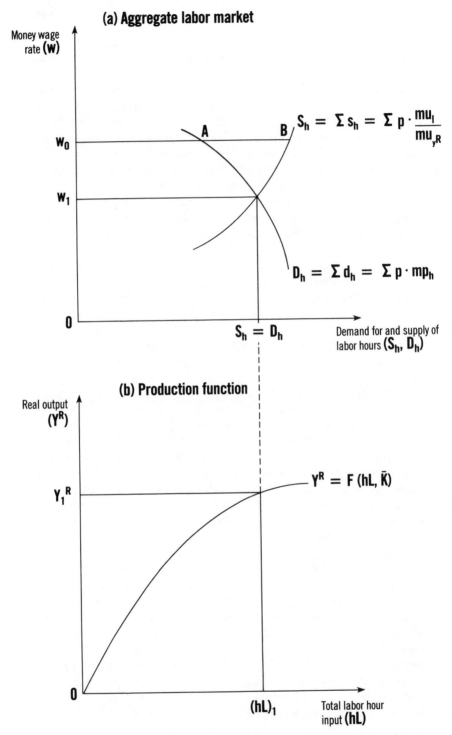

Figure 2.20. Derivation of employment and real output from the labor market.

Consider, for example, the previously discussed aggregate labor market, depicted once again in figure 2.20(a). Suppose there is significant unemployment there, as indicated by AB in the diagram. According to neoclassical theory, the proper solution is for money wages to fall from w_0 until that excess labor supply of AB becomes zero at the equilibrium wage, w_1, in the diagram.

Whatever so-called unemployment remains at that equilibrium wage may be thought of either as transitional in nature or as strictly voluntary. The former idea indicates the possibility of temporary unemployment due to an individual's being in transition from one job to another. The latter idea refers to individuals who have decided of their own free will to choose leisure rather than income from working at the wage w_1. Clearly, this "unemployment" is quite voluntary; it is not a social problem, for it is freely chosen by individuals.

This full-employment level in the labor market also tells us what will be the corresponding level of full-employment output in the society. To see this clearly, consider figure 2.20(b), which presents our previously specified neoclassical production function. We have lined up employment in the two diagrams so that by reading off the full-employment point at which the aggregate demand for and supply of labor hours equal one another in figure 2.20(a), we can derive as well the full-employment output level of Y_1^R in figure 2.20(b). The logic of this determination means that the neoclassical essences—preferences (the choice of individuals between real income and leisure) and scarcity (the marginal product of labor)—govern the final equilibrium output in the economy.

The stark implication of this reductionism is that the aggregate supply of goods and services, and by logical extension the full-employment level to which it corresponds, are completely unaffected by changes in the aggregate demand for those goods and services. For example, suppose the demand for all goods and services increases because the state increases the money supply. Since, as shown, the supply of goods and services must be fixed by these essences (which by assumption have not changed), the only effect of such a change by the state will be for prices to rise as individuals try to purchase more of a given supply.

Now, consider the labor market again. An increase of prices will only act to shift both the aggregate supply and the aggregate demand for labor hours so that there is no net effect on the full-employment level, $(hL)_1$, and, therefore, none on the implied full-employment output level, Y_1^R. To see this, consider that the rise in prices, because of an increased money supply, shifts the aggregate demand for labor hours upward and to the right. The reason for this demand shift in the labor market is that for any given money wage, producers will demand more labor at the higher prices because that given money wage corresponds to a lower real wage. In addition, the same rise in prices acts to shift the aggregate supply of labor hours upward and to the left. The reason for this supply shift in the labor market is that for any given money wage, laborers will supply fewer labor hours at the higher prices because that given money wage corresponds to a lower real wage. We show these respective demand-and-supply shifts in figure 2.21 from D_h^1 to D_h^2 and from S_h^1 to S_h^2. At the original money wage, w_1, there will now be an excess demand for labor hours, as measured by xy in figure 2.21. Money wages will therefore rise to w_2 in the figure at the point at which the excess demand for labor hours becomes zero.

Thus, an increased money supply produces an increase in the money wage, but the increase in prices exactly offsets it, so that the real wage remains at its equilibrium level. Since the real wage remains unchanged, so must employment and real output. In other words, higher prices caused by an expansion in the money supply would induce an increase in real output only if producers' money-wage costs did not rise

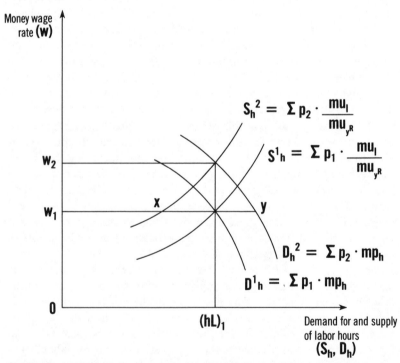

Figure 2.21.   Shift in both supply of and demand for labor hours as a result of price change. Both curves shift upward by the same proportion so that total hours of employment, on the horizontal axis, remain the same.

proportionately. Since they did, however, real output, Y_1^R, remains unchanged.

Let us summarize this neoclassical logic by considering the aggregate supply of and demand for commodities as shown in figure 2.22. There the supply is drawn as a perfectly inelastic line. The reason for this is that only so-called real factors—that is, labor-versus-leisure choices and marginal productivity of labor—govern it. The aggregate supply of commodities is given, as it were, by the play of these forces or, as we have been calling them in this book, these essences. It is thus unaffected by changes in aggregate demand.

Of course, this still leaves open the question of what determines the price level in a society. Stated differently, the question is, What determines the position of the aggregate-demand curve in figure 2.22? The neoclassicals answer this question by specifying a new equation in which price level is related to the money supply.

The Fisher, or Cambridge, equation thus completes our explanation of the neoclassical system. In its Cambridge version, we may write the equation as

$$P = \frac{M}{k \cdot Y^R},$$

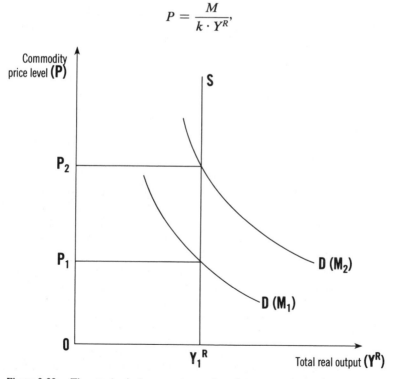

Figure 2.22.   The neoclassical aggregate-supply and aggregate-demand curves.

where P represents the absolute price level; M, the demand for money to finance market purchases of commodities; k, the proportion of real income individuals want to hold for these transaction purposes; and Y^R, real income. Since Y^R is given by the so-called real side of the economy (i.e., by the labor market and the production function), and k is assumed to be given by mass human psychology, we have a simple relationship between prices and the demand for money in a society.

To see this clearly, suppose the citizens of a state empower it to supply money to them. Consider now a given state-supplied stock of money, $\bar{M}$. To derive the aggregate neoclassical demand curve, let us rewrite the above Cambridge equation in the form

$$\bar{M} = k \cdot P \cdot Y^R.$$

Suppose real income rises in the society. A rise in real income means, according to this equation, that the demand for money will rise to finance these increased real transaction needs (assuming here no change in k). If, however, the state does not alter the money supply ($\bar{M}$), there will be an excess demand for money in the society. An excess demand for money is equivalent to saying that there will be an excess supply of commodities as individuals try to build up their cash balances.

This excess supply of commodities will tend to depress prices (P in the above equation). Prices will fall until the real cash balances individuals desire to hold are equal to k times the new Y^R. (Note that here the only change in the fraction $\bar{M}/P$ occurs in the denominator.) Consequently, we have a negative relationship between the price level and real income as shown by the negative slope of the aggregate-demand curve in figure 2.22.

The aggregate-demand curve, however, will shift if the state decides to increase the supply of money. Suppose, for example, the state decides to increase the supply of money even though there has been no change in real income or in k. In this case, there will be an excess supply of money at the current level of real income and prices. This means that individuals will begin to spend their excess holdings of money on the given supply of commodities ($\bar{Y}_1^R$), thereby bidding up their prices. This process will continue until the real cash balances are once again in line with the unchanged k times the unchanged $\bar{Y}_1^R$. (Note that in contrast to the previous example, both numerator and denominator change in the fraction M/P.) This shift in aggregate demand as a result of an expansion of the money supply is shown in figure 2.22. Prices will thus rise from P_1 to P_2.

Let us now see exactly why in neoclassical theory an expansion of state expenditures can affect only the composition but *not* the level of aggregate demand. Suppose the state expands its purchase of commodities in the society by selling government bonds to citizens. This will have absolutely no effect in the just described aggregate demand-and-supply market. Since the money supply has not changed, the aggregate-demand curve does not shift. Since there is no change in the real side of the economy (i.e., in the productivity of labor or in labor-versus-leisure decisions), there can be no change in the aggregate-supply curve.

It follows that change occurs only in the capital market. To the private demand for savings, we may now add this new public demand. These demands compete with each other, thereby driving up the rental rate on capital. This increased rate, in turn, acts to decrease the real demand for new capital. And this induced decrease in private investment allows resources to be shifted from the production of commodities for the private sector to the production of goods for the state.

According to neoclassical theory, the expansion of state expenditures has a purely redistributive effect on the economy; it does not alter the existing level of real output, demand, or employment in the society. Neoclassicals thus conclude that there is no role for the state to play in determining employment and real output, for these are *already* determined within the society's competitive markets and ultimately by the real forces (essences) that govern those markets. If left alone, competitive markets will correct whatever temporary disequilibria may occur in the society.

D.2. The Keynesian Answer to Capitalist Recessions

Keynesian economists criticize this neoclassical view and the implied policy of no state intervention. They argue that if neoclassical markets do not adjust properly or if their adjustment is too slow, involuntary unemployment will persist. In such a situation can the state, via its spending, be a substitute mechanism for the improperly functioning or too-slow market adjustment? Keynes clearly answered in the affirmative.

To prepare the ground for his answer, Keynes challenged the contending neoclassical determination of output and employment. Following the logic of neoclassical theory, he criticized the role of markets as automatic stabilizers and questioned their underlying determinants, especially the role of utility.

We may therefore begin with Keynes's position on the supply of labor hours. His notion is that workers are generally endowed with a psychological propensity to resist declines in their money wages. They also use the power wielded by their unions to maintain these wages. This Keynesian thesis produces a perfectly elastic supply of labor hours at a psychologically and union-determined money wage. In figure 2.23(a)

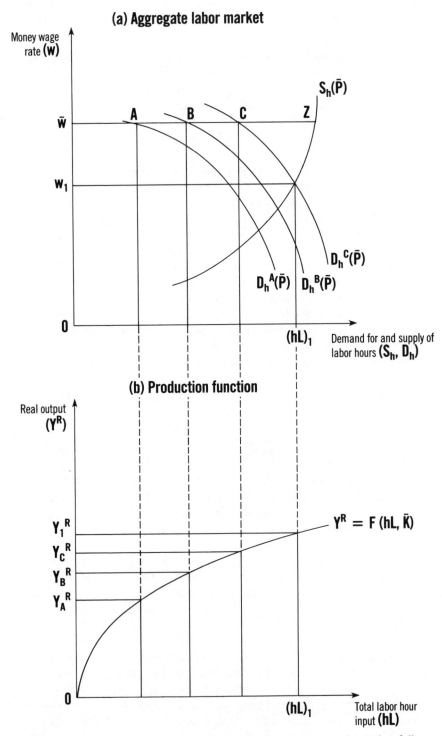

Figure 2.23. Involuntary unemployment in the labor market and less-than-full-employment output in the economy, with money wages and prices assumed to be constant.

this supply is indicated by the horizontal line drawn from the fixed money wage, $\bar{w}$, to the point of intersection of that line with the demand curve $D_h^c(\bar{P})$. In sharp contrast to the previous neoclassical concepts, Keynes has now created the possibility of involuntary unemployment of an amount CZ at the money wage $\bar{w}$.

Two observations are in order. First, this involuntary unemployment results from Keynes's new assumption about how human nature reveals itself in this market. The neoclassical utility calculus of the choice between real income and leisure no longer governs the supply behavior of laborers. In its place is a new kind of human rationality derived from what Keynes takes to be given human psychology and power. Presumably, the latter are as plausibly rooted in our genes as are the neoclassical axioms about nonsatiation, consistency, and so forth. In that sense, Keynes is as much a humanist as are neoclassical economists. Of course, from the perspective of the neoclassical economist, the "Keynesian human" may appear to act in a quite irrational way. The reason is that individuals in the neoclassical world are assumed to calculate decisions in terms of real wages and not this Keynesian money wage.

Second, this perfectly elastic supply of labor at the fixed money wage amounts to a kind of market imperfection such as those discussed earlier in this chapter. In a sense, Keynes has found a barrier that prevents the labor market from self-correcting. An excess supply of labor is not competed away by having money wages fall; it is a market imperfection introduced into an otherwise neoclassical world.

Now let us examine carefully the condition of the labor market when the demand for labor falls. We will also assume for the moment that prices remain constant. The reasons for the latter assumption will be given after we explore the effects produced by a fall in the demand for labor.

Given the assumption of constant prices, suppose a fall in the demand for labor is caused by a decrease in investment. The latter may decline because of increased business uncertainty about future prospects for profitable sales. Shifts in the demand for labor to the left will trace out a series of different employment points along the given money wage line $\bar{w}$. These points are shown in figure 2.23(a) as C, B, and A. Each of these employment points will be below that of full employment at $(hL)_1$.

At each point along the line CBA, there is involuntary unemployment. Individuals are willing to work additional hours at the wage $\bar{w}$, but they are prevented from doing so by the very forces that set the money wage at that level. Clearly, market competition is not working properly in this labor market. Consequently, the equilibrium employment that results with any given demand-for-labor curve is not that of the full-employment curve at $(hL)_1$.

If we now take into account the production function as shown in figure 2.23(b), we can derive the real output in this economy for each of these less-than-full-employment points. This is shown in figure 2.23(b), where Y_1^R indicates the full-employment output.

Given these less-than-full-employment real outputs, the aggregate-supply curve is easily derived. Since prices have been assumed to be constant, the supply of real output must be perfectly elastic at whatever the given price level is assumed to be. The different employment levels in figure 2.23(a) produce different real outputs in figure 2.23(b). Each of these employment levels, however, corresponds to the same given price level ($\bar{P}$ in figure 2.23(a)). Since these different outputs are also related to the same price level, the aggregate-supply curve must be a horizontal line. Such a Keynesian supply curve is shown in figure 2.24. We have also noted there the previously derived neoclassical, perfectly inelastic supply at the full-employment income Y_1^R.

It is worth noting that this neoclassical, perfectly inelastic supply curve is based on two key assumptions: (1) that all markets, including the labor one, are assumed to be completely flexible, and (2) that all agents of supply and demand are assumed to be perfectly informed about price and wage movements. In fact, we have assumed implicitly that all laborers in the labor market are perfectly informed about price and wage movements and that the operation of this market is not hindered in any way by market barriers. In stark contrast to these neoclassical assumptions, Keynes's way of looking at the labor market produces a constant money wage there and a perfectly elastic aggregate-supply curve. This constancy of money wages persists in the face of significant involuntary unemployment, the possibility of which neoclassical theory rules out.[15]

There is another reason for this Keynesian, perfectly elastic aggregate-supply curve. It, too, is based partly on the previous assumption that changes in the demand for firms' output do not produce changes in their prices. One might think of this assumption in terms of a given and constant marginal cost of output whenever firms operate significantly below their potential capacity. Over that relevant range of their supply curve, the marginal product of labor may be assumed to remain more or less constant when additional labor is hired. This constancy of the marginal product, along with the unchanged money wage, produce a constant marginal cost and thus a constant output price. (Recall that

---

15. A further discussion of some of the differences between the neoclassical and Keynesian conceptions of the labor market appears in the appendix to this chapter.

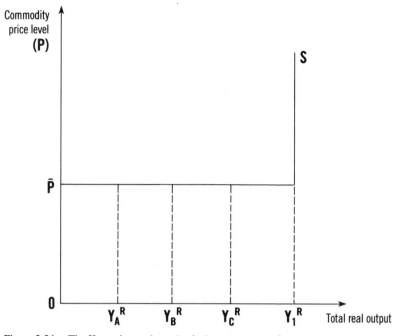

Figure 2.24.   The Keynesian and neoclassical aggregate-supply curve.

$mc_q = w/mp_{hL}$, and that for profit maximization $P = mc_q$; if both numerator and denominator in this mc_q fraction are constant, then prices also will be constant.) In a sense, the recession itself could be a cause of this situation for producing units because it creates so much excess capacity in the economy.

Let us now turn to the demand side of the Keynesian theory. With his new assumptions about supply conditions, Keynes produced the theory that demand is the essential determinant of aggregate output and employment. For the neoclassical essentialization of supply Keynes substituted an essentialization of demand. According to neoclassical theory, changes in demand have absolutely no effect on real output or employment. The supply or real output and the level of employment are essentially effects of utility and scarcity. Changes in demand do not touch those essences. In contrast, Keynes stressed that these neoclassical essences do not matter at all in situations of less than full employment. Their irrelevance is expressed geometrically by the Keynesian, perfectly elastic supply curve.

Thus, space was created for Keynes's new theory of aggregate-demand behavior. There are basically two parts to this demand theory.

One deals with the savings-versus-consumption behavior of individuals, and the other concerns the demand of individuals for money. We will begin with the savings-versus-consumption decision.

Keynes rejected the neoclassicals' preference determination of the supply of new capital or savings. For him the supply of new capital was influenced not so much by the rental rate on capital as by the real income of potential savers. In other words, given any rental rate, individuals will save money because of some given psychological propensity to put aside some of their real income for the future. This propensity, taken to be more or less constant, is called the "marginal propensity to save." Like all of Keynes's other psychological propensities, this one, too, seems to be grounded in our nature as human beings.

The other side of this psychological law of savings is the law that determines real consumption: whatever individuals do not save, they must consume. Thus, the total consumption by individuals is also a function of their real income. This dependence has been called the Keynesian consumption function. It specifies a more or less fixed relationship between added consumption and added income. That relationship has been called the "marginal propensity to consume."

To better appreciate the Keynesian alternative, consider the neoclassical analysis of the capital market. There the supply of and demand for new capital determines the rental rate on capital and the amount of savings and investment in the economy. The market works as follows: If investment increases, an excess demand for new capital will develop. This will bid up the rental rate until sufficient new savings are forthcoming to once again clear the market by establishing a new equilibrium at a higher rental rate. Consequently, consumption will fall by just enough to release the necessary resources to produce the increased investment goods desired by the society. We may thus conclude that increased investment creates its own increased savings by changing the price of future relative to current consumption.

Keynes's consumption function introduces a new and rather important change in the neoclassical idea that adjustments within the capital market alone produce an equality between savings and investment. If savings are a function of income, then in a situation of less than full employment a change in investment spending will also change that income and savings. The amount saved will no longer be independent of the amount invested. In the capital market, a shift in the investment function to the right will also shift the savings function to the right. It is quite possible that the new equilibrium rental rate will remain the same as before rather than necessarily rise (as in the neoclassical theory).

This dependence of savings on income means that continued changes in investment will trace out a series of different rental rates as both curves shift in the capital market. Therefore, we no longer have an un-ambiguous solution for the equilibrium rental rate in the savings-and-investment market alone, as claimed by neoclassical economists. Only if income is given can the rental rate alone determine the equilibrium be-tween savings and investment. But, of course, Keynes's emphasis was on the impact of investment on income in a less than fully employed society.

Keynes next expanded his theory for determining the rental rate on capital in the so-called money market. He introduced still another new psychological determinant: individuals have a propensity to hold money not only for the traditional reason, to make transactions, but for liquid-ity or speculative purposes as well. Consequently, he theorized, in a money market the demand for money becomes a function not only of real income (as in the previously specified Cambridge equation) but of the rental rate as well, because of speculative or liquidity needs. For-mally, the total demand for money in the economy became a function of both real income and the rental rate on capital.

Keynes's theory of liquidity preference suggests that as the rental rate rises, an individual's demand for money will decrease because of the increased cost of holding cash balances idle when attractive high-yielding assets could be purchased. In addition, as rates rise, expecta-tions tend to build that they will eventually fall. Given that expectation, it makes sense for an individual to try to lock into higher-yielding assets now and thus be in a position to take advantage of any possible capital gains when rates do drop. In that eventuality, the previously purchased assets could be sold at much higher prices.

With Keynes's changes, the savings-and-investment decisions in the capital market and the transaction-and-liquidity decisions in the money market both came to depend on the rental rate and on real income. This differed from the neoclassical dichotomy, in which savings-and-invest-ment decisions depended only on the rental rate, and the demand for money depended only on real income. By bringing together this modi-fied behavior in both the capital market and the money market, Keynes was able to determine simultaneously the equilibrium real income and the equilibrium rental rate on capital. Logically, these equilibrium lev-els were determined by the given marginal propensity to save and by the inherent marginal product of capital in the capital market, and by the propensity to demand money for both transaction and speculative needs and by the state-given supply of money in the money market. These determinants became the new essences within the Keynesian theory.

Given the resulting determination of the equilibrium real income in terms of these essences, we can find the corresponding employment level by examining the production function. Clearly, this equilibrium employment level can be anywhere between zero and full employment.

If we now compare the neoclassical and Keynesian theories of employment and real output, we can see how in the neoclassical view, employment determines what will be the real output in society, whereas in the Keynesian view, spending determines what will be real output and thus employment. For neoclassical economists the rental rate is determined without regard to what happens in the money market, while aggregate demand is determined in the money market without regard to what happens in the capital market. In sharp contrast, for Keynesian economists the rental rate *and* real income are determined simultaneously by the interaction of forces emanating from both of these markets.

In figure 2.25 we consider once again the Keynesian and neoclassical supply segments of the aggregate-supply curve. To these we add the Keynesian aggregate-demand curve. A change in spending by either or both consumers and investors will shift the aggregate-demand curve to the right, thereby increasing real income in the society from Y_A^R to Y_B^R, as shown in the diagram. This result is exactly what Keynes set out to show; it presumes the Keynesian supply curve in figure 2.24.

The precise quantitative impact of this change in spending on real income and thus employment depends on the size of the marginal propensity to save; that is, the proportion of income saved determines the magnitude of the Keynesian multiplier. Its impact depends partly on the existence of unemployed resources so that a change in spending will not merely bid up prices and wages (that is why the perfectly elastic supply curve becomes so important). Its impact also depends on the effect of increased spending on the rental rate of capital. Increased incomes generated by an increase in spending produce a rise in the transaction demand for money. With an unchanged supply of money, this rise in the transaction demand for money creates an excess demand for money, and rental rates are bid up. If investment is at all sensitive to such an increase in this rate, then the multiplier impact on real income will be smaller, the more important the link becomes between an increase in spending, an induced increase in the rental rate, and a consequent fall in investment. Yet if prices and wages are more or less constant or are slow to change, and if changes in investment spending are not that sensitive to changes in the rental rate, then a change in aggregate spending in society will have a significant impact on the level of real incomes.

A problem arises: there is no reason to expect investment demand to increase when business prospects are so poor. Indeed, poor business expectations are part of the problem causing a lack of effective demand. In addition, since consumption spending is tied to real income and since incomes are depressed, there is not much hope that consumption will

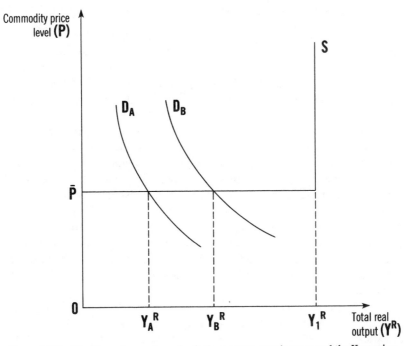

Figure 2.25.   The Keynesian and neoclassical aggregate-supply curve and the Keynesian aggregate-demand curve.

rise somehow. However, since increased spending is the essential Keynesian solution to the depression, the obvious candidate to undertake that spending becomes the state. It must increase its spending and the supply of money in order to shift the aggregate-demand curve to the right and thereby secure a full-employment equilibrium.

However, suppose that in times of depression, the propensity of individuals to hold their wealth in the form of cash balances is high. Then any increase in the money supply will have only a minimal impact on lowering the rental rate (the so-called Keynesian liquidity trap). In this case, the ultimate determinant of real output and employment becomes state spending. The key to achieving full employment is for the state to run deficits that are sufficient to push the otherwise inert economy to full employment.[16]

16. The typical textbook model of demand, which is based on these assumptions of fixed prices and wages in commodity markets and a liquidity trap in the money market, can be written as

$$Y^R = cY^R + I + G,$$

D.3. Reactions to Keynesian Theory

Perhaps the previously mentioned three main forms of reaction to the
Keynesian critique of neoclassical theory and Keynes's alternatives can
now be better understood. For those who, for whatever complex reasons, wish to maintain neoclassical theory's two essential organizing
ideas—scarcity and preferences—the Keynesian contribution is seen
mostly as an attack, for it subtracts that which is deemed to be essential
(preferences and scarcity) and substitutes unexplained new essences
(psychology, power, and institutions). Such economists quickly go to
work to show how the new essences can be explained by (reduced to)
human preferences (and/or scarcity). Thus they reestablish the basic
structure of neoclassical theory, and the Keynesian critique becomes
merely one of the many that neoclassical theory has encountered and
overcome. Certain new ideas or emphases remain, of course (such as
Keynes's uncertainty principle), but these, too, are understood as secondary complications within the context of the neoclassical tradition of
self-adjusting markets based on the rational behavior of suppliers and
demanders.

For those who wish to supplant neoclassical theory with any approach save Marxism, Keynesian theory offers the way. Such economists seize upon the new entry-point concepts of mass psychology,
power, and institutions to develop ever-new concepts, or "macromod-
els," to extend Keynes's contributions and continue the challenge to
neoclassical theory.

Economists who advocate a middle position attempt to synthesize
these two extremes. Consequently they swing from one to the other, depending on the times. They can be found at one moment embracing the
Keynesian contributions and at another rejecting them. It almost seems
as if the neoclassical theory is the one in which they truly believe. Yet
they hold the Keynesian view as well in order to assuage their social
concern about the bothersome neoclassical explanations of unemployment and poverty as voluntary, as well as the theory's complete reliance
on the effectivity of self-correcting markets.

In recent years, economic theory has witnessed all these reactions.

---

where c is the Keynesian marginal propensity to consume, I stands for investment, and G
represents government spending. Solving the equation for Y^R yields

$$Y^R = \frac{1}{1-c} \cdot I + \frac{1}{1-c} \cdot G,$$

where $1/1-c$ stands for the multiplier. If I does not change, then $\Delta Y^R = 1/1-c \cdot \Delta G$.
The essential determinant of Y^R has become the state.

One popular approach relaxes the Keynesian assumption of fixed prices, but leaves money wages fixed, as before, by the psychology and power of laborers. The result of this approach has been the creation of an aggregate-supply curve that is neither perfectly elastic nor inelastic. This is the dream of those who advocate taking a middle position. Such a curve is shown in figure 2.26.

A shift in aggregate demand will still cause an increase in real income and employment, but the size of the multiplier will be diminished the more important the induced price rise becomes owing to the expansion of demand. In such a world, there is room for the concerns of both neoclassicals and Keynesians: state spending, changes in the money supply, and market adjustments can all have their respective effects on the level of real income and employment in the society.

Thus, for example, if demand falls from its full-employment level, then an automatic offsetting tendency will be set in motion. The fall in prices of commodities due to the excess supply in the markets will create an increase in the real cash balances held by individuals. This will put

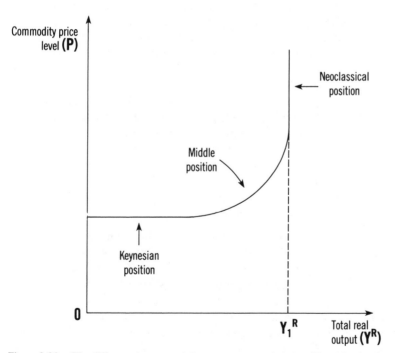

Figure 2.26.   The different segments of the aggregate-supply curve offered by the three different positions provoked by Keynes's theory.

downward pressure on the rental rate for new capital in the money market (assuming no liquidity trap is operating there). This decrease in rental rates may then stimulate investment spending. Also, the rise in real cash balances may stimulate consumption spending, assuming that real consumption of commodities is a function not only of real income but of the real money balances of individuals as well. An increase in the latter will then stimulate consumption spending. The upshot of these two effects is that real income will not fall as much as it might otherwise.

However, with money wages still rigid, the economy can remain locked in a new less-than-full-employment equilibrium. Thus there is room for increased state spending and/or an increased money supply to shift the aggregate-demand curve back to its former full-employment level. Clearly, the need for state intervention is reduced the more important these automatic market adjustments become.

The next step may seem obvious. Why not let wages as well as prices be flexible? That is precisely what has happened during the past few years in the new macroeconomics that has developed. If wages and prices are completely free to adjust to whatever changes occur in demand and supply, then we are back to a perfectly inelastic aggregate-supply curve. In other words, we have rediscovered the neoclassical theory in which there is no space for the state to influence aggregate real income or employment. We have also reaffirmed the underlying importance of preference calculations and scarcity in determining the value of all commodities produced, the employment generated, and the aggregate real income of individuals in society.

The latter approach has recently been called the "new classical theory." It is an appropriate label, for the content of that new theory is precisely what has been presented in much of this chapter. And what of the Keynesian criticisms of and alternatives to neoclassical theory? Basically, by reaffirming the inherent market rationality of all individuals, Keynesian economics disappears.[17]

D.4. The Role of the State in Capitalist Society

Keynesian theory claims that of the two main components of private spending, consumption and investment, consumption spending is the more stable. It follows that the essential reason offered by the theory for why an economy might be operating at less than full employment is a fall in investment spending by private businesses. This raises the question of why investment declines. The Keynesian answer is that the expected marginal product of, or return to, capital falls off. This causes

17. See the appendix to this chapter.

the demand for new capital to collapse in the capital market. Consequently, we have the above-mentioned problem of a deviation of expected investment from expected savings.

The reason for this decline in the expected return to capital is found in our inability to foresee the future. Business investors must make investment decisions that are unavoidably dependent on predictions and expectations about an inherently unknowable future. They are born with this uncertainty, and one effect of this "natural" phenomenon is the inevitable possibility of a disruption between the more or less stable savings in a society and the levels of investment rendered volatile by uncertainty. In this sense, declines in investment spending are not anyone's fault; their cause is ultimately reduced to our imperfect human nature.

In such a world of natural imperfections, the state steps in to heal the society. Because of other market imperfections, such as Keynes's liquidity trap and his wage-and-price rigidities, the economy is not able to correct itself and restore the full-employment equilibrium it would otherwise be destined to achieve. Therefore, the state's visible hand guides the economy to that full-employment, Pareto-optimum point where individuals finally have the freedom to choose whether or not they want to be unemployed and whether or not they want to be rich or poor.

It follows that the cause of a less-than-full-employment economy and thus that economy's decline in wealth is not to be found in the capitalist structure itself. Instead, the ultimate cause can be traced to limitations in our nature as human beings and thus to our need to form investment plans that are uncertain and volatile in nature. In addition, existing market imperfections can be traced to limits in our nature: the will for power by laborers and business, which produces wage and price rigidities; and the uncertainty in the money market, which produces a possible liquidity trap.

In this sense, the Keynesian understanding of society is parallel to the neoclassical view: both embrace a kind of humanist view of the workings of the economy and the inevitability of human development. Neither theory has any place for an alternative view that focuses on complex structural relations within capitalist economies which might, in a wide variety of circumstances and for quite heterogeneous reasons, generate a crisis, in the sense of a decline in investment spending. Specifically, neither theory sees how the existence and reproduction of capitalist classes can generate capitalist crises.

A number of Keynesians would disagree with our characterization. While they do not embrace the class approach and analysis of the next chapter, they have grave doubts about the capacity of the capitalist institutions of private property and markets to achieve a fully employed society. The combination of an institutional structure, distribution of income, and uncertainty promises continually to plunge a capitalist society into deep and recurrent crises.

Aside from the important qualification just noted, for both the Keynesian and the neoclassical theory the ultimate cause of capitalist crises is found in nature—human or otherwise. The state, for the Keynesians, and the market, for the neoclassicals, generate social effects that are similar to those attributed to religion. Each reforms whatever evil is given to society by our nature. However, both Keynesians and neoclassicals share the view that capitalist economies represent the optimum social arrangement for producing and distributing the fruits of labor. Marxists do not share that view. Nor do they believe in the theoretical systems of the neoclassicals and the Keynesians. Their different theory offers an altogether different interpretation of the structure and problems of capitalist economies.

E. Suggested Readings

Friedman, Milton. *Capitalism and Freedom.* Chicago: University of Chicago Press, 1962.

A classic and clear statement of the basic philosophy informing conservative neoclassical thinking.

Froyen, Richard. *Macroeconomics: Theories and Policies.* New York: Macmillan, 1983.

An intermediate text in macroeconomics that presents a good overview and summary of the various theories at play in current neoclassical and Keynesian economics.

Hicks, J. R. *Value and Capital.* London: Oxford University Press, 1957.

An advanced and sophisticated summary of the structure of neoclassical theory.

Katzner, Donald. *Walrasian Microeconomics: An Introduction to the Economic Theory of Market Behavior.* Reading, Mass.: Addison-Wesley, 1988.

An advanced but very clear treatment of the logical structure of neoclassical theory which comprehensively incorporates recent developments.

Keynes, John Maynard. *The General Theory of Employment, Interest, and Money.* London: Macmillan, 1936.

The classic statement of macroeconomics and its differences from traditional neoclassical theory.

Klamer, Arjo. *Conversations with Economists: New Classical Economists and Opponents Speak Out on Current Controversy in Macroeconomics.* Totowa, N.J.: Rowman and Allanheld, 1984.

The title captures nicely the message of the book.

McCloskey, Donald. *The Applied Theory of Price.* New York: Macmillan, 1985.

An intermediate text that develops the tradition of Stigler's *The Theory of Price.*

Phelps, Edmund. *Political Economy.* New York: W. W. Norton, 1985.

An introductory text that attempts to present a new coherent picture of modern neoclassical thinking about micro- and macroeconomics.

Samuelson, Paul, and Nordhaus, William. *Economics.* New York: McGraw-Hill, 1985.

A classic text on neoclassical theory: the progenitor of almost all introductory texts in economics.

Stigler, George. *The Theory of Price.* New York: Macmillan, 1942.

A classic intermediate text in microeconomics that presents a concise overview of that theory.

Appendix. Rational Expectations

One might expect neoclassical economists to worry about the assumption that human beings somehow possess perfect information about price and wage movements. As we have already noted, humans foresee the future imperfectly. Consequently, for this reason alone, deviations from the full-employment equilibrium are always a possibility since individuals will make mistakes in foreseeing future prices and wage changes. In recent years, the issue of imperfect individual forecasts has occupied many neoclassical economists.

A so-called rational-expectations school has developed to deal with the problem. Neoclassical economists working on this new approach have modified the basic neoclassical theory presented so far in this chapter by introducing new concepts into the theory in regard to how individuals form expectations of future price and wage movements. As might be expected in any logical extension of the concepts informing neoclassical theory, individual expectations or forecasts are made in a rational way. This extension amounts to a new attack on the Keynesian approach. In particular, it is an attack on the Keynesian assumption that at least in the short run, with money wages fixed, a shift in the demand for labor to the right (caused by a change in the money supply) will increase the level of employment in the economy.

Suppose, for example, individuals expect the supply of money to increase. The expected rise in the money supply will shift the aggregate-demand curve to the right, and prices will then be expected to increase. In turn, this rise in prices will shift the demand for labor hours in the labor market. Now, in the Keynesian world, in response to this rise in prices, the supply of labor hours will *not* shift upward and to the left, at least not in the short run. Thus, a rightward shift in the labor-demand curve, combined with an unchanged supply-of-labor curve, indicates that employment and real output are on the rise in the economy.

However, in the world of modified neoclassical rational expectations, we obtain a very different answer. According to this approach, the supply curve of labor hours will shift upward and to the left in the short run because rational labor suppliers fully expect that a rise in this money supply will increase prices in the economy. Therefore, being rational, these labor suppliers demand higher money wages, unlike their irrational Keynesian counterparts. The labor market thus reaches a new equilibrium at a higher money wage and price level, but no change takes place in the real wage. In effect, the result pictured in figure 2.21 is reproduced here. Thus, the labor market returns to its initial full-employment level, and, consequently, real output in the economy does not change.

Comparing the two approaches, we can see how in the Keynesian world, laborers are "fooled" by or react slowly to price increases induced by changes in the money supply, whereas in the rational-expectations world, laborers are never systematically fooled by policy changes. The rational reaction to an expected increase in the money supply is to demand higher money wages to offset higher expected prices. It follows that the rational-expectations school has in effect returned us to the neoclassical world, in which the state, even in the short run, cannot affect any real part of the economy—for instance, its level of employment or its real output.

3 Marxian Theory

A. The Marxian Tradition and Its Theories

We mentioned in chapter 1 that Marxian theory is a class theory. The originality of this theory lies not in its claim that classes exist, but in its proposition that they have a particular structure—exploitation—and that this structure shapes what we see, think, and do. Marxian theory concludes that class exploitation occurs in our society and that our political system, literature, family structure, sports, television programing, religions, and incomes are all complexly shaped by such exploitation. In particular, economic outcomes in the United States today (prices, incomes, and wealth) are shaped by class exploitation.

These are bothersome conclusions to consider. They force us to contemplate a relationship, a connection, between those things in life we may hold dear—political freedom, the family, private enterprise, baseball, religion, and the like—and something we typically find bad—namely, exploitation. They also suggest the possibility of an endless tension and perhaps even of struggle and revolution in our society: exploiters versus exploited. On the one hand, such ideas are unsettling. On the other, they can be liberating, in the Marxian view, by permitting people to see exploitation in our society and work for the social changes needed to eliminate it.

Parallel to neoclassical theory, Marxian theory conveys its own ethical messages. One of the most significant messages concerns the class process itself. Those laborers who produce goods and services should own them and decide what to do with them. The laborers who produce more than they consume, who create the surplus so central to Marxian theory, should control and distribute that surplus as their own. If and when this does *not* occur in a society, Marxian theory claims that a kind of social theft takes place: some individuals "steal" the surplus labor (or its fruits) from those who have produced it. The term "social theft" seems warranted because the thieves (the receivers of surplus) *take* what others (the performers of surplus labor) have produced; they give nothing in return. Marxists label the two sides "exploiters" versus "exploited."

Just as we become angry when personal theft strikes our families, so, too, Marxism exhorts us to become angry at this social theft of the labor of one group by another. Just as society establishes laws, morals, teachings, and customs that oppose and condemn personal theft, so Marxism calls for the establishment of a society rid of social theft. Marxism's recognition of exploitation as social theft aims to awaken anger and to direct attention to social changes that would eliminate exploitation.

Marxian theory also underscores how capitalist society has produced ideas, politics, and economic structures that not only repress knowledge of exploitation as social theft but also encourage the growth and development of exploitation as "economic progress." Indeed, classical and neoclassical economics are two idea-systems that, in the Marxian view, help make exploitation possible in society. This situation provoked Marx and Marxists after him to direct their work toward a criticism both of capitalist society and the theories that support it by denying or ignoring the existence and social consequences of class exploitation. The Marxian tradition has developed around these twin critical objectives.

The Marxian economics presented in this chapter forms part of the overall Marxian tradition. The context of Marxian economics is that tradition, just as the context of neoclassical economics is the philosophical and political tradition with which Americans are most familiar. We need briefly to sketch the history of the Marxian tradition precisely because it is not familiar. Otherwise, students would understandably confuse matters by attempting to cram Marxian economics into the non-Marxian tradition they are most familiar with. Before anyone attempts to bridge the distance separating Marxian from neoclassical economic theory, we need to know just what that distance is. Placing Marxian theory within its broader tradition will help us do that.

Karl Marx (1818–1883) did both theoretical and practical political work throughout his adult life. The child of "comfortable" parents (his father was a middle-level German state bureaucrat, and his mother was from an educated Dutch family), he became radicalized as a university student. He responded to, and joined movements for, democratic changes away from the monarchies of Central Europe, for free thought instead of religious dogmatisms, and for economic well-being distributed to all rather than reserved for rich minorities. His legacy has been a growing tradition of both theoretical output and practical political organizations.

The tradition that Marx's work inaugurated has since extended into many areas not touched by Marx himself. Marx did not theorize much about how parents interact with children or about the way artists' works impact on society or about the economic problems of lawyers and doctors. Indeed, he said little about how a socialist or communist economy would operate or what problems it would face. However, in the one hundred years since he died, thinkers influenced by Marx have contributed their thoughts on these and many other topics. Similarly, the revolutionary movements for basic social justice in Europe which drew Marx's enthusiasm have since grown and changed in geographic terms as well. Today such movements exist on every continent, and Marx's name and writings play some role in nearly all of them.

A.1. Marx's Contributions

From his days as a German university student, Marx matured into a full-time activist in the ongoing European movements for social change. He shared their excitement at the possibilities for democratic societies promised by the French Revolution. The intellectual shift from concern with God and piety to concern with the social and economic conditions for human happiness attracted his enthusiastic participation. He traced many of the miseries of his time to the great inequalities of wealth and power he saw everywhere around him. He further linked these inequalities to the institution of private property, which he therefore opposed. He joined various organizations that were working to transform capitalist Europe into a cooperative commonwealth of freethinkers, something which those organizations often referred to as "socialism" or "communism." Marx's 1840s shared something of what the 1960s meant to many Americans in their twenties.

But the upheavals of 1848 across Europe, which had inspired Marx to hope for the realization of his revolutionary expectations, failed to usher in socialism or communism. True, the shock waves of 1848 altered Europe fundamentally. Feudalism never recovered, and capitalism exploded across the Continent at an accelerating pace. But the revolutions of 1848 did not bear the fruits Marx had hoped for. Instead, capitalism established itself as the dominant system, and Marx was forced to reassess his thinking, to determine what had gone wrong and why the revolutionary movements had been unable to realize a socialist transformation.

The 1850s were years of exile in Britain, and there Marx would remain for the rest of his life. He was exiled not only from his native Germany but also, for many years, from practical revolutionary activism. He decided to reevaluate his own way of thinking and the ideologies of the movements in which he had participated. He and his close colleague Friedrich Engels reexamined and criticized the social theories used by the revolutionary movements, seeking thereby to gain new insights that would bring success when history ushered in the next wave of revolutionary upheavals. During the last two decades of his life, Marx published the results of that period of reflection. He wrote several volumes of analysis of capitalism as an economic system.

The originality of Marx's analysis was and remains his lasting contribution to social theory and to modern revolutionary movements for social justice. Marx believed that he had found an important flaw in the way revolutionaries understood European society. That flaw concerned their underestimation of the significance of economics in shaping societies and their histories. More precisely, the revolutionaries of 1848 had neglected the role of class, by which Marx meant the production and distribution of surplus labor within the economy. This neglect blinded them to the class aspects of European society, and that blindness weakened their analyses of capitalism and contributed to the failure of their revolutionary projects.

Marx's writings were aimed directly at correcting this flaw. He proposed an analysis of capitalism which emphasized class. His major work, *Capital,* focused attention on the complex interdependence between the production and distribution of surplus labor (the class structure) and every other aspect of modern capitalist societies. He stressed class, made it his entry point into the analysis of society, precisely because he saw his task as one of overcoming the neglect of class among his fellow revolutionaries.

Not only did Marx write theory, but he also later resumed his organizing activities. He intended to use his new class theory to define new strategies and tactics for revolutionary movements in Europe and America. The passionate commitments of his youth resurfaced in his writings and in his intense participation in revolutionary politics (including his antislavery articles on the Civil War in the United States). He ridiculed the idea of "dispassionate analysis," which he suspected was the disguise of analysts who preferred to excuse rather than expose social injustices. Every analyst, Marx believed, makes a particular commitment to social values and to a particular kind of future society. Both Marxists and neoclassicals have their particular values, passions, and visions of a better society. What distinguishes these theorists from one another is the *difference* in their commitments or passions and in their correspondingly different theories.

For Marx, capitalism was a mass of contradictions. On the one hand, he praised capitalism for a technological dynamism whose productivity promised plenty to all on a scale unimaginable to prior generations. On the other, he criticized capitalism for tearing peasants from the land, working them ruthlessly in factories, and generating needless suffering on an equally massive scale worldwide. The promise of plenty contradicted the reality of degradation as chronicled by such novelists of nineteenth-century capitalism as Dickens, Zola, Dostoevsky, and Balzac. On the one hand, capitalism celebrated human relationships based on free, voluntary contracts between adults. On the other, it put people into such unequal situations that the poor and oppressed entered voluntarily into exploitative relationships since their alternatives were even worse. On the one hand, Marx readily acknowledged, capitalism stimulated vast new developments in human knowledge and cultural creativity. On the other, most people were reduced to performing routine, menial production tasks that earned them relatively low incomes, and they could therefore not enjoy most of those developments.

Marx's theory, like the Marxian tradition it engendered, understood itself to be an attempt to save and enhance the positive contributions of capitalism while overcoming the negative ones. The point was to analyze capitalism in order to transform it, to liberate its potential by removing its oppressive components. In Marx's view, to liberate the possibilities of capitalism required a revolution to communism. Capitalism itself was too hopelessly mired in contradictions that condemned the vast majority of people to unjustifiable denial and suffering. Communism, by contrast, would liberate the fruits of technology and cultural creativity so that they could be shared equally by everyone.

Marx did not spend time or effort analyzing communism; he seems to have frowned on speculation about the future. He did concentrate on capitalism. His analysis focused on class because Marx believed that without a full appreciation of class, society could not be liberated from the negative consequences of capitalism. Class had to be added to the analysis of capitalism, and class changes to the agenda for social transformation, if revolutionary projects were to succeed.

This liberational context for Marx's theories parallels that of another original theorist who focused on liberation. Sigmund Freud began as a physician seeking to free certain patients from intense personal suffering. He soon confronted his failure and the failure of other doctors to relieve that suffering. Deciding to reexamine critically the basic theories of the relation between mind and body used by his profession, he arrived at his new theory of "the unconscious."

Freud developed an original theory in which something overlooked by his fellow doctors, this unconscious, was shown to play an important role in the life and suffering of patients. He developed a psychoanalytic technique based on his concepts of the unconscious, and he organized others to use it to treat patients. In short, Freud contributed a new theory of the individual mind and body which enabled people to see their personal suffering in a new light. The goal of his theory and of its practitioners since has been to liberate individuals from their suffering by alerting them to their unconscious and its effects throughout their lives.

A.2. Marxism since Marx

When Marx died in 1883, no society was yet governed by a state calling itself socialist or communist. The brief attempt at establishing a workers' state in the Paris Commune of 1871, which deeply impressed Marx and Engels, had lasted only a few months. Marx's theory retained the status of a framework for analyzing capitalism and determining revolutionary strategies. It did gradually attract adherents among radicals in Europe and America, but this was a slow process that depended on individual contacts and the spread of small editions of the works of Marx and his followers.

Marxism grew in Europe most markedly in Germany. There a political party whose base was primarily workers in capitalist enterprises became increasingly involved with Marx's theories. In the years before World War I, this party, the German Social Democratic Party, became a major contender for political power. This situation brought new and different pressures and influences to bear on Marxian theory. No longer was the theory developed chiefly by small groups of revolutionaries. Now a large, established political party with elected officials to protect and an electoral image to maintain left its imprint on Marxian theory.

The German Marxists extended the theory to groups and issues Marx had barely touched. Marxian analyses of the legal system, of the social role of women, of foreign trade, of international rivalries among capitalist nations, and of the role of parliamentary democracy in the transition to communism drew animated debates. Extending the theory in these ways attracted many new adherents to socialism. It also produced changes in Marxian theory. Ambiguities in Marx's writings were found and resolved in different ways by the different sides in the debates. Marxian theory (singular) gave way to Marxian theories (plural).

The Russian revolution of 1917 added another shock to Marxian theory. For the first time, men and women inspired by Marxian theory seized state power at the helm of a massive social revolution. Their leaders, especially V. I. Lenin (1870-1924), struggled to adapt Marxian theories to the urgencies they faced. The Russian civil wars of 1918-1922, the attempt to reorganize the shattered Russian economy, and the campaign to collectivize the country's agriculture were officially analyzed using Marxian terminology and concepts. Putting Marxian theory to such tests altered it in all kinds of ways. Moreover, Marxists around the world disagreed about the significance of the new state, the Soviet Union. Some thought it represented the fulfillment of Marx's ideas and of the Marxian tradition. Others evaluated its development negatively, as a perversion of Marxism which was all the more troublesome because it clothed itself in Marxian language.

Both sides of this debate added changes to the ways in which Marxian theory was understood and extended. Some Marxists elaborated the theory into an official explanation and justification for Soviet policies at home and abroad. Others developed it to criticize and attack those policies. Both sides pushed Marxian theory into such new areas as analyses of socialist economic development, analyses of the conflicts between capitalist and communist economic systems, and debates over the definitions and relations between socialism and communism. All this added new Marxian theories to the tradition.

World War II, the growth of the Soviet Union to superpower status in the modern world, its split with China, the growth in political and economic importance of Asian, African, and Latin American societies, and the emergence of more or less independent communist political parties around the world—all these developments added still more variations to the theories making up the Marxian tradition. Recently, broad movements to alter the oppressive social conditions of women and various racial and ethnic groups have stimulated yet other Marxian theoretical innovations. Marxism is now a rich and diverse tradition. Its diversities and debates are comparable to those in other traditions—the Judaeo-Christian, the neoclassical, the republican, and so on.

It is thus unacceptable to single out one theory within the tradition and then act as if the whole tradition equaled that theory. For example, because one kind of Christian theory in South Africa endorses apartheid, that does not mean that Christianity equals apartheid. Because one kind of neoclassical theory supports government policies in Chile and South Korea, that does not mean that neoclassical theory equals right-wing dictatorships and torture. Because the Catholic church once mounted an Inquisition in Spain does not mean that Roman Catholicism can be equated with such practices. Similarly, because some Marxists, too, employed violence to silence their political opponents does not mean that Marxian theory equals dictatorship, and so on. The Marxian tradition is complex. To treat it or any other tradition as simple or unidimensional is inaccurate and misleading.

A.3. Which Marxian Theory Shall We Present?

The diversity and complexities of Marxian theories pose a problem for the writers and the readers of this book. How shall we proceed? To attempt to present a Marxian theory that somehow encompassed everything in the tradition would produce a long, tedious survey. To present one particular theory would open us to criticism that we have left out alternative Marxian theories.

Nevertheless, we have chosen the second path. We do present one particular Marxian theory. It is the one we have found to be most coherent, systematic, and persuasive, especially as an alternative to neoclassical theory. Since it is one Marxian theory and since we do not pretend that it is Marxism in general, we are obliged to explain and justify its place at the center of our attention.

In the last fifteen years, the Marxian tradition has matured enormously. There are many reasons for this. The pro- versus anti-Soviet pole around which Marxian debates swirled after 1917 has receded. Marxists around the world no longer measure one another's legitimacy and arguments against the acid test of one's attitude toward the U.S.S.R. The upsurge of new kinds of revolutionary movements in modern capitalist societies (feminism, environmentalism, antiracism, etc.) induced Marxists to reexamine and reformulate their theories. In Third World countries, social conditions provoked new departures from a Marxian theory that still largely reflected its European origins. Finally, theoretical work by non-Marxists reacting to modern capitalism and socialism generated important new insights into how societies develop. Many Marxists recognized the need to study these insights and critically incorporate them into a Marxian framework.

We have tried to choose and present here a Marxian theory that responds to all of these developments. It begins on the solid and systematic logical foundation set by Marx. However, it does not slide into the dogmatisms that trapped many Marxists in the focus on the U.S.S.R., pro or con. A basic strength of this Marxian theory lies in its concern to demonstrate the interdependency between the class and nonclass, economic and noneconomic, aspects of society. Finally, this Marxian theory emphasizes class as Marx did. We emphasize this Marxian theory because we think that what Marx aimed to achieve still remains the contribution Marxian theory has to make: to teach people about the existence and implications of class in modern society.

What follows is a particular Marxian theory. It is drawn from the works of Marx as well as from the works of many Marxists since. We have benefited from those who work with this Marxian theory and also from those who work with different Marxian theories. We believe that the Marxian theory stressed in this book incorporates important non-Marxian insights (such as those of Freud mentioned above) that need to find some place within Marxism too. Finally, this theory serves to clarify sharply the differences between Marxian and neoclassical economics.

The value of the Marxian theory that we present here will be tested in the success or failure we achieve in helping our readers distinguish Marxian from neoclassical economics. If we can sharpen the intelligence that students bring to assessing the claims of both theories, we will be satisfied. We hope that students will learn to go beyond the simple notion that there is a right and a wrong economics. If some students realize that the study of economics is like the study of any other group of theories and requires attention to the differences among them rather than the search for some finally and absolutely correct one, we will be pleased indeed. Our intent is to lead students to see theoretical differences in economics and to see how those differences matter in the world today.

B. The Logical Structure of Marxian Theory

The knowledge of economics produced by Marxian theorists depends upon Marxian theory. This knowledge differs from neoclassical knowledge. Our task is to examine in detail the specific distinguishing characteristics of Marxian theory. These will enable us to see why and how Marxian theory produces its distinctive understanding of the modern capitalist economy.

B.1. The Basic Concepts of Marxian Economics

The first step in Marxian thinking about economics concerns the relationship between the economy and the society as a whole. By "economics," we understand Marxian theory to mean all those processes in any society which involve the production of goods and services and their distribution among producers and consumers. The summary term "noneconomic" then refers to all the other kinds of processes which, together with the economic processes, form the totality called "society." There are three different kinds of noneconomic processes: the natural, the cultural, and the political.

Marxian theory works with general definitions of these noneconomic types of processes. It defines natural processes as those involving the transformation (biological, chemical, etc.) of physical properties of matter. Political processes are those concerned with the control (legislative, judicial, administrative, etc.) of individual and group behavior within society. Finally, it regards cultural processes as all those in which people construct meanings for themselves—for example, language, arts and letters, music, religion, science, and so on.

One way to think of the relationship between economic and noneconomic aspects of society is to make one the cause and the other the effect. For example, some people think that economics is what makes the world move. Such phrases as "money talks" or "the business of society is business" embody the idea that economic aspects of life are the final determinants of everything else. How often have you heard someone insist that "it was not love nor politics nor religion nor nature" that caused some event, "it was economics."

This kind of thinking is called "economic determinism." Determinist reasoning is equivalent to what we have already encountered in neoclassical theory: there are some basic causes in society which determine its daily life and its history. In particular, economic determinists generally feel that the final or essential causes of social events are found in the economic foundation of society. Often Marxism is equated with economic determinism. Yet that reasoning is just as frequently found among non- and anti-Marxists. A former president of General Motors, Charles E. Wilson, is famous for having said, "What's good for GM is good for America." That is a kind of economic determinist thinking.

Although there are Marxists and non-Marxists who theorize in economic determinist ways, there are also many on both sides who do not. The Marxian economic theory analyzed in this book is strictly opposed to economic (or any other kind of) determinism. Instead of a determinist linkage between economy and society, this Marxian theory is committed to a linkage called "overdetermination." As noted in chapter 1, we will use this term rather than the traditional term "dialectics" to describe the existence of and interaction among all aspects of society.

B.2. Overdetermination and Process

From an overdeterminist perspective, the economic aspects of society influence the noneconomic, and the reverse holds true as well. For example, economic considerations certainly influence decisions about marriage and family, and family considerations likewise influence the economic decisions people make. Economic calculations affect U.S. foreign policies, and foreign policy decisions make their marks on our economy as well. In short, the Marxian view assigns no priority to economic over noneconomic aspects of society as determinants of one another. *All the different aspects shape and are shaped by all the others.* No one part of a society, neither the economy nor any other part, determines the whole society. Every aspect of society, including the economic, is overdetermined by all the others. Economic or any other kind of determinism is rejected here in favor of overdetermination.

The notion of overdetermination is central to Marxian theory. This unique way of understanding causation clashes with the reductionism presented as the logic of neoclassical theory in chapter 2. The two theories explain the existence or causes of individuals, institutions, and indeed everything in society in radically different ways.

Thinking in terms of overdetermination means that each aspect of society is approached as the combined effect of all the other aspects of that society. This idea is best described by the word "constitutivity." Each aspect of society is constituted—literally created—as the combined effect of all the other aspects. Thus no aspect can exist independently of the others, which create it. No one aspect can exist prior to the others as, for example, their ultimate cause.

It follows that each aspect owes its existence to the others. Each is the result of the interactions among all the other aspects of society. If you think about this, you can see that this idea of overdetermination must also mean that every aspect of society is always a cause *and* an effect. Each aspect plays its particular role in shaping—that is, in causing the existence of—every other. In contrast to overdetermination, the neo-classical concept of causation assumes that some aspects (scarcity and preferences) are causes but are *not* also effects. These causal aspects have a prior existence; they occur first and serve as the ultimate deter-minants of other aspects of society. They do not constitute their effects while being simultaneously constituted by them, as the logic of overde-termination would require.

In this overdeterminist Marxian approach, the economy is shaped by the influences flowing from all the other natural, political, and cultural aspects of society. The economy is literally pushed and pulled in all di-rections by all of the different determinations emanating from the non-economic aspects of society which combine to overdetermine it. This in turn implies that the economy is always in a state of tension and change. A change in climate will favor some kinds of production and distribu-tion and inhibit others. Changing political trends will favor and inhibit certain kinds of production and distribution. Changing cultural pat-terns too will stimulate some kinds of production and distribution and stifle others.

There is no reason to expect all of those changes to impact on the economy in the same way, pushing it in the same direction at the same pace. Rather, the economy is full of contradictory impulses, tensions, and uncertainties. These reflect the many different influences that over-determine any economy.

Let us consider an example that suggests the rich play of diverse in-fluences combining to cause the existence of any one aspect of the soci-ety, in this case the economy. Suppose that you are considering what courses to take to prepare yourself for a career. Your feelings propel you toward the arts. Your parents favor law or medicine for you. Changing university priorities discourage you from considering certain majors that may be phased out soon. Your sense of the political future suggests that you do something which will not require that you seek a govern-ment job. Your mounting student loans influence you to consider a ca-reer that will put money in your pocket quickly. Your process of decid-ing is overdetermined, pushed and pulled in conflicting directions by all of these (and many more) diverse influences.

Your ultimate course and career choices will be the complicated product of the diverse influences overdetermining you. Your choices are in part economic events. They determine whether you and millions of other students like you will enlarge the supply of this kind of labor or that one. If many choose computer or health sciences, that may depress wages and salaries in those fields. This in turn will affect the investment decisions of companies who hire people trained in computer sciences. This in turn will affect the pattern of exports and imports of computer components, and so on. The economy is nothing other than the total of all such overdetermined events of production and distribution.

In the Marxian view, the economy is ceaselessly changing. This follows from the overdetermination of the economy, since a change in any noneconomic aspect of society will necessarily impose a change upon the economy. For example, when the presidency passed from Carter to Reagan, university priorities changed. Some departments won more money to hire faculty, expand course offerings, and the like, while other departments withered. This change affected students' course and career choices and so changed the economy. To take another example, changes in the science of birth control and cultural changes in attitudes toward family planning continue to have momentous economic effects. Couples with fewer children are changing their demands for housing, entertainment, and automobiles, to name just a few commodities. Declining population growth induces further changes in all kinds of economic supplies and demands, and so on.

Each change in a noneconomic aspect of society exerts its particular effects upon the economy. Since the many noneconomic aspects of society are changing in different ways all the time, they are also changing their diverse impacts upon the economy. The resulting changes in the economy are the outcome of many conflicting pressures. Changes in the economy in turn generate changes in the noneconomic aspects of society. The changes in any one part of society are simultaneously the causes *and* effects of changes in every other part.

The Marxian theoretical commitment to overdetermination thus leads directly to the view that everything in society is forever changing. This theory rejects any notion of stasis, the idea that some aspects of life are fixed. Rather, every event, person, institution, and relationship is understood as always changing. Theories, governments, economies, nature, music: all things are in the ceaseless movement of coming into being, changing, and passing out of existence. These changes are sometimes barely perceptible and sometimes dramatically revolutionary.

To underscore the endless change it sees in every aspect of every society, Marxian theory conceives of every aspect as a "process." Each process is a basic building block of the Marxian analysis of society, including all its economic aspects. Processes, then, are the infinity of aspects or things or parts of our social and natural life.

Marxian theory constructs its sense or knowledge of societies by examining how they are composed of a variety of different interacting and changing processes. Each society is thus conceived to be a mass of theoretical processes, governmental processes, economic processes, natural processes, musical processes, and so on. Marxian theory groups all the processes of any society under four broad headings or types: natural, political, cultural, and economic. As noted, each process exists only as the result of the determinations emanating from every other process in the society: each and every one is constituted by all the others. All the qualities of any one process, as well as its very existence, depend completely on (are constituted by) all the other processes in society.

For example, economic processes do more than merely influence cultural processes. They help "constitute" cultural processes—literally bring them into existence. Thus advertising expenditures not only shape the cultural creations on television; they literally make their existence possible. Similarly, the climate of North America does not merely influence crop yields; it makes them possible, it creates them. Political processes of lawmaking not only influence economies; their effects help bring into being the specific economic processes (buying, selling, importing, lending, producing, etc.) that will exist.

To take another example, consider people engaging in the economic process of saving money. They do so because of (as the complex effect of) all the other processes in society. The cultural processes that help constitute savings include ideas about frugal living, fears and expectations about the future, religious convictions, articles in newspapers, and the like. Political processes play their role; for instance, laws declare our right to own and control what we save, disciplinary processes deter others from taking such savings, rules govern inheritance, and so on. Natural processes also participate in overdetermining the process of saving; uncertainties of climate and health provoke savings, deteriorating tools necessitate saving to pay for their replacement, and so on. Finally, other economic processes also overdetermine savings: paying interest induces savings; price fluctuations sometimes provoke savings as insurance against market downturns, while in times of inflation they discourage savings; central bank management of supplies of money influences savings decisions, and the like.

These and all the other processes in society produce diverse effects that together bring into existence the one particular process of saving. They give it whatever particular features it displays in a society at a particular time. Change or remove any one of them, and the consequence will be to change or remove the saving process. It only exists because they do. It is overdetermined by all of them. No one of them causes saving; they all do. Saving is not merely the effect of any one or a subset of the other processes in society; it is rather the overdetermined effect of them all as they interact with one another. And the same is true of every other process.

Overdetermination functions within Marxian theory as the logical connection among the processes that together form any society. It is the glue that links the parts into the social whole. Its centrality in Marxism has two profound consequences for that theory. We have already noted the first one: a change in any one process leads to changes in all the other processes, which then impact back on the first process to change it, and so on. Marxian theory summarizes this implication of its commitment to overdetermination by stressing the ceaseless change that characterizes every process in society and hence the society as a totality.

B.3. Contradictions

The second consequence of the Marxian idea of overdetermination is its notion of contradictions. Since every process exists as the effect of all other processes, each is quite literally a bundle of contradictions. That is, each social process contains within itself the pushes and pulls emanating from all the other processes that make it what it is. As those processes change, so do the pushes and pulls they exert, and so too does the process they overdetermine.

For example, the process of loving another person is contradictory. It contains within itself the different effects of sexual desire, ego gratification, financial considerations, religious taboos, parental preferences, peer-group pressures, fears of loneliness, and so on. Indeed, the process of loving another person is constituted by—it is the effect of—all of the other processes surrounding both people. Since these processes push and pull both in all manner of conflicting directions, Marxian theory refers to the process of loving as contradictory, as the effect of many different and some conflicting determinations. As those other processes change and thereby exert different determinations upon the process of loving, that process too will change, and so on.

Every social process is contradictory in the sense that its existence is the overdetermined effect of all other social processes. Changes in processes engender new ways in which they affect other processes. This means that new contradictions are generated in those processes. These new contradictions impart new kinds of change in those processes, which thereby change the ways in which they influence other processes. Contradiction is, for Marxian theory, the consequence of overdetermination, the mechanism whereby change becomes the universal mode of existence of society and all its parts. Therefore, each part of society and the society as a totality exist in change.

Marxian theory generally proceeds in its analysis of any society by (1) identifying the processes in it; (2) detailing their overdetermination; and (3) then demonstrating the resulting contradictions in those processes. The point is to explain social changes as the outgrowth of the contradictions in the society. Marxian economic theory focuses on the economic processes within the society, seeking to locate their contradictions. To identify those contradictions is to pinpoint the tensions from which economic and thereby social changes evolve.

By comparison, neoclassical theory is not committed to overdetermination. Rather, it is determinist or essentialist in nature, as discussed in the previous chapter. According to the neoclassicals, social changes are usually reduced to being effects of economic changes. Economic changes are comparably reduced to being determined by a very few essential causes, such as individuals' preferences, their productive capabilities, and their privately owned resource endowments.

As demonstrated in the previous chapter, the geometric diagrams used by neoclassical economists to portray economic relationships typically make some economic phenomena causes and others effects, an essentialist idea. Other neoclassical models, whether simple linkages of effects to causes or more complex systems of simultaneous equations, also cannot represent overdetermination, because overdetermination means that all economic aspects are simultaneously causes *and* effects, in the sense of constituents, of one another and of all the noneconomic aspects of society too. The conventional mathematical models of neoclassical economics do not express relationships of overdetermination, because that theory does not connect the different aspects of the economy and the society in that way. As chapter 4 will show, the difference between neoclassical theory's determinism (essentialism) and Marxian theory's overdeterminism (antiessentialism) has major consequences when the two kinds of theorists generate their concrete economic analyses and policy recommendations.

B.4. Processes, Activities, and Relationships

In the Marxian approach, processes never occur by themselves in society. They always occur in groups. For example, a person who reads (cultural process) also breathes (natural process). Someone who orders another person to follow a rule (political process) also thinks (cultural process) and digests (natural process). An employer hiring workers (economic process) talks to them (cultural process) and directs workers' behavior during the working day (political process). Such groupings, often of many processes, are what Marxian theory defines as "relationships" or "activities" or "practices."

An activity or practice by any person can always be broken down analytically into the basic processes of which it is composed. For example, when a person runs down the street, he or she may also be perspiring, thinking, earning interest on investments, and obeying someone's order to run, all at the same time. Those processes together constitute the activity of running. Indeed, it is not quite accurate to call this activity merely "running," since that one-word label does not take into account the many different processes simultaneously involved. Similarly, the practice of organizing a trade union is a composite of processes: talking to people, thinking through strategies, perhaps changing laws, buying paper for leaflets, and so on. Marxian theory analyzes all activities and practices precisely in terms of the processes that compose them.

As with activities and practices, relationships among people are decomposable into their constituent processes. When you and I talk, we also look at each other, possibly touch each other, possibly transact some economic business with each other, and so on. Each particular relationship is a complex grouping of specific processes. As with activities and practices, it is never quite accurate to give relationships a single name or qualifying adjective, such as a "business" relationship, a "love" relationship, or any other. Relationships are always complex groupings of specific processes. You can often avoid grief in your relationships if you avoid the mistake of interpreting them unidimensionally.

The complete set of activities of a group of people and the relationships that exist among them form a society (which Marxists often call a "social formation"). The Marxian analysis of a society thus amounts to a detailed specification of which processes are grouped in what ways into the relationships that distinguish that social formation. These differ from one society to another. For example, in one society, buying and selling processes never occur. Instead, goods and services pass from their producers to their consumers by means of religious processes of distribution following sacred rules. In another society, processes of praying accompany every economic process according to elaborate rituals. In still another society, sexual processes never occur without rigid political controls by parents over children throughout life.

From the standpoint of Marxian theory, in order to understand any society, we must pay systematic attention to the particular processes that occur within it and to the particular ways they are grouped into the activities and relationships of the members of that society. The objective is to grasp and express the contradictions that give that society its particular pattern of qualities, tensions, and changes. Since Marxists usually favor certain kinds of social change, they seek an understanding that will guide their personal and organizational decisions about how to act politically to facilitate those social changes.

B.5. A Theoretical Dilemma

But a dilemma is posed by Marxian theory's view that societies and economies are immense collections of diverse processes, activities, and relationships intertwined in complex contradictions. To fully unravel them all in a systematic exposition would take huge numbers of Marxian theorists vast amounts of time. Moreover, by the time the task was done, all the theorized processes, activities, and relationships would have changed. The analyzed society would have become a historical relic superseded by the new, current society in which the Marxists lived and which they presumably wanted to change. They would have to start all over. The dilemma would remain as before.

This dilemma is still more troubling given the idea of overdetermination. If any one social process exists and has its specific qualities and contradictions by virtue of all the other social processes whose effects overdetermine it, a theorist would have to study them all to ever completely understand that one social process. And such completeness is not practically possible.

From the Marxian standpoint, the task of a comprehensive social analysis is in principle not achievable, neither for Marxian nor for any other kind of theory. It is rather like human beings' achieving birdlike flight or avoiding death or eliminating all loneliness from a lifetime. Like those impossibilities, the human incapacity to produce complete social analyses need not and should not bother us very much. To deny or dwell morosely upon our limitations promises little beyond bitter disappointments or bouts of depression or both. The point is rather to recognize the limitations that influence but do not prevent our efforts to build productive personal and social situations.

In this spirit, Marxists recognize that all social analyses, no matter which theoretical framework is used to produce them, are partial and never complete or finished. No one can understand or write the whole story about how a society is structured and how it is changing. Every theory involves an inevitably partial stab at social analysis. Marxists reject as vain any hope that one analysis will be complete while others remain partial. Nor should anyone credit the claims of those who are frightened by the limits of our theoretical capacities into insisting that they have found some miraculous way to completeness, the truth, the final explanation.

This recognition of the partiality of all theories and the social analyses they can produce is controversial among both Marxists and non-Marxists. Many Marxists find it unacceptable; they remain committed to the idea that somehow, someday, a complete analysis will be accomplished and that they are working toward that end. However, the kind of Marxian theory being discussed in this book, based as it is on overdetermination, contradiction, and process, logically arrives at a direct affirmation of its own partiality as well as that of all other social theories.

Is this admission of partiality debilitating? Does it mean that there is no point in trying to explain anything since we can explain nothing fully? Is Marxian theory's insistence on its partiality tantamount to an invitation not to bother listening to what such Marxists have to say? Are these Marxists stymied by their own theory from having anything important to add to human knowledge?

B.6. Marxian Theory and Its Entry Point

The answer to all of these questions is no. Marxists committed to overdetermination and the inevitable partiality of their theoretical output do not hesitate to generate that output. They accept partiality as a quality common to all theories. No social analysis, in their view, is other than partial. What distinguishes one theory from another is precisely that they are partial in different ways. Different theories produce different partial analyses. Marxian and neoclassical economic theories generate different economic analyses, and each analysis is partial.

That no theory can produce a complete analysis does not bother the Marxists. They argue that all theories, however partial, exert specific effects on the societies in which they occur. When neoclassical theorists produce their economic analyses (whose partiality they rarely admit), those analyses are socially influential. They participate in overdetermining everything else in that society. Similarly, when Marxists generate their different partial analyses, those analyses likewise participate in overdetermining everything else in that society. The point is that the two kinds of theory influence, push, shape, the society in different ways and different directions.

How is one theory partial in a different way from another theory? As we have seen, part of the answer lies in the important notion of entry points. All theories of society confront a totality: a complex, multidimensional mass of diversity. Every theory has to begin somewhere, with some selected aspects or part of society, to make its particular sense (knowledge, understanding, truth) of society. A social theory is always partial: it is unavoidably limited in proceeding from a part of its topic—its entry point—and it is likewise limited by the impossibility of theorizing about every aspect of the totality.

Neoclassical theory displays its partiality in three broad entry-point concepts: individual preferences, technology, and initial endowments. Neoclassical theory builds up its particular analysis or knowledge of modern economies by entering into that analysis from these distinctive entry points. By contrast, Marxian economic theory has a very different entry point: class. Marxian economics builds its distinctively partial analysis by entering into the study of the economy via its concept of class process.

Our analysis of Marxian theory requires that we examine carefully what is meant by the Marxian entry-point concept of class. Doing so will enable us to clarify this basic difference between Marxian and neoclassical economic theory, after which we will be in a position to clarify more of the differences between them by tracing how their different entry points lead them to sharply divergent understandings of economics. The final chapter of this book explores the contrasts and divergences between the two theories.

B.7. The Class Process

Marxian theory generally begins its study of any society by first inquiring into the class processes (aspects) of that society. It then proceeds to examine how the society's class structure is overdetermined by all of its nonclass processes. Finally, Marxian theory aims to show how, in turn, class participates in overdetermining all of the nonclass aspects of society.

Class is the entry-point concept of Marxian theory. It is that particular aspect of society which this theory aims to highlight and understand. Class operates in Marxian theory rather like the concept of individual human nature operates in neoclassical theory. Each theory begins with definitions of its respective entry point(s) and elaborates from there its complex understanding of how any economy works and interacts with the rest of society.

To say that Marxian economic theory has class as its entry point requires us first to examine how the theory defines the term. As stressed originally by Marx, "class" refers to a particular social process— namely, the production of surplus labor. More precisely, class is actually two particular economic processes: in one, people perform surplus labor; in the other, the fruits of that surplus labor are distributed. This specifically Marxian concept of class is different from other concepts of class which were popular before Marx and remain popular today.

The Marxian concept of surplus labor is complex. Every society of human beings is assumed to require that at least some of its members interact with nature and one another to produce goods and services.

This interaction is called "the labor process": the expenditure of human muscles, nerves, and brain power to transform objects in nature into goods and services satisfying human needs and wants. Those members of society who do this labor are called "direct laborers." These are the assumptions that lie behind the Marxian concept of surplus labor.

What then is "surplus labor"? Marx answered his own question in two steps. In the first, he noted that all labor takes time. Part of the time spent by the direct laborers goes to produce the goods and services that they themselves will consume in order to be able and willing to continue laboring. This portion of their labor time Marx called "necessary labor." It was "necessary" in the precise sense of being required to meet the direct laborers' demands for goods and services (and thus to keep them working).

Second, Marx insisted that the direct laborers always perform more labor than the necessary labor. They participate in the labor process for a longer period of time than that which is needed to supply their own needs and wants. This extra time of labor is what Marx called surplus labor. Thus, direct laborers participate in two distinct processes: the labor process of transforming nature, and the class process of performing surplus labor. It is one thing to transform nature through human labor; it is another and different thing to be involved in the production of surplus labor. The class process of producing surplus labor has existed in all societies, from the earliest known to the contemporary.

"Class" is thus defined as the economic processes of producing and distributing surplus labor. Class processes exist alongside all the natural, political, cultural, and other economic processes—nonclass processes—that constitute any society. Class processes are overdetermined by all those other, nonclass processes. Like any other processes, class processes are contradictory and constantly changing. Similarly, they participate in overdetermining all the nonclass processes and hence in shaping the contradictions and changes of the entire society.

Notice that Marxian theory, by making class its entry point, arranges the complexity of the society it seeks to understand into two contrasting parts or aspects: class and nonclass. The theory thereby organizes the topics it will treat around the task of thinking through the relationships in any society between its class and nonclass aspects. As we will show, the analyses generated by Marxian theory focus upon the interdependence between the class and nonclass parts of the social whole.

C. The Marxian Concept of Class

Overdetermination and contradiction refer to the logic and method of Marxian theory, while class refers to its basic entry-point concept. The definitions and uses of these terms distinguish Marxian theory from other theories of how societies are organized and how they change. Having explored how the first two of these concepts figure in the Marxian theoretical framework, we turn now to the third concept, class. As we shift our attention from societies as a whole to a more narrow focus on economics, Marxian theory's complex conceptualization of class is again the logical first step for us.

Several different concepts of class have long appeared in the works of both Marxists and non-Marxists. The same word, "class," is used to mean very different things. For example, since at least the time of the ancient Greeks, the term has been used to classify people according to the wealth or property they have or do not have. In this approach, the class of "haves" confronts the class of "have nots." The "rich classes" confront the "poor," the class of high-income earners confronts the class of low- or no-income earners. In all these variations, the basic definition of "class" concerns the grouping of people who either do or do not own or possess wealth. A second definition of "class," as old as the first, refers not to ownership of wealth or income but to power. This concept of class distinguishes people according to whether they wield power over others—give orders—or are powerless and have power wielded over them—take orders. Variations on this definition of "class" speak of "the ruling class" or "the power elite" or "the class of the powerless."

These two concepts of class—as a matter of property or of power—are probably the most widespread understandings of the term (although there are still others). However, the concept of class in the specific Marxian theory discussed in this book is different from both of them. It classifies people not according to the wealth or power they have or lack, but according to their participation in the production and/or distribution of surplus labor. In short, this Marxian concept of class is not a matter of wealth or power. Since such notions of class will be uppermost in many readers' minds, we need to underscore here Marxian theory's distinctive concept of class. Of course, all Marxists are concerned about the distribution of wealth and power in society. The point in light of the Marxian theory discussed here is simply that class is a different and important matter, one that has lacked the attention and understanding needed to bring about successful social change.

According to this view, Marx originally contributed the new concept of class to his contemporaries—who also worked with the old property and power notions. The Marxian theory discussed here stresses what it sees as Marx's innovative concern with the production and distribution of surplus labor. Since this unique concept of class will be used in all of the subsequent propositions and arguments made about Marxian economics in this text, we need to give it close attention here.

C.1. The Fundamental Class Process and Exploitation

In his writings, Marx attached the adjective "fundamental" to the class process. This followed from his theoretical strategy of focusing readers' attention on the process of producing surplus labor. However, he seems also to have wanted to distinguish such a fundamental class process from another kind of class process. Marx's major theoretical writings in economics present two kinds of class process. Indeed, as this section will show, Marxian theory works with a complex notion of class processes (note the plural).

Let us look more closely at the term "fundamental class process." It refers to the process whereby some members of all communities (or societies)—the direct laborers—perform not only necessary but also surplus labor. Their necessary labor results in the produced goods and services they consume. Their surplus labor results in a further quantity of goods and services which we will call "surplus product." One question arises immediately: Who gets the surplus product? In their act of performing surplus labor, the direct laborers produce surplus product, but for whom? In Marx's language, who appropriates (receives directly into his or her hands) this surplus product? The answer is, It depends.

One possibility is that the direct producers themselves will appropriate their own surplus product. They will keep it for themselves to consume, or save, to use for producing other things, or for still other purposes. They might do this collectively. For example, a community of agricultural and industrial laborers might periodically stop working, gather together and decide how to use their total surplus product, what remains after they take care of their own direct needs.

Another possibility is that the direct laborers will appropriate their own surplus product, but do so individually, not collectively. In this case, each individual laborer, no matter what particular kind of work is done, will appropriate his or her own surplus product and decide individually what to do with it. For example, consider an individual producer of computer software programs. She produces a quantity of these programs, sells them, and uses the money to purchase the goods and services she consumes to maintain her standard of living. This quantity represents her necessary labor. However, she normally produces more than this quantity of programs. This extra quantity is hers to sell and reap the rewards from. She is the individual appropriator of her own surplus labor; she decides what to do with it.

These are not the only possible answers to the question of who gets the surplus. In some cases the direct laborers who perform the surplus labor may not appropriate their own surplus product, neither collectively nor individually. Picture, for example, a society in which the direct laborers are also slaves. When the slaves perform surplus labor, their surplus product is appropriated by people who are not slaves. To be precise, the slaves produce a surplus product that passes automatically and immediately into the hands of persons other than the slave laborers. Note that the nonslave appropriators in this example do not perform the labor. Rather, they receive the surplus product of the labor of others, the slave laborers. They give no product to the slaves, but they receive product from them.

This situation, when the direct laborers do not appropriate their own surplus labor, is what Marx called "exploitation." One person exploits another, in Marxian theory, if and only if he or she appropriates the surplus labor of that other. Exploitation is a basic concept in Marxian economics to which we will devote considerable attention.

However, we have not yet finished cataloging the possible answers to the question of who gets the surplus product. Another possibility is that the direct laborer is not a slave, but is rather an employee of a capitalist in a factory or office. In this case, the direct laborer—usually a wage or salary earner—helps produce capitalist commodities. These commodities are automatically and immediately the property of the capitalist, not the employed direct laborer. The capitalist normally sells them for money. Part of this money is used to pay the direct laborer's wage or salary. This part represents the laborer's necessary labor. Another part is kept by the capitalist as his or her profit. This represents the direct laborer's surplus labor.

Think of it this way. During part of the time that such employees work, they produce commodities whose sale gives the capitalist just enough money to pay their wages and salaries. This is the employed direct laborers' necessary labor. But if they worked only that much time, nothing would be left as profits for the capitalist. Few capitalists would exist under such circumstances. What actually happens, according to Marxian theory, is that direct laborers work an extra portion of time doing surplus labor. The commodities that result from this surplus labor are sold alongside those produced by their necessary labor. However, the money realized in the sale of this surplus product remains with the capitalist, who thereby appropriates the surplus labor of the employed direct laborers.

Here again, note that the capitalist appropriates the surplus product of his or her direct laborers without giving any product in return. Wages or salaries are given by the capitalist to direct laborers in exchange for their necessary labor. These laborers give their surplus product to the capitalist—who thereby obtains profits—without obtaining any product in exchange. Marx and Marxists refer to this class process as exploitative. This is what they mean by capitalist exploitation.

There are still other possible arrangements whereby the people who perform surplus labor do not appropriate their surplus product. The different possible arrangements will be discussed further below in the section entitled "Different Forms of the Fundamental Class Process." Consistent with their theory, Marxists often divide the histories of societies into periods according to which form of the fundamental class process prevailed over a given span of time.

Marxian theorists analyze a society by looking first at the forms of the fundamental class process that may exist within it. Their aim is to identify which of the several possible forms coexist in that society—that is, which particular arrangements of performers and appropriators of surplus labor are in place. Pursuing this aim is part of what Marxists refer to when they describe their theoretical work as "class analysis."

C.2. The Subsumed Class Process

Just as the logic of the fundamental class process led to the question of who gets the surplus product, so the answer Marxists give generates the next question: What do the appropriators of surplus product do with it? Do they gobble it up in a frenzy of luxury consumption? Do they hoard it in miserly fashion? Do they use it to induce or force still more people to produce still more surplus product for them in a dizzying spiral of surplus accumulation? Do they distribute it to the masses in periodic festivals and carnivals? Do they use it to feed and arm a special group of people who do no productive work but rather engage in wars?

These are just some of the possible ways for appropriators to dispose of the surplus product they gather into their hands. Which ways are actually chosen in any society will influence how life is lived by all the people in that society. How the appropriators dispose of their surplus will help shape the structure, contradictions, and changes characterizing that society. Marxian theory therefore analyzes the complex causes that together overdetermine the particular uses of appropriated surplus product in any society. It likewise analyzes the consequences of those uses for the structure and changes in that society.

In arriving at his theory about the uses of appropriated surplus, Marx stressed the remarkable contradictory position of the appropriators. On the one hand, they receive into their hands the surplus, the fruits of human labor above and beyond what was needed to meet the desired standard of living of the direct laborers. The appropriators of the surplus dispose of goods and services that are in some sense the discretionary fund of the society. This puts them in a heady position of power. On the other hand, their hands are also tied. As Marxian theory explains it, they are always under pressure to pass the appropriated surplus to others, whether they wish to or not.

The point here is that no sooner do appropriators receive the surplus product into their hands than they realize that they have to distribute it to other people right away. If they do not, they immediately risk that their appropriation of surplus will stop. That is the pressure they are under. Marx gave many examples to illustrate his point; we will build upon some of them here.

Consider a slave master who exploits some slave direct laborers. They do necessary labor, the product of which the slave master allows them to keep to enable them to continue working. They also do surplus labor, the product of which the slave master appropriates. However, the slave master's happiness at being the recipient of this surplus is quickly overshadowed by anxiety. He or she worries about many things. For example, it is always possible that the slaves may rebel against constantly delivering their surplus product to the slave master and refuse to do so. The slave master risks losing the position of appropriator. To prevent this, he or she must take a portion of the appropriated surplus and use it to prevent the slaves from rebelling.

There are various ways to do this. One way is to maintain standing military or police forces to coerce the slaves to perform surplus labor. The slave master would have to distribute a portion of the appropriated surplus to feed, clothe, house, transport, train, and arm such forces. No sooner would surplus product be received than part of it would have to be distributed to maintain such people. Not only would these people produce no surplus for the slave master; worse still, they would siphon off part of the surplus appropriated from the slave direct laborers.

Another way to prevent slave rebellions is to educate slaves along particular lines. For example, schools or religious institutions could be established to administer classes, rituals, and ceremonies designed to convince slaves that efforts at rebellion were futile, or intolerable to deities, or both. To the extent that slaves could be so convinced, the risk of rebellion would be reduced. However, the men and women who operated such schools and religious institutions would have to be fed, clothed, housed, and equipped to perform the educational and religious processes in question.

Many other nonclass processes—beyond policing and educating—may be required for the slave fundamental class process to continue providing surplus to slave masters. Slaves who die must be replaced. If this necessitates that slave masters arrange shipping expeditions to secure new slaves, the costs of those expeditions are claims upon the slave surplus. The appropriators of that surplus must use part of it to obtain new slaves or they risk losing surplus as the number of slaves falls.

Slaves who work may need supervisors, individuals who make sure that they work efficiently rather than inefficiently and that they do not have opportunities for unproductive relaxation. Such people do not themselves produce surplus, but they are indispensable if the slaves are to continue providing surplus to the appropriators. Their costs are covered from that surplus; the appropriators use shares of the surplus to pay supervisors for helping ensure that there is a surplus.

Our examples from a slave form of the fundamental class process are perfectly parallel to examples that might be taken from a capitalist form of the fundamental class process. Indeed, we will be using such examples throughout the rest of the chapter. However, the slave example is enough to permit us to draw some initial conclusions here about the distribution of surplus by appropriators.

The distribution of the surplus by appropriators is called "the subsumed class process." It is a class process because it directly concerns surplus labor and its fruits. It is called "subsumed" because it seems logical that we consider the distribution of the surplus after we consider its production, which is the fundamental class process.

The subsumed class process occurs after the fundamental class process. It is motivated by the appropriators' aim to continue the fundamental class process and their position in it. The subsumed class process is the way appropriators pay for the performance of certain nonclass processes without which the fundamental class process could not exist. In our example of slave labor, the police and military processes, the educational and religious processes, the shipping and supervisory processes, were precisely nonclass processes. The people who provided these nonclass processes to the appropriators did not themselves produce or appropriate surplus labor. Instead, they received distributed shares of the slave surplus from the appropriators. They did therefore participate in a subsumed class process; they were subsumed classes.

In all societies, according to Marxian theory, fundamental and subsumed class processes occur. They coexist with the vast array of nonclass processes in constituting any society. Given the logic of overdetermination, Marxists argue that in any society, the various forms of the fundamental and subsumed class processes help shape one another and all of that society's nonclass processes. They also argue that simultaneously the nonclass processes together overdetermine the class processes, fundamental and subsumed.

This permits us to formulate a summary statement of the goals and structure of a Marxian theory of society. The theory aims to analyze what the class processes in the society are, why they exist, and what consequences they have. One prime purpose of Marxian theory is to identify the fundamental and subsumed class processes in any society, but especially in one's own. Another prime purpose is to analyze how nonclass processes in that society overdetermine the identified class processes and vice versa. Finally, Marxian theory aims to show how interacting class and nonclass processes give the society its particular contradictions and patterns of change.

C.3. Different Forms of the Fundamental Class Process

Marxian theory recognizes that societies differ from one another in their class structures. While all societies exhibit some class processes, fundamental and subsumed, they differ in the mix of the particular forms they contain. The rich diversity of human communities has produced a wide variety of arrangements whereby men and women perform surplus labor and distribute its fruits. Marxian theorists have constructed sketches of some historically important forms of the fundamental class process, but have examined exhaustively only the modern capitalist form.

One form is commonly called "the primitive communist class process." In this form, the direct laborers themselves collectively discuss and decide upon their working conditions, how much surplus they will perform, and how they will dispose of the fruits of their surplus labor. The primitive communist subsumed class process occurs when the direct laborers, who collectively appropriate their own surplus, distribute it to others—for example, to special groups of people acting as warriors, spiritual counselors, teachers of children, and so on. These recipients of distributed shares of surplus constitute the primitive communist subsumed classes. Their received shares enable them to defend, pray for, and teach the specifically primitive communist form of the fundamental class process and thereby help reproduce it.

A second form of the fundamental class process is that which Marx called "ancient." In this social arrangement, individual direct laborers appropriate their own individual surplus. They too will usually distribute shares of their surplus to various persons who perform nonclass processes that are needed if the ancient fundamental class process is to survive. The individual producer of computer software programs is an example of the ancient fundamental class process discussed earlier.

Earlier we discussed the slave form of the fundamental class process, but we have not yet described the feudal form. The feudal arrangement most typically involves possessors of land, called "lords," and direct laborers on that land, often called "feudal peasants." The direct laborers, who are not slaves, work the land part of the time for themselves. They keep the fruits of this labor; it is their necessary labor. The rest of the time they work for the lord, who appropriates the fruits of that work. A complex personal relationship involving loyalties and obligations intertwines the performers and appropriators of this feudal surplus labor.

Capitalism differs from all other forms of the fundamental class process in that it is remarkably disconnected. The direct laborers are connected to the appropriators neither as slaves nor through personal ties of loyalty. Instead, the capitalist form of the fundamental class process inserts a novel institution between direct laborers and appropriators: the market. Direct laborers are required to sell as a commodity on the market their ability to work; they sell their "labor power."

The appropriators appear first as buyers of labor power. Following a market exchange process—in which appropriators promise to pay wages in exchange for the direct laborers' labor power—the appropriators set the direct laborers to work. The products that result belong immediately to the appropriators, who sell them for money in the market. Part of this money is used to pay the direct laborers their promised wages. This part of the money represents necessary labor. Another part represents the raw materials and equipment used up and hence embodied in the products sold.

The remainder, that portion of receipts from commodity sales which the appropriator retains as "profit," represents the surplus labor. A person who "makes a profit" by retaining a portion of the values produced by employees is called a "capitalist." This is the name given to an appropriator of surplus labor when the form of the appropriation involves the existence and purchase of labor power as a commodity as well as the sale of produced objects as commodities in markets.

Notice that the differences in the forms of the fundamental class process refer to the differing social contexts in which the class processes occur. Collective decision-making and the absence of private property loom large as contexts of the primitive communist form of the fundamental class process. The social conditions that support the treatment of human beings as property, as slaves of others, help determine another particular form of the fundamental class process. Complex patterns of land dispositions and interpersonal loyalties shape the feudal form, while commodity markets in both produced objects and human labor power help generate the specifically capitalist form of the fundamental class process.

Lastly, Marxian theorists have sketched a communist form of the class process. In such a form the social context is thought necessarily to include the collective ownership of all means of production, the allocation of labor power not by market exchange but rather by collectively designed economic planning, and the collectively determined disposition of the surplus. Generally, modern societies whose governments aim explicitly to establish the communist form of the fundamental class process refer to themselves as "socialist." This term is meant to suggest a period of social transition from the capitalist to the communist form of the fundamental class process.

C.4. Social Formations and Social Transitions

Marxian theory approaches society as a complex bundle of interacting class (fundamental and subsumed) and nonclass processes. Considering the class processes first, it seeks to determine precisely which forms of the fundamental class process are present in any society it chooses to analyze. In this society do people perform and appropriate surplus labor within the capitalist form or the feudal form or the ancient form, and so on? Or, as Marxists would expect, does the society exhibit more than one form? How are the forms present in the society changing? Are some disappearing? Are new forms coming into existence and possibly into prominence?

As noted earlier, Marxists prefer the term "social formation" to "society" because it underscores their particular way of approaching society as a set of several forms—a formation—of the class processes.

Within any social formation, some of the forms of the fundamental class process will be more socially prominent than others. More goods and services emerge from some forms than from others. For example, the United States today is seen by most Marxists as a capitalist social formation. This means that the capitalist form of the fundamental class process overshadows the other forms in accounting for total output and in shaping the nonclass processes of the society. However, noncapitalist forms of the fundamental class process also exist in the United States. Millions of individual, self-employed persons perform and appropriate their own surplus labor in classic examples of the ancient form of the fundamental class process. Some Americans today live in religious and nonreligious "communes" that exhibit sometimes the primitive communist and sometimes the feudal form of the fundamental class process. However, when looking at the United States as a whole—its complex of cultural, political, and economic processes—most Marxists agree that the capitalist form of the class process is the most prominent.

For this reason, Marxian theorists refer to the United States as a "capitalist social formation." The label attached to the social formation is the name of the particular form of the fundamental class process that is most prominent in that social formation. However, after specifying the most prominent and the other forms of the fundamental class process in the United States, Marxian theorists confront the equally important task of assessing the changes or transitions occurring in those forms.

We will use the word "change" henceforth to describe the constant alterations occurring within the various forms of the class process that coexist within a social formation. We will reserve the word "transition" to describe a situation in which the prominent form of the fundamental class process in a society is losing its prominence, is giving way to another form that is becoming the most prominent. Thus, we will see, changes are always occurring in all of the forms of the fundamental class process in every society. However, transition is a different and rarer occurrence.

In the United States today, the capitalist fundamental class process is changing. Changes in all of the nonclass processes are impacting, via overdetermination, upon the capitalist fundamental class process to change it continually. Similarly, the ancient and primitive communist forms of the fundamental class process are changing in the United States too. However, a transition does not seem to be under way. The predominance of the capitalist fundamental class process does not now seem to be giving way to another form, not to the ancient or the primitive communist or the communist. Neither a socialist nor any other transition seems imminent in the United States.

On the other hand, in places like the Soviet Union, the German Democratic Republic, and Cuba, Marxists can more readily argue for the existence of a social transition. In social formations where capitalist or feudal forms of the class process were most prominent until a few decades ago, those forms may indeed have lost their prominence in favor of new and different forms. We say "may" here because whether transitions have occurred and whether they are socialist transitions to communism remain matters of intense and still unsettled debate among Marxists.

Marxian theory is premised on the critical stance that Marxists adopt toward capitalism and their general preference for socialism and/or communism. It is therefore quite consistent for Marxists to be concerned with transition. Their focus on class structures leads logically to their inquiries about whether and what kind of transition may be under way in any society chosen for scrutiny. Since they are motivated in particular by the desire to achieve transitions to communism in contemporary societies, they seek to determine whether such a transition is possible and how Marxists might act to facilitate it in the particular circumstances of each social formation.

D. The Capitalist Fundamental Class Process and Commodities

Marx's three-volume work, *Capital,* provides the foundation and the broad logical structure of Marxian economics. In volume 1, Marx concentrated on the capitalist fundamental class process. In volume 2, he stressed the uniqueness of his theoretical approach to economics by differentiating it from others. He did this by concentrating on a class analysis of the market circulation of commodities and money. In volume 3, he focused chiefly on the capitalist subsumed class process. There he showed how the interdependence of these fundamental and subsumed class processes constituted the specifically capitalist class structure of the West European social formations he aimed to analyze.

While we will explore how Marxian economic theory has evolved beyond Marx's beginnings, it still makes good sense to start as he did in *Capital,* volume 1. Thus, our goal too will be to describe the capitalist fundamental class process. Like Marx, we will begin by defining and discussing commodities and then move from there to the capitalist fundamental class process.

D.1. Products, Markets, and Commodities

In all human societies, people take objects given in nature (land, water, plants, animals, etc.) and transform them to meet human needs and wants. We referred to this previously as the labor process. The results of this process are produced goods and services. Usually some members of society produce them while all members get distributions of them since survival is rarely possible without access to at least a minimum of such products. In short, the useful fruits of human labor are called "products." They are not necessarily "commodities," however. For a product also to be a commodity, it must not only be useful; it must also be exchanged (for money or for another commodity) on some market.

What is striking about modern societies is the fact that the products of human labor usually pass through a market in their journey from producer to consumer. In the long history of the human race, products have normally made that journey without going through markets and without having prices (market exchange ratios) attached to them. When production was completed, most societies arranged for the distribution of the products by means of customary rules. Sometimes certain elders of the community decided who was to get what share of community output. Sometimes religious rules sufficed to guide producers in deciding where to deliver what they had harvested. Sometimes community-wide councils existed to deliberate over each year's distribution of the fruits of community labor among community members.

In short, most societies distributed their products rather like most families today distribute the goods and services they make or buy with their incomes. The parent who cooks dinner does not usually charge children a price to buy it. One parent does not charge the other for taking out the garbage. Instead, complex rules of family interaction govern decisions about who does what labor and how the fruits of that labor get distributed among family members. Similarly, most communities of people throughout human history determined production and distribution without establishing markets, prices, and the like, as means for such distribution.

True, the markets through which the products of labor pass before reaching their final consumers did exist at various times and places in history, but most products did not go through them. Only very recently, in terms of historical time, have *most* products gone through markets and in that process acquired prices. This remarkable feature of modern society struck all early economists, not only Marx, as especially significant. They all appreciated the historically new problem of explaining why one product fetched a high price on the market while another did not, or why the price of a product was high now but low earlier or high in this market but low in a market a few miles away. Of course, it was not only economists who wondered about prices; the rest of modern society wondered and worried too.

When markets were inserted among and between producers and consumers, everyone had to be concerned about prices. Making or doing something well to meet community needs no longer sufficed to assure a person a comfortable place in the community. Now another test had to be passed. Could that individual's product be sold in the market, and would the price it fetched allow him or her in turn to buy enough of the products of others to lead the sort of life he or she desired? Market conditions became central to everyone's life, yet no one had any clear ideas about what determined those conditions. What caused prices to be high or low, to rise or fall?

D.2. Commodity Values

Most early economists commenced their economic reasoning with attempts to unravel the mystery of markets. They invented theories of value. In the sixteenth and seventeenth centuries, Europeans wrote many articles, pamphlets, and books proclaiming their various theories of what determined prices in markets. Toward the end of the eighteenth century, two English writers sifted critically through that literature and arrived at a general theory that has been part of economics ever since. Adam Smith (1723-1790) wrote first, and then David Ricardo (1772-

1823) corrected and condensed this theory, which was later named "the labor theory of value." Smith and Ricardo were the two major contributors to what we now refer to as "classical economics."

Their basic idea was relatively simple. The price of a good or service in the market was thought to be determined by the amount of labor devoted to its production. If a pair of shoes required an average of two hours of labor to produce, it would be priced twice as high as a vase that took only one hour. In the market we would observe that one pair of shoes would be equal in value to two vases. If shoes cost $10 per pair, then vases would be expected to cost $5 each, and so on.

Neoclassical theory, as explained in the previous chapter, grew logically out of this concern with markets and prices. It entered into its analysis of the total economy by studying the individual participants in markets: their preferences for the various goods and services available in markets, the endowments (goods and services and resources) they bring to market to sell, and the technology available for producing commodities in the markets. From the days of Smith and Ricardo until the present, individuals acting in markets have been the focus of neoclassical economic theory. However, neoclassical theorists reject labor as the major determinant of commodity values, choosing instead to explain these values as the results of market demands and supplies. In so doing, they reduce demand and supply to preferences and productive capabilities as the ultimate causes of commodity values.

Marx had a different theoretical agenda. He did not enter into economic analysis by focusing on individuals, markets, and prices. His entry point was class. However, he knew that the audiences he hoped to reach with his different theory were accustomed to thinking about economics in terms of markets, commodities, and prices. So he made the tactical decision to begin *Capital* with commodities and markets too. His plan was to take readers rather quickly from there to his preferred entry point, class, and then to use the bulk of the book for his class analysis of the capitalist economy.

Marx began *Capital* much as Ricardo had begun his *Principles,* with a discussion of commodities and the labor theory of their values. Unlike the neoclassical school, Marx remained faithful to the original Smith-Ricardo idea of linking values to labor rather than utility. However, Marx's version of the labor theory of value departed in very basic ways from the Smith-Ricardo original. Marx's labor theory of value, unlike theirs, provided a direct bridge from the issue of commodity values to the issue of class understood as the production, appropriation, and distribution of surplus labor. We will similarly cross this bridge into the formal structure of Marxian economics.

D.3. Commodities and Fundamental Class Processes

In Marxian theory, commodities are the fruits not only of the processes of labor and exchange but also of the fundamental class process. This Marxian addition of the class process transforms the classical labor theory of value. When people participate in the labor process, transforming nature into useful goods and services that are exchanged in markets on their way to consumers, such people also participate in fundamental class processes. Some perform necessary and surplus labor, and some appropriate that surplus. Which individuals perform and/or appropriate and how they do so depends upon what particular form of fundamental class process is involved.

For example, if the people who produced a commodity were laboring slaves and appropriating slave masters, we would speak of the product of their labor as a slave commodity. The adjective "slave" would designate the particular fundamental class process involved in the existence of that commodity. If feudal peasants and lords were the performers and appropriators of surplus labor involved in producing some goods sold in markets, these goods would be feudal commodities. If capitalists and wage workers were respectively the appropriators and performers of surplus labor, the resulting products would be capitalist commodities since the capitalist fundamental class process was part of their existence.

Marx and Marxian theory concentrate attention on capitalist commodities precisely because the capitalist form of the fundamental class process serves as the entry point into their economic analyses. After leading readers from commodities in general to the capitalist form of the fundamental class process, Marx and Marxian theory can proceed to elaborate their system. This they do by moving theoretically from commodity values in general to capitalist commodity values to surplus value.

D.4. Marx's Labor Theory of Commodity Values

When direct laborers sell their ability to work, as commodities, they exchange their labor power for money. The buyers of labor power set it to work with equipment and raw materials in the production of saleable goods and services. These in turn are exchanged in the market for money. There are then three distinct commodity values to compare: the value of the labor power, the value of the other inputs to production (the equipment and raw materials), and the value of the products finally sold.

The values of used-up equipment and raw materials and of the commodities sold are clearly understood in terms of the labor theory of value: the values of commodity inputs and outputs are determined by the amount of labor embodied in them. Of course, the meaning of "labor" here is the average amount of work needed to produce each commodity. The different skill levels of individual workers are averaged to determine what Marx called "the socially necessary" labor needed to produce any given commodity. That average, not each individual worker's productivity, is what determines each commodity's value.

Theorizing about the value of labor power is somewhat more complicated. The value of labor power is understood to be equal to the value of the goods and services that laborers require to keep selling their labor power day after day. In other words, the labor embodied in the commodities that direct laborers consume determines not only the values of those commodities but also the value of the labor power that the laborers reproduce by means of their consumption.

To illustrate Marx's theory, consider a simple example of the value of a commodity—say, a chair. We will look first at the value of the labor power needed to produce that chair. Suppose that the bundle of goods and services purchased and consumed in an average day by a wage-earning direct laborer embodies a total of six hours of labor by community members. In other words, it takes six hours of socially necessary labor to produce the wage commodities required by workers. Now suppose further that in one day of production a direct laborer hired to make chairs uses up equipment and raw materials embodying four hours of labor. In other words, it takes four hours of socially necessary labor to produce the nonwage commodities (saws, lumber, glue, etc.) required for the production of chairs.

The values of labor power, equipment, and raw materials are the costs of production. They are sums paid to purchase all of the commodity inputs needed for daily chair production to occur. In this example, they total ten hours. That leaves the third value for us to consider, the value of the commodities—in this example, chairs—that daily emerge from the production process.

Suppose that the direct laborer works for eight hours per day. Although he or she works for these eight hours, we have assumed that only six hours' worth of commodities are paid to him or her in the form of wages. As we shall soon see, this assumed difference between x hours' worth of wages paid and y hours' worth of commodities produced is key to the Marxian theory of the capitalist fundamental class process. As noted, the direct laborer uses up four hours' worth of equipment and raw materials. The total labor embodied in the commodities produced during those eight hours must then equal twelve hours.

Eight hours' worth of *living labor* is embodied in the final commodities: the number of chairs produced per day. We will label this factor

LL. Additionally, four hours' worth of previously *embodied labor* (in equipment and raw materials) is transferred into the chairs during each day's production. We will label this factor *EL*. Finally, Marxists use the letter *W* to designate the value of commodity outputs: the value of the chairs produced each day.

The relationship between values going in and values coming out of the commodity production process can then be written as

$$EL + LL = W,$$

where embodied labor, *EL* (4 hours), plus living labor added, *LL* (8 hours), equals the total value of commodities produced, *W* (12 hours).

This apparently simple summary of the labor theory of value in capitalist commodity production affords Marxian theory the ideal context in which to ask its key questions. What is the connection between commodity production and exchange, on the one hand, and the capitalist fundamental class process on the other? To prepare its answer, Marxian theory first asks another question: How shall we understand the difference between the value added in commodity production by living labor (*LL*) and the value of labor power?

In our chair example, the value of labor power was six, since it took an average of six hours of socially necessary labor to produce the bundle of goods and services required for consumption by direct laborers (to reproduce their labor power for sale). Also in our example, the daily value added by the direct laborers in working eight hours was eight. The difference between these two values is two. Marxian theory refers to this difference as "surplus value."

Surplus value is a central part of Marxian theory. It is the particular form taken by the surplus labor appropriated in the capitalist fundamental class process. When surplus labor is embodied in products that are also commodities, the values of those commodities include a surplus value corresponding to that surplus labor. In Marxian theory, commodity exchange values need to be decoded to reveal the class process from which they emerge.

D.5. The Surplus Value of Capitalist Commodities

Surplus value is the extra value produced by hired direct laborers over and above the value of their labor power, what they obtained for selling their labor power. In our chair example, the eight hours of living labor performed by hired laborers, *LL*, can be broken down into two parts. During the first part, the laborers add a value exactly equal to what their employer must pay them for purchasing their labor power: six hours' worth. During the second part, the laborers add a value that is extra, more, or surplus to the value paid to them for their labor power. In our example, this was two hours' worth. As Marxists put it, part of living labor is paid for and part is not.

We can now rewrite our earlier equation to take account of the division of living labor (LL) into its two parts, the paid (LL_p) and the unpaid (LL_u):

$$EL + LL_p + LL_u = W,$$

where $LL = LL_p + LL_u$.

Marxian theory can now assert the conclusion it draws from this analysis of commodity values, a conclusion that is intended to take us over the theoretical bridge from commodity values to class analysis. Commodity production under conditions in which direct laborers sell their labor power as a commodity (capitalism) involves the direct appropriation of each laborer's surplus labor by his or her employer.

The argument is that surplus value, part of the produced commodity's value, is surplus labor appropriated by the person who buys labor power. Using our chair example again, this person is understood to spend a certain quantity of value (ten hours' worth) to buy both labor power (LL_p) and the equipment and raw materials needed to enable the labor power to work (EL). This person is also understood to receive the commodities produced by the laborers and to sell them at their embodied twelve hours' worth of value (W). Finally, this person keeps as his or her own, the difference between the twelve hours' worth of revenues (W) and the ten hours' worth of costs $(EL + LL_p)$:

$$W - [EL + LL_p] = LL_u.$$

This two-hour difference is surplus value from the standpoint of the person who incurs the costs of production, the one who buys labor power and equipment and raw materials. LL_u is an extra value over what this person had at the outset of the commodity production process. Surplus value is LL_u, the portion of the labor that hired laborers perform which is unpaid and whose fruits flow directly into the hands of the employer when he or she sells the commodity outputs. Surplus value is the form taken by surplus labor in the capitalist fundamental class process.

The fundamental class process occurs together with the labor process in production. It is also closely intertwined with the market exchange processes in which both commodity inputs and commodity outputs are involved. One of the aims of Marxian theory is to unravel the complex interconnection of all three processes—class, exchange, and labor—in order to highlight the fundamental class process that others have missed and that Marxian theory makes its entry point.

D.6. A Summary of Marxian Value Theory

Marxian theory explains the value of a capitalist commodity in terms of the embodied and living labor materialized in it. The living labor is further divided into paid and unpaid labor. Finally, the source of the unpaid labor is shown to be the capitalist fundamental class process. Thus, the value of a capitalist commodity is explained in relation to the conceptual focus of the theory, which is class.

The overdeterminist logic of Marxian theory is also at work in its explanation of commodity values. The amount of labor that is socially necessary to produce chairs or any other capitalist commodity is overdetermined by all the processes existing in society. Economic processes of exchange, competition, and lending, for example, will influence how much labor will be required to produce chairs. So too will political and cultural processes ranging from legal factory regulations to technological inventions. In their unique ways each will participate in overdetermining how much labor will be socially necessary to produce chairs. Throughout *Capital,* Marx showed how various economic, political, and cultural processes exercised their influence on commodity values.

The logic of overdetermination can be further illustrated in terms of the basic equation connecting embodied and living labor to the value of commodity outputs. This is meant to be a two-directional relationship:

$$EL + LL_p + LL_u \longleftrightarrow W$$

It is *not* Marxian theory's idea to reason that value inputs determine value outputs in a unidirectional way. That would be a kind of essentialism; it would reduce the determination of commodity values to socially necessary labor inputs. Instead, Marxian theory insists that outputs also participate in overdetermining inputs.

For example, production of a new commodity output might induce laborers to admire and demand that such commodities be included in their consumption. This, then, would be an output (W) that influences inputs (LL_p). Another example would be the output of a new piece of machinery for making chairs. Suppose that this machine altered the efficiency of both lumber utilization (fewer board-feet needed per chair) and labor utilization (fewer workers needed per machine and so per chair as well). In that case, an output (W) would again exercise its influence on various inputs (EL and LL_p). To take a different example, a change in some commodity output's value could well provoke changes in buyer's attitudes toward this and related commodities. Buyers' reactions to a changed value of outputs (W) could and would likely alter the quantities and values of the inputs (EL and LL) used in production. Here commodity output values influence inputs. Such examples could be multiplied endlessly, for it is clear that every output in society exercises its unique effects on everything in its environment, including, of course, inputs to commodity production.

This overdeterminist quality of Marxian arguments and explanations contrasts with the reductionism of neoclassical theory. The latter utilizes a unidirectional explanation of values, reducing them to its three governing essences. Marxian theory not only stresses labor rather than utility and scarcity as the source of value but it insists that labor inputs and their values are themselves overdetermined by output commodities and their values.

E. Capitalists and Laborers

The subtleties and richness of the Marxian theory discussed in this book are well displayed in its economic analysis of capitalists and laborers. No simple dichotomies between good and bad, strong and weak, rich and poor, or powerful and powerless are acceptable to this Marxian theory. Rather, capitalists and laborers are shown to be of diverse kinds and to be involved in many different sorts of relationships to one another. Marxian theory's analysis of capitalists and laborers is unique among modern social theories. Its equally original insights into the complex workings of capitalist economies will be introduced in the subsequent sections of this chapter.

E.1. What are Capitalists?

Marxian theory focuses on "capitalists" as individuals who occupy the class position of appropriators of surplus labor in the form of surplus value. It emphasizes one kind of capitalist, the one who buys labor power and who owns and sells the commodities produced thereby. Yet the theory also recognizes other kinds of capitalists, who do not appropriate surplus labor. We can introduce Marx's own notation to clarify the different kinds of capitalists.

All capitalists start with a sum of values, usually in the form of money, M. Their goal is to use their money to "make money"—to secure an increment, ΔM, as an addition to their original M. Mathematically this can be stated as $M \longrightarrow M + \Delta M$. Capitalists of the sort we have been discussing convert their original M, via market purchases, into labor power, equipment, and raw materials. Marx calls the expenditure on labor power "variable capital," or V; his choice of term expresses the idea that this component of the capitalist's capital will grow or vary. As noted above, the purchase of paid living labor (LL_p) grew into the living labor (LL) embodied in commodity output value. Marx calls the expenditure on equipment and raw materials "constant capital," or C, and his choice of term reflects the idea that the value of these commodities passes unchanged (unvaried) into the final commodities produced from them. Thus, the purchase of EL and its utilization in production added precisely EL and no more to the value of the produced commodity output. The following incomplete expression summarizes this Marxian approach:

$$M = C + V \longrightarrow W = M + \Delta M.$$

This equation begins with a sum of value, M, and ends with a larger sum of value, $M + \Delta M$. ΔM refers to the variation, the growth, accomplished by the capital as it passes through the fundamental class process. ΔM is the surplus value that attaches itself to capital in the course of capitalist production. Marx defines this variation as the "self-expansion of capital." He then completes the equation of capitalist commodity production as follows:

$$C + V + S = W.$$

This equation precisely parallels our earlier equation, because $C = EL$, $V = LL_p$, and $S = LL_u$. Capitalists achieve the expansion of their capital, from $C + V$ to W, by appropriating the surplus labor embedded in the commodities they sell. The initial capital, $C + V$, grows to W because of the addition of S during production and because the capitalists appropriate that S. A measure of the rate at which capital self-expands would be

$$\frac{\Delta M}{M} = \frac{S}{(C + V)}.$$

If this rate rises, capital is relatively successful in expanding; if it falls, it is having problems.

Marxian theory attaches the label "productive" to such capitalists to distinguish them from other kinds of capitalists. All capitalists appropriate surplus value, but only productive capitalists do so by appropriating the surplus labor of direct laborers. This raises two closely connected questions. What other kinds of capitalists exist? How can a person appropriate surplus value without at the same time appropriating surplus labor?

In general, Marxian theory defines "capital" as a sum of values—money—which expands itself by going through some social process. The word literally means "self-expanding value." The fundamental class process is one way for a sum of values, M, to expand itself into $M + \Delta M$. However, the fundamental class process is not the only way that values expand themselves.

For example, lending money at interest is another way for a sum of values to expand itself—to function as capital in the economy. You start with M, lend it to a person at interest, and eventually receive back your original sum plus the interest, $M + \Delta M$. The interest, ΔM, is surplus value for you, the amount of self-expansion accomplished by your capital through the lending process. Another example is the process of renting out land. In this case, you begin with a sum of values, M, with which you buy a piece of land. Then you grant use of this land to a person for a set length of time in return for a rental payment, ΔM. At the end of this time, your original capital invested in land, M, which you still own, has grown by the amount of your rental receipts to $M + \Delta M$. The rent is a surplus value to you; it is the expansion of your initial capital. A third kind of capital is merchant capital. In this case, a merchant begins with an amount of capital, M, and uses it to buy commodities for resale at a higher price. The revenues from such a resale will equal $M + \Delta M$, where ΔM is the surplus value for and goal of the merchant. The latter's capital has expanded simply through the process of buying and selling commodities.

Such kinds of capital—sums of value that generate surplus value—are called "unproductive" capital, because no surplus labor is involved in them. Their expansions do not occur by means of production. When I lend money to you at interest, I am not employing you or obtaining any commodities from your labor. You simply have to give me back more money than I lent to you. All that happens is that I end up with more money than I had at the beginning, while you end up with less. My sum of value is increased exactly as much as yours is diminished; your loss is offset by the surplus value I gain. No new value is produced in the process, no labor or surplus labor is done, no new commodities are created: hence the notion of unproductive capital. The same applies to surplus value obtained through renting out land or through merchanting activities.

Productive capitalists are those individuals who obtain surplus value (expand their capital) by appropriating surplus labor in the capitalist fundamental class process. Unproductive capitalists expand their capital by means of certain nonclass processes—processes other than surplus labor appropriation, such as a lending at interest, merchanting, and renting property. Unproductive capitalists have existed for thousands of years. Records of ancient societies demonstrate the existence of moneylenders, merchants, land renters, and the like. Productive capitalists may have existed sporadically before the seventeenth century, but only since then have they become the powerful, socially prominent group typical of modern history.

Marxian theory, given its entry point of class, stresses the differences among capitalists. It does this to pinpoint the specific social role and

importance of productive capitalists since it is chiefly they who appropriate surplus labor in modern society. For Marxian theory, productive
capitalists represent the individuals who sit atop the fundamental class
process. They are therefore key objects of a class analysis of modern
capitalist social formations.

E.2. What are Laborers?

Like capitalists, laborers may be either productive or unproductive.
Productive laborers are those who sell their labor power to a productive
capitalist and also perform surplus labor appropriated by that capitalist. The direct laborers that we have been discussing in this chapter are
productive laborers. Unproductive laborers also sell their labor power,
but they do not perform surplus labor. Marxian theory not only stresses
the difference between productive and unproductive capitalists; it similarly distinguishes unproductive from productive laborers.

The following is an example of unproductive labor. Suppose that I
sell you my ability to do work in your garden for two hours next Satur-
day. You agree to pay me $30 for my time and effort. When I get there,
you direct me to help you clear brush from your garden. I am a laborer;
I sell my labor power. I also participate in a labor process and may also
use implements to aid my labor. However, I produce no commodity for
my employer, you, to sell. I perform no surplus labor; you realize no
surplus value. In this relationship between us, my labor is unproductive; the labor power I sell is unproductive. (Were the relationship to
alter, for example, by having my two hours of gardening become part of
your commercial production and sale of vegetables, then my labor
power would be productive. In other words, by adding the fundamental
class process to the relationship, the same labor changes from unproductive to productive.)

Consider a second example. I sell my labor power to a productive
capitalist. However, the productive capitalist does not combine my labor power with equipment and raw materials to produce commodities.
Rather, the productive capitalist uses my labor power to provide certain
conditions that enable productive laborers to perform their surplus labor. One such condition is disciplinary supervision. The productive
capitalist directs me to supervise productive laborers, to make sure they
perform the maximum possible surplus labor. In this case I do unproductive labor since my labor power is not a direct part of the production
of capitalist commodities. I am an unproductive laborer, as I would also
be if I performed any other nonclass process needed to make sure that
the fundamental class process occurred according to the productive
capitalist's objective: to gain surplus value.

Unproductive labor is every expenditure of human brain, nerves, and muscles which is not directly involved in the capitalist fundamental class process of performing surplus labor. Therefore, labor power purchased by anyone other than a commodity-producing productive capitalist is automatically unproductive. And even if the labor power is purchased by a productive capitalist, Marxian theory still must determine whether that labor power is directly involved in surplus labor production (in which case it is productive labor power) or is rather set to work to perform nonclass processes needed for the fundamental class process to occur (in which case it is unproductive labor power).

Capitalist commodity production usually involves productive capitalists purchasing both productive and unproductive labor power. To understand Marxian theory it is vital to note that the difference between productive and unproductive laborers is *not* a matter of their importance to the survival and reproduction of the capitalist structure. Both kinds are indispensable, although in different ways. The productive laborer produces the surplus that the productive capitalist appropriates. The unproductive laborer provides the conditions without which the productive laborers could not or would not produce that surplus.

The adjectives "productive" and "unproductive" are Marxian theory's way of distinguishing between workers who participate in the fundamental class process from those who do not. The two kinds of laborers are subject to different conditions and play different roles in capitalist economies. This distinction parallels the role played by these words in differentiating among capitalists. In both cases the purpose is to highlight the existence and uniqueness of the fundamental class process and its overdetermined connections to the many different nonclass processes occurring in modern capitalism.

E.3. Exploitation

People have used the word "exploitation" in many ways for many years. Positively, the word sometimes means "to make good use of some resource," as in "the pioneers who exploited the opportunities of virgin forests and streams." More often it carries a negative connotation, meaning "to take advantage of or abuse some person or resource." Phrases such as "those parents exploit their children" or "that government exploited its minority citizens" illustrate this negative usage. Differing from all of these meanings, Marxian theory attaches a specific definition to "exploitation."

"Exploitation" refers to a type of fundamental class process in which the person who performs surplus labor is not also the person who appropriates it. The latter is then understood to exploit the former. It follows that the primitive communist and ancient forms of the fundamental class process are not exploitative, since performers collectively or individually appropriate their own surplus labor. However, the slave, feudal, and capitalist forms are exploitative.

The capitalist fundamental class process involves the exploitation of productive laborers by productive capitalists. Marxian theory is concerned with both the quality of exploitation (is it feudal, capitalist, etc.?) and its quantitative dimensions (the size of the surplus produced and available for social distribution). In terms of our earlier notation, the size of the surplus, S, depends on the difference between the value added during the work time of productive laborers and the value of their labor power. To see the significance of exploitation in Marxian theory, it is necessary to look more closely at these two values.

In general, the value of labor power, V, depends on two social circumstances. First, how many of which commodities do laborers require in order that they be able and willing to keep on selling their labor power? Second, how much labor is socially necessary to produce those required commodities? Each of these circumstances varies constantly from one economy to the next and from time to time within any economy. The higher the standard of living to which laborers are accustomed (sometimes called "the real wage" by economists), the more commodities they will require and the higher the value of their labor power will be. On the other hand, as commodity production becomes more efficient, it requires fewer hours, on the average, to produce each commodity. This means that each commodity will have less value (will require less socially necessary labor to produce it). This in turn will lower the value of labor power since the individual commodities consumed by laborers will contain less value. At any particular moment, the value of labor power in an economy will reflect both the quantity of commodities laborers require and the value of each of them.

A simple equation can make this point clear:

$$V = e \cdot q.$$

Here, $e \cdot q$ is the sum of all the quantities (q) of wage commodities required multiplied by the value of each per unit (e). If e should fall (because of a drop in the per-unit value of wage commodities) more than q rises (owing to an increase in workers' real wages), then the value of labor power would fall despite the increase in the standard of living of those workers. Such a circumstance may well have characterized capitalist economies since Marx's death. This would mean that increased exploitation *and* increased real wages have been the experience of productive workers over the past hundred years. This remarkable insight and lesson is unique to Marxian theory; it is not possible in alternative theories.

Given some particular value of labor power, V, the size of the surplus value will depend on how much value laborers add on average during the labor process. Since "value," in Marxian theory, is another word for "socially necessary embodied labor time," the value laborers add depends directly on how long they work. The more hours per day they work, the greater the value they add; the fewer the hours they work, the less value they add. The surplus value produced by workers will be as large or as small as the difference between the value added and the value of labor power:

$$S = [S + V] - V.$$

Another way to state this is to focus attention on the value added during the working day. The length of the working day is represented by the following line, AB:

$$A\text{\rule{4cm}{0.4pt}}B$$

The distance AB represents all of the value added in one day by a productive laborer—say, eight hours' worth. Now we can divide this line into two parts:

$$A\text{\rule{3cm}{0.4pt}}X\text{\rule{1.5cm}{0.4pt}}B$$

The length AX represents an amount of value added that exactly equals the value of labor power in this particular economy at this time, $AX = V$. Since the laborer is paid for his or her labor power an amount $AX = V$, it follows that this portion of the working day's labor is called "paid labor." XB must then represent the surplus labor performed and the surplus value appropriated, S. XB is that portion of the day during which the laborer adds value that is not paid for.

The ratio between the two parts of the day, S and V, is Marx's "rate of exploitation":

$$\frac{XB}{AX} = \frac{S}{V} = \text{rate of exploitation.}$$

This rate measures the quantitative dimension of the capitalist fundamental class process: just how effectively productive capitalists are appropriating surplus value from productive laborers. The rate of exploitation measures the ratio of the surplus to the necessary labor performed by productive laborers.

Using the numbers from our original chair example, where paid labor was six hours and unpaid labor was two hours, we can calculate the rate of exploitation in the chair enterprise: $LL_u/LL_p = 2/6$. If the length of the working day, LL, were to be increased, say, to nine hours, while the value of labor power (LL_u) remained unchanged, the surplus value (LL_u) would rise to three hours. In this case, the rate of exploitation would rise to $3/6$.

Marx used his theory to interpret the continuing social conflicts over the length of the working day and work week. In the eighteenth and nineteenth centuries in Europe, as capitalism spread there, productive laborers were often required to work twelve-, fourteen-, and sixteen-hour days as a matter of course. The novels of Charles Dickens in Britain and Emile Zola in France offer detailed descriptions of workers' living conditions under such circumstances. These long days served productive capitalists by increasing the ratio XB/AX. For the same wage, workers were pressured to work longer hours, with the fruit of those longer hours accruing to the employing capitalists. In Marxian terminology, productive capitalists lengthened the working day to increase the rate of exploitation of labor, to make their capital expand faster. Not surprisingly, productive laborers eventually began to fight back, utilizing laws and/or trade unions to restrict the length of the working day. Major social struggles erupted, leading to laws that eventually limited the length of the working day to eight hours and the work week to forty—the basic law in the United States today.

However, the logic of the capitalist fundamental class process, according to Marxian theory, compels capitalists constantly to reopen the question of the length of the working day or week. Thus, in the United States today, employers of productive laborers seek to obtain agreement to "voluntary or compulsory overtime," as the arrangement for a lengthened working day or week is now called. Capitalists keep pressing to lengthen work times, not because they are insensitive or obsessed by greed, but because the survival of a productive capitalist depends in part on how effectively he or she exploits productive laborers. Lengthening work times is one way to enhance exploitation.

Indeed, the pressure that makes productive capitalists seek to increase the rate of exploitation is nothing other than capitalist competition. As each capitalist acts to secure his or her own position as a surplus labor appropriator, these actions threaten the abilities of other capitalists to secure their positions. The result is a constant state of tension among capitalists. Each fears the consequences of the others' attempts to survive. Each struggles to offset those consequences and to survive, which then provokes new reactions and new dangers for other capitalists and so on. In Marxian theory, competition is understood to be this interdependent network of risks and dangers imposing all kinds of actions upon productive capitalists. However, before turning to a discussion of capitalist competition, we need to consider the effects on productive laborers of a capitalist seeking to enhance their rate of exploitation.

E.4. Class Struggles

How do productive laborers react when confronted with a capitalist who seeks to increase their rate of exploitation? Depending on the complex circumstances they face, such workers may simply accept doing more unpaid labor. They may even accept ideas and arguments that disguise their growing exploitation. On the other hand, it is also possible that they will decide not to accept this situation. By themselves or with all kinds of allies—spouses, the unproductive employees of the capitalist, professionals involved in the ancient class process, and so on—they may cause a social conflict to erupt over the quantitative dimensions of the capitalist fundamental class process—for example, over the length of the legal working day or week.

A struggle ensues over the capitalist fundamental class process, in this case over the ratio between XB and AX, the rate of exploitation. All kinds of people involved in all manner of different class and nonclass processes take sides in this struggle. One side fights for a higher S/V, the other for a lower S/V. Because this is a struggle over the class process, it is called in Marxian theory a "class struggle."

Unions of productive laborers pressing for higher wages is a class struggle. Management pressing productive laborers to accept compulsory overtime is a class struggle. The fight between two groups of representatives in Congress over a law that would raise the legal minimum wage is a class struggle. Each of these instances is a class struggle because of what the struggle is about. The groups struggling include persons involved in all manner of class and nonclass processes, but their struggle is a class struggle because of the specific nature of the object of their struggle.

When complex groupings of people fight over nonclass processes such as school curricula or medical ethics or criminal justice procedures, we refer to these as nonclass struggles. Any society involves an ever-changing pattern of both class and nonclass struggles. Because of Marxian theory's focus on class, it has always been most concerned to locate, identify, and connect class struggles to the other processes and struggles occurring in any society under scrutiny.

Class struggles concern not only the quantitative dimensions of the fundamental class process, such as the rate of exploitation in capitalism. Groups of people also struggle over the qualitative dimensions of class processes. For example, the issue may be the qualitative form of the fundamental class process rather than the ratio of paid to unpaid labor time. One side may want to preserve the capitalist form of surplus labor production. The other side may want to change to another form of the fundamental class process—say, a communist form. This too is a class struggle because the object of the struggling is the class process. This time the struggle is over the qualitative form of the fundamental class process rather than its quantitative dimensions. Of course, nothing prevents people from struggling simultaneously over the quantity and quality of the fundamental class process.

The class struggles discussed here have so far been limited to struggles over the fundamental class process, but social groups fight over the subsumed class process as well. In this case the conflict will concern the size and form of distribution of appropriated surplus from the appropriators to the receivers. Section G below shows how capitalism includes struggles over the size of the interest payments productive capitalists have to make to bankers to secure the credit required to appropriate surplus value. Section G also details struggles over the size of the tax payments productive capitalists have to make to the state and over the salary payments they make to the unproductive laborer they hire to supervise their productive laborers.

Without delving further into the complex analyses of class struggles initiated by Marx, one preliminary conclusion is already warranted. Marxian theory clearly works with an array of different class struggles that occur in, and help shape the history of, any society. These class struggles may concern either fundamental or subsumed class processes or both. They may concern either the quantitative or the qualitative dimensions of either class process or both. In Marxian theory, class struggles are like class processes: both are overdetermined by all the other processes occurring in a society. Likewise, class struggles affect every other process in society, including the class processes being struggled over.

Traditionally, Marxists distinguish their perspective from that of other social reformers by stressing the need for a qualitative change in the fundamental class process. Marxists see the capitalist fundamental class process as a major barrier to the construction of a just, peaceful, and democratic society. Marxists address this sort of declaration to other reformers: "Unless you take into account the capitalist fundamental class process and subsumed class process and understand how class interacts with the rest of modern society, you will neither understand nor successfully transform that society in the directions we all want." Marxists present and develop Marxian theory as precisely the indispensable analytical tool for producing the needed understanding and transformation.

E.5. The Complexity of Industrial Capitalist Firms

The productive capitalist who appropriates surplus value from his productive laborers may be an individual or a group of individuals (as in a modern corporate board of directors). In either case, the appropriation of surplus value occurs quite literally at places in society usually called "enterprises" or "firms." Commodity-producing firms are the main sites in modern society where the capitalist fundamental class process occurs. They are likewise the sites of distribution of already appropriated surplus value, which we have called "the capitalist subsumed class process." We will henceforth refer to the productive capitalists as "industrial capitalists" to distinguish them from the unproductive capitalists (such as merchanting, moneylending, and land-renting capitalists).

Many nonclass processes occur together with the capitalist class processes at the site of a firm. Cultural processes in a firm include speech among persons, the writing of all sorts of business reports, the decoration of buildings, and so on. Political processes include the giving and taking of orders among the persons working in this firm, the writing of behavioral rules for employees, the adjudication of disputes among people present in the firm, and the like. Natural processes include the transformation of natural materials during the production of commodity outputs, climatic changes occurring where the firm is located, various forms of pollution of the environment inside the firm, and so on. Other economic processes occurring at the site of the firm, besides the capitalist class processes, include all of its buying and selling, borrowing and lending, saving and investing, and the like.

For any given capitalist firm to last through time, the processes that define it—natural, cultural, economic, and political—must somehow be reproduced. Otherwise the firm might cease to exist. For example, if a natural process changed such that average temperatures dropped to $-100°$, the firm would probably expire. If a virus thrived in the bodies of the firm's employees and deprived them of hearing, the firm might disappear. For the firm to survive, natural processes such as "normal" temperatures and virus-elimination would somehow have to be reproduced. The firm itself might seek to facilitate their reproduction, even though there might be little or nothing it could do to reproduce many of the processes its life depended upon.

The capitalist firm also depends upon the reproduction of cultural processes. If its employees shifted from their traditional religions to a belief in nonwork as a value esteemed by a deity they worshiped, the firm's existence might well be jeopardized. The firm could respond to such a cultural development by expending funds to counteract that religion in various ways, but it might or might not succeed in this, depending on what other social forces shaped its employees' religious convictions.

Political processes inside the firm—for instance, the adjudication of disputes among employees—must be maintained to ensure work discipline. Otherwise the firm's survival will be at risk. Thus, the firm must make sure that employees continue to use and obey such adjudication processes. If employees' home lives or fear of punishment suffice to produce such obedience, the firm need expend little or none of its own funds to secure labor discipline. If not, the firm will need to expend energy and probably money to alter the adjudication procedures and/or convince or compel compliance by employees. One way or another, the political process of adhering to the firm's rules governing interpersonal behavior must be reproduced if the firm is to survive.

The firm likewise needs the many economic processes that provide the conditions of its existence. For example, the firm would be at risk if the conditions for it to buy and sell its inputs and outputs were threatened or not reproduced over time. These processes of commodity exchange are only partly, if at all, under the firm's control. They could be jeopardized by factors beyond the firm's control (a war that disrupts exchange, a monopolist who corners a market, a massive depression, etc.). Under such conditions, the firm could try to use its own resources to re-create the old or organize the new exchange processes necessary for its survival. It might or might not succeed.

If the nonclass processes inside and outside the firm are more or less reproduced or at least are not changed in dangerous ways, then the industrial capitalist firm will survive. Depending on just how all of these nonclass processes change, the capitalist class processes in the firm will expand or shrink or otherwise change. These nonclass changes combine to overdetermine the changes in the class structure of the firm.

However, it is always possible that the many diverse changes that occur in the nonclass processes will combine to threaten or destroy the capitalist class processes in the firm. Industrial capitalists might well wish to survive, to maintain their firms intact in the face of the threatening changes taking place around them. Of course, under some circumstances, they might not wish to survive as industrial capitalists, preferring to participate in other social processes rather than the capitalist fundamental class process. Then they would respond to the threatening changes by eliminating the capitalist class processes in their firms by closing the firm altogether. Those reactions are always occurring in all societies where industrial capitalist enterprises have existed.

Here, we are going to focus on industrial capitalist firms whose surplus-appropriating capitalists do wish to continue in their positions, to maintain the capitalist class structures of their firms. For each of them, actual or potential changes in all the nonclass processes on which their firm's survival depends are continuing issues of intense concern. Indeed, to continue being a capitalist appropriator of surplus labor requires constant vigilance. If and when changes in those processes appear to threaten the firm's capitalist class processes, the industrial capitalist must take action to deflect the threat, to reverse some change in nonclass processes, to set in motion new nonclass processes. The goal in this case is to protect and secure the firm's capitalist class processes.

Any industrial capitalist needs a regular flow of resources to be able even to try to secure the firm's capitalist class processes. Such a flow of resources is the surplus value appropriated from productive laborers. The capitalist who receives the surplus distributes it in such a way as to secure or change in specific ways the nonclass processes on which the firm's capitalist class processes depend.

Indeed, we have already made this point by defining the distribution of the surplus as a subsumed class process. The industrial capitalist receives (appropriates) the surplus value produced by productive laborers. Then, he or she distributes the appropriated surplus to other people as payment for their performance of the various nonclass processes needed to sustain the firm's capitalist class processes. This amounts to a chain of interdependence. The capitalist fundamental class process provides the surplus that ensures the firm's survival. The subsumed class process distributes that surplus to a variety of people. These people in turn perform the nonclass processes that overdetermine—that is, reproduce over time—the capitalist fundamental class process, which renders the chain of interdependence complete.

Thus, to return to some of our specific examples, an industrial capitalist might distribute surplus to certain persons inside or outside the firm to get them to remove troubling religious commitments, or to enforce company conflict rules, or to deal with viruses that are disrupting employee efficiency. These persons are said to occupy subsumed class positions because they obtain distributed shares of surplus in return for providing conditions of existence for the firm's capitalist class processes and hence for the capitalist's ability to occupy a fundamental class position.

E.6. Competition

Competition arises among industrial capitalist firms because the ways in which any one firm seeks to secure its own reproduction often have the side effect of jeopardizing the reproduction of another. This does not necessarily reflect the intentions or will of either capitalist. Rather, the structure of class and nonclass processes within which all capitalists function makes certain efforts at self-reproduction by one capitalist a threat to the survival of others. The resulting struggles among industrial capitalists, as each seeks to survive the consequences of others' efforts to survive, are collectively labeled "competition."

Marxian theory attaches great significance to industrial capitalist competition for several reasons. First, these competitive struggles continue to exert deep and lasting impacts on the history of all modern societies. Second, neoclassical theory claims that competition is a positive force that generates optimum economic efficiency—a claim which Marxists wish to refute. Third, competition among industrial capitalists can and often does provoke various sorts of class struggles. Marxists seek to understand and transform such class struggles into movements for fully just and democratic societies built upon nonexploitative fundamental class processes.

Industrial capitalist competition takes many forms. For example, one capitalist, concerned about flagging discipline among his or her productive laborers, decides to distribute more surplus toward supervision of the laborers. This capitalist hires several additional supervisors. The strategy works and enables this capitalist to induce the productive laborers to manufacture more commodities (say, chairs) than before. That is, the same amount of labor is now embodied in more chairs. This means that each chair has a lower value than before.

Meanwhile, consider the other capitalists who are making identical chairs. How do they react to what the first capitalist has done? They panic. They instantly recognize that the first capitalist, who is now getting more chairs from his or her laborers per hour, will lower what he or she charges per chair toward its now lower value. They cannot do likewise since they have not likewise lowered the value of each chair they produce. They fear that buyers will desert them in favor of the first capitalist's cheaper chairs. Unable to sell their chairs at actual value, they find that their existence as capitalists is in jeopardy. And should they go out of business, the innovative first capitalist might not only pick up their former customers but also buy up their machinery, and so on. This story implies great incentives (profits and growth) for the first capitalist to improve his or her productive laborers' efficiency, and serious threats to all others producing the same commodity.

Knowing how sadly this story might end for them, these other industrial capitalists try quickly to reproduce what they think is the effective strategy of the capitalist who hired the extra supervisors. Or they try any other available strategy for improving their workers' productivity, or at least find some way to lower the value of their chairs without losing their profits. Indeed, all industrial capitalists come to understand that their survival depends on how quickly they can match the lower values of other producers (of the same commodity) who improve their workers' efficiency. Likewise, all industrial capitalists come to understand that if they innovate first—try some new machine, new process of supervision, new style of management, or new source of cheaper inputs—and can therefore lower the value of their commodity, great economic gain will accrue to them.

Thus industrial capitalists strive for value-reducing innovations, not only as a defense against their competitors' possible innovations, but also as an offensive strategy aimed to induce growth and prosperity. The capitalist class structure happens to be organized in such a way that the gains of one industrial capitalist immediately threaten all the others who produce the same commodity. However, it is important to stress that competition is not primarily a matter of personal wills. Because it is a structural requirement imposed on all industrial capitalists, some individuals internalize this requirement and adjust their personalities to fit what their environment demands. Capitalist competition is not the result of some innate human competitiveness. If anything, the reverse makes more sense. In any case, whatever competitiveness industrial capitalists display is in no small part a product of the conditions of their existence.

To take another example, one competing capitalist might invent a new piece of machinery or buy a newly invented piece of machinery that allowed his or her productive laborers to make many more chairs per hour than they had been able to make previously. The same panic would grip all the other chair capitalists, and for the same reason. In still another example, an industrial capitalist might discover a new, cheaper source of lumber, an input to chair production, which would allow him or her to lower the value of each chair. This gain would likewise spur another round of competition for all the other chair producers.

E.7. Competition and the Accumulation of Capital

Perhaps the most famous example of capitalist competition concerns the decision by one chair capitalist to "accumulate capital." This decision deserves careful examination. Consider again the basic equation for a capitalist firm producing a given commodity:

$$C + V + S = W.$$

The capitalist sells the chairs produced by his or her productive laborers and thereby obtains a value equal to W. Presumably this capitalist uses a portion of the W to replace the tools and raw materials used up in producing the chairs. This equals the C in the equation. Likewise the capitalist uses another portion of the W to pay for the productive labor power purchased from the laborers. This equals the V. That leaves the capitalist with an appropriated surplus value, S, which must be distributed to secure the various conditions that are necessary if he or she is to continue to appropriate S.

Now suppose that this capitalist decides to use part of the S to buy extra tools, raw materials, and productive labor power. This process is called "accumulating capital." The extra C and V purchased out of S will generate extra S for the capitalist. By accumulating capital, he or she will be able to appropriate more surplus because more productive laborers will be performing surplus labor. We can show this in terms of two consecutive time periods in the process of accumulating capital:

$$\text{Period 1: } C + V + S = W,$$

where S is used to buy additional C and V (denoted as ΔC and ΔV, respectively).

$$\text{Period 2: } C + V + \Delta C + \Delta V + S + \Delta S = W + \Delta W.$$

This second equation indicates that the capitalist must now replace more tools and raw materials absorbed into production ($C + \Delta C$) as well as pay for more hired labor power ($V + \Delta V$). These expanded input costs result from capital accumulation. However, because variable capital creates new value, the capitalist also appropriates a new surplus value (indicated by the term ΔS in the value equation). Thus the accumulation of capital augments the mass of surplus value from S to $(S + \Delta S)$.

The reasoning of the accumulating capitalist is quite straightforward: the more surplus the capitalist appropriates over time by means of accumulation ($\Delta C + \Delta V$), the more resources he or she will have to secure the conditions of his or her existence. And, again, the reaction of the other chair capitalists is panic. They see the danger immediately. The accumulating capitalist might use the additional surplus to buy an expensive new machine that nonaccumulating capitalists might not be able to afford, or to hire supervisory personnel that nonaccumulating capitalists might not be able to afford, and so on.

It does not matter that the chair capitalist who first adds supervisors, or buys new machines, or accumulates capital does not intend to trouble the existence of other chair capitalists, but simply acts to secure the conditions of his or her own existence. Nonetheless, all the other chair capitalists feel threatened. They see the possibilities and probable dangers occasioned by the first chair capitalist's actions.

Moreover, their only logical response to the actual or potential threats posed by the first capitalist's actions is to take comparable steps.

They too will hire more supervisors, and/or buy new machines, and/or accumulate capital. Indeed, they may take yet other steps to enhance their security by finding new ways to distribute their surplus value to subsumed classes. And, of course, whatever they do to enhance their security will similarly threaten the first capitalist, who in turn will take more steps. Competition is this never-ending struggle to survive in the face of the dangers flowing from other capitalists' parallel efforts to survive.

One of the most interesting and perhaps paradoxical results of this competition among industrial capitalists is the driving down of the value per unit of commodity as industrial capitalists distribute surplus value to enhance their laborers' productivity. In terms of Marxian value theory, the amount of socially necessary labor to produce each commodity is overdetermined by this competition among industrial capitalists. That amount can continue to fall as competition continues.

In that event, competitively successful industrial capitalists discover that their efforts to survive have generated a decline in the per-unit values of the commodities they produce and sell. Such a decline may well induce further reactions on their part, perhaps altering their accumulation of capital, which in turn will react on their competitive strategies and so on. We will begin to explore Marxian theory's treatment of these and other consequences of competition in the section on the cycles or crises of capitalism (section F.3 below).

F. Capitalist Economies and Social Development

From the standpoint of the Marxian theory elaborated here, the interaction of the capitalist fundamental class process and commodity exchange processes plays an important role in shaping the modern history of capitalist social formations. Marx is understood to have begun the analysis of that role. Although he never reached his goal of writing a full analysis, he did produce some sketches of an analysis which were extended in various directions by later Marxists. These Marxists wanted to demonstrate the significance of their class analytics by using them to construct explanations of the growth of the modern international economy, the distribution of income in capitalist societies, and the boom-bust cycles that afflict capitalist economies. By briefly considering their arguments here, we can gain a more comprehensive feel for the structure and implications of Marxian theory.

F.1. Growth of a Capitalist World Economy

The competition among industrial capitalists can and typically does drive down the per-unit prices of commodities for the reasons we have been discussing. This has had awesome historical effects. Ever-cheapening commodities present ever-widening opportunities for selling these commodities. Marx attached great importance to this remarkable feature of capitalism. Wherever it took hold, the productive capitalists eventually realized that falling commodity values suggested new markets where these ever-cheaper commodities might be sold. In the eighteenth and nineteenth centuries, for example, the falling values of their textile commodities led British capitalists to seek and find worldwide markets for them. British textiles fell enough in their unit values that continental Europeans, Asians, Africans, and Americans eventually purchased them instead of locally produced textiles, whose values had not fallen comparably.

In this sense, capitalist competition directly contributes to the securing of one of the conditions of existence of the capitalist fundamental class process—namely, expanding markets in which to sell capitalist commodities. The effect of competition on unit values generates a growing market for such commodities. Capitalism's relatively early arrival in the nations of Western Europe and North America and in Japan allowed these nations to acquire powerful economic positions because their capitalist commodities eventually displaced locally produced commodities in many parts of the world. The profitable export of commodities from capitalist economies engendered wealth and prosperity there. Indeed, those nations eventually carved up the rest of the world into colonial properties that were operated as protected territories partly to enhance commodity sales and partly to allow direct labor exploitation by capitalist enterprises. Food and raw materials were produced all over the world in a variety of different fundamental class processes (capitalist, feudal, slave, and ancient). The produced capitalist and noncapitalist commodities were then exported to the nations of Western Europe and North America and to Japan.

The last two centuries might well be called the era of capitalist growth toward world dominance. However, outside of Western Europe, North America, and Japan, vast social dislocations took place as imported capitalist commodities disrupted traditional economies. Traditional livelihoods were destroyed as these imports displaced local produce and local producers. This had occurred earlier in Europe during the long transition from feudalism to capitalism. Then new capitalist industries in urban centers had sold their commodities to mostly feudal agricultural hinterlands. One result had been waves of displaced rural people moving to cities and selling their labor power to industrial capitalists. As capitalist competition spurred further growth, vast international migrations began in which people looked desperately for new ways to survive. Often moving toward work in capitalist industries, the migrations continue to this day. The history of the United States is a continuing testament to the complex and profound impacts of those migrations. In the nations that the migrants left behind, patterns of political life were undermined as these governments struggled over how to react to the economic, social, and psychological disruptions occasioned by capitalist commodity imports.

The disruption became still more intense in the later nineteenth and in the twentieth century. Then capitalist commodity exports were joined by exports of capital itself. Capitalist enterprises in Western Europe, North America, and Japan established investments in the rest of the world. They found and exploited sources of raw materials and food, and shipped these commodities back to the capitalist centers. They erected factories in Asia, Africa, and Latin America to exploit lower wage levels there. Colonial governments dutifully obliged by establishing and maintaining profitable conditions for such investments. Even after colonial power had given way to local, independent regimes, the desperate economic circumstances of these governments led most of them to try to ameliorate their social crises by continuing to invite and protect foreign industrial capitalist investments.

On the other hand, in some of these societies the social crises promoted by capitalist commodity exports and later by capital exports interacted with domestic social tensions to fashion a different response. In these societies, the link to European capitalism was itself identified as the source of social crisis. Hence the solution would be to break away from the capitalist world market. The Soviet Union, China, Cuba, and many other countries pursued this alternative. Their strategy was to create the space for rapid internal economic development by largely cutting themselves off from capitalism. They did this by replacing privately owned factories, land, and equipment with collectivized, publicly owned property, by minimizing or strictly controlling trade with capitalist countries, and by rejecting any foreign capitalist investment in their countries.

Such actions closed off a growing part of the world to capitalist enterprises from Western Europe, North America, and Japan. Ironically, then, capitalist competition and accumulation produced their own limitations and obstacles via the reactions they provoked. Where socialism and communism did not literally close parts of the world to capitalist enterprise, many so-called Third World countries, especially after 1960, began to demand better economic relations between themselves and the capitalist enterprises they dealt with. Some tried to change their economic conditions by controlling the prices of their exports through cartels like OPEC or the International Coffee Agreement. Or they threatened to discontinue paying off some or all of the massive debts they had incurred as part of their economic dilemmas before 1970. In the last twenty years there have been discussions in a growing number of international organizations—the United Nations, the World Bank, and the International Monetary Fund, among others—about a new international economic order. Widespread demands have been made for some massive reorganization of the world economy to alleviate the disruptive, accumulated tensions of two hundred or more years of the development of a capitalist world market.

Despite the tensions, conflicts, and uncertainties that cloud the modern world economy, however, Marxian theory acknowledges that the capitalist fundamental class process did much to provoke the formation of a truly world or global economy for the first time in human history. Industrial capitalist competition provoked firms to produce lower-valued commodities, to seek markets ever farther afield, to search the globe for new, cheaper sources of food and raw materials, and to seek foreign opportunities for higher rates of exploitation where labor power could be bought cheaply. The competition also provoked the technical innovations in metal manufacture, engines, shipping, and weaponry. These made possible the transportation, trade, and warfare that accompanied the foreign economic activities of industrial capitalist firms. Indeed, the rapidly rising surplus value appropriated by European industrial capitalists provided the resources for their tax payments to European governments: resources which they demanded should be used to provide military security to the capitalists' growing overseas ventures.

In Marxian theory, there is the most intimate connection between the capitalist fundamental class process and the histories of colonialism, imperialism, and the contemporary world economy. In elaborating that connection, Marxian theory produces insights into the contradictions and dynamics of the world economy which are different from the analyses constructed by all other theories.

F.2. Capitalism and Real Incomes

As capitalist expansions (chiefly from Europe) disrupted societies elsewhere, real incomes—actual goods and services consumed—dropped drastically for most of the people in these societies. Usually only a relatively few local appropriators of surplus labor and some subsumed classes could accommodate capitalist expansion and thereby secure or even enhance their incomes. These included local feudal lords, some ancient classes, and some native small industrial capitalists among the fundamental classes. Local subsumed classes typically included merchants, landlords, moneylenders, and various levels of bureaucrats.

In the centers of capitalist enterprise, the movements in real incomes were more uneven. In the early stages of capitalist enterprise in Western Europe, North America, and Japan, laborers, who were usually drawn from rural areas to industrial centers, experienced extreme privation. However, as generation after generation of productive and unproductive laborers worked in capitalist enterprises, their real incomes rose. Today, such employees typically look back over past generations and conclude that their real incomes have risen impressively.

Yet, as suggested earlier, for Marxian economic theory, rising real incomes can be consistent with a simultaneously rising rate of exploitation. And this has important implications for the structure of modern capitalist economies, especially those in Western Europe, North America, and Japan. Did those economies achieve relative social stability because they were able to provide industrial capitalists with rising rates of exploitation and to simultaneously provide workers with rising real incomes? How was this possible? Can it last? In generating its answers to these questions, Marxian theory explains how higher real incomes did indeed coexist with rising rates of exploitation.

Recall the division in Marxian value theory between V and S in the $C + V + S = W$ equation for all industrial capitalist enterprises. V is the value of labor power. It is the value of the goods and services that productive laborers require in order to be able and willing to keep on working for their capitalist employers. The latter pay their laborers a money sum of value—the wage—which they in turn use to buy commodities for their consumption. That sum, V, when subtracted from the total value added by the laborers during any day that they work, yields S, the surplus value appropriated by the industrial capitalist.

If we suppose for the moment that this sum, V, and the length of the working day are fixed, then S must also be fixed. Hence the rate of exploitation, S/V, must likewise be fixed. Yet we have noticed that capitalist competition generates a tendency for the per-unit values of commodities to drop over time. This means that even if the value paid to productive laborers is fixed over time, this constant V will permit them to purchase a growing bundle of goods and services whose individual unit values trend downward. Thus we can see that a constant rate of exploitation can be perfectly consistent with an increase in the real incomes of workers.

It is a simple next step to see how a rising rate of exploitation can coexist with rising real incomes. All we need to do is compare the rate at which V falls in relation to S, on the one hand, with the rate at which the per-unit values of commodities purchased by productive laborers fall, on the other. If industrial capitalists pay their laborers a reduced sum of value—say, 10 percent less—while maintaining the length of the working day, then the S/V ratio will necessarily rise. If the unit values of wage commodities fall further—say, by 20 percent—these laborers will be able to buy more of them despite the reduced wages they receive (see appendix 2 to this chapter).

According to Marxian theory, this situation has existed in the centers of capitalist enterprise for the last hundred years. The value of labor power fell faster than the length of the working day was shortened, so that the surplus portion of the day's labor rose relatively. The S/V ratio rose, delivering to industrial capitalists an ever-growing surplus to use to secure their conditions of existence. At the same time, the unit values of commodities purchased by workers fell even faster. This was partly the result of the capitalist competition we noted above. It was also partly the result of capitalist expansion to the rest of the world, where new, cheaper sources of food and raw materials were colonized, exploited, and brought back home to permit cheaper commodities to be produced. The last hundred years thus brought rising real incomes for most workers in the capitalist centers even as workers' real incomes in the rest of the world moved in the opposite direction.

Capitalist class relations were reproduced and extended on the basis of rising rates of exploitation combined with rising real incomes for most workers in Western Europe, North America, and Japan. These societies adjusted politically, culturally, and psychologically to a prosperity based on rising exploitation and rising real incomes. On the one hand, this yielded unprecedented wealth, power, and global predominance for the industrial capitalists and governments of these societies. On the other hand, these societies became dependent on being able to continue to combine rising real incomes with rising rates of exploitation.

If, for whatever reason, threats arose to such societies' ability to enjoy rising real incomes and rising rates of exploitation, extreme social reactions would likely occur. Thus, when workers inside advanced capitalist societies organized to demand changes in wages and working conditions which would have lowered the S/V ratio, they were usually met with repression ranging from political attack to physical destruction. Socialist and communist organizations and revolutions were treated as the scourge of the earth wherever they arose. Movements for political independence and economic modernization in Asia, Africa, and Latin America, which might disrupt sources of cheap inputs into capitalist commodity production, were ruthlessly suppressed. As two world wars attest, the advanced capitalist countries also waged wars upon one another partly because some felt that the others were undermining their ability to assure the combination of rising rates of exploitation and rising real incomes.

The responses of these societies to all such possible threats to their prosperous capitalist social structure contributed to local social disruptions and the cataclysm of world war. These in turn generated new and formidable obstacles to the continuation of those societies' capitalist structures. Thus, the two world wars played major roles in forming the communist group of nations. The repression of independence movements in Asia, Africa, and Latin America provoked the current determination in many countries there to improve their economic conditions if necessary at the expense of advanced capitalist economies. The world wars destroyed vast numbers of workers as well as capital equipment and infrastructure that had been built up over many years. Smaller, localized conflicts across the globe did likewise.

The arresting irony in this history of capitalism seen through the lens of Marxian theory is that the strivings of industrial capitalists to secure their conditions of existence had the effects of undermining them as much as reproducing them. These are some of the specific internal contradictions of capitalism. Another set of capitalist contradictions, to which Marx devoted considerable attention in *Capital,* concerns the disruptive cycles or crises that result from capitalist competition and the accumulation of capital inside the advanced capitalist economies. Marxian theory's treatment of these cycles permits yet another demonstration of the insights such class analysis makes possible.

F.3. The Cycles or Crises of Capitalist Economies

Marx was not the first observer to note tendencies in capitalist economies toward cyclical ups and downs, the fluctuations that economists call "recessions" and "recoveries" and that most people call "booms" and "busts." However, Marxian theory offers a distinctive explanation for their occurrence. We will here begin to sketch the complex overdetermination of cycles, building upon certain preliminary notions first presented by Marx in *Capital* and further developed in the earlier parts of this chapter.

Cycles are periods of time in which capitalist economies undergo a phased shift from one set of conditions to a roughly opposite set. In the boom, prosperity, or upswing phase, the distinguishing economic phenomena include falling unemployment, rising quanta of output, capital accumulation, growing commodity sales, and rising incomes. In the other phase, the distinguishing signs include rising layoffs, falling output, disaccumulation, shrinking sales, and diminishing incomes. Over the history of capitalist economies, both phases show varying durations and degrees of movement. Upswings can be larger and last longer than downswings (capitalists speak of such periods as long-run booms), or, alternatively, the opposite can occur (in which case the word "depression" is often heard). The cycles of capitalist economies have persisted despite the varied policies invented to eliminate them. They have provoked many economists to interpret and explain their recurrence.

Nor is this merely a matter of specialists' interests. Urgent practical issues motivate the efforts at explanation. Economic downswings generate all manner of socially troublesome consequences in capitalist societies. As economic activity declines, tax revenues to governments fall and cause government programs to contract. Competitors in economies that are not experiencing such downturns often gain crucial advantages. Unemployed workers become angry and may even begin to question the desirability of a capitalist organization of the economy if it subjects them to the privations of unemployment so recurringly. Here is another sign of the consequences of denying workers the rising real incomes they have come to expect. Unemployed workers may emigrate and not return even when the next upswing occurs. The personal damage suffered by unemployed workers, bankrupt entrepreneurs, and their families may have lasting and costly social effects long after the downturn has passed over into the next upturn. To avoid these and other negative consequences of downturns, explanations for them are needed that will guide policy makers to minimize those consequences or, if possible, to eliminate the cycles altogether.

A capitalist downturn might trigger a social movement aimed not merely at hastening the shift to an economic upturn but also at radically altering the existing economic system, including its class structure. As suggested in chapter 2, the fears of capitalists and those who favored the capitalist system during the depression of the 1930s concerned the costs of the economic downturn. These costs might have led to the overturning of the capitalist system. Such fears continue today. People hurt by one or more of these cyclical downturns—unemployed workers, bankrupt entrepreneurs, students who have had to abandon their career hopes, farmers who have been unable to sell perishable crops and animals, and so on—might well develop preferences for different, noncapitalist economic systems.

If they believed that noncapitalist systems could be free from cycles and their social costs, they might organize themselves politically. Swelled in number at the bottom of a downturn, they might move radically to transform the economic class structure. The preferred transformations range from kinds of feudalism or fascism, on the political right, to kinds of socialism and communism, on the left.

How to prevent such transformations has motivated many neoclassical studies of cycles and their causes, consequences, and possible remedies. We noted this in chapter 2, in our discussion of neoclassical and Keynesian solutions to such unwanted cycles. Indeed, an explicit goal of many Keynesian theoretical statements was to lessen the duration and intensity of capitalist cycles so as to counter Marxian treatments of and proposals for dealing with cycles. Marxists have studied cycles as well, but with different motivations. Their purpose has chiefly been to demonstrate that cycles are intrinsic, unavoidable aspects of capitalism. Their point has been to transform dissatisfaction with cycles into a particular kind of political dissatisfaction with capitalism, which they link closely with cycles. In short, Marxian treatments of cycles form one part of the Marxian critique of capitalism and argument for socialism. Partly for that reason, cycles are often referred to in Marxian literature as the "crises" of capitalism.

Using the term "crisis" emphasizes the Marxian notion that cycles are critical moments in the life of capitalist economies. They are critical because downturns lead people to question the causes of their suffering and sometimes to consider radical critiques of capitalism as a class structure. Some Marxists took the notion of crisis still further to argue that cyclical downturns would worsen over time and eventually bring about the economic collapse of capitalism. This Marxian crisis theory then became a theory of capitalism's inevitable collapse under the weight of its own internal economic contradictions.

The Marxian theory at work in this chapter offers a different interpretation and explanation of cycles or crises. It sees them as overdetermined effects of the contradictions of the capitalist economy, but not as guaranteed to produce the collapse of capitalism. Whether, and if so, when, a particular cyclical downswing will eventuate in a transformation of the class structure of some capitalist society is itself dependent on all the class and nonclass processes of that society. In other words, just as cycles are overdetermined as to their occurrence, duration, and intensity, so too are any possible transitions from cycles to social revolutions.

Cycles do not result from some essential cause or group of causes; the Marxian theory at work here does not reduce them to mere effects of one or another quality of capitalism. Nor does it reduce them—in the manner of the neoclassicals and Keynesians—to limitations found in human nature or given exogenously by physical nature. Rather, it claims that social processes interacting in varying combinations and patterns generate (overdetermine) cyclical downturns and upturns. The task of Marxian analysis is to explore some of these processes and thereby establish the tendencies toward recurring cycles that are generated by capitalist class structures. Marx commenced the task in *Capital*. Other Marxists took it further. Continuing their work, we will sketch the crisis argument we find persuasive in Marxian theory.

One mechanism that contributes to the generation of cycles is capital accumulation. As we noted earlier, industrial capitalists typically utilize a portion of their appropriated surplus value to secure their conditions of existence by accumulating capital. This means that such capitalists increase their purchases of and hence their demand for both the physical means of production and labor power ($C + V$). No problem is generated by such capital accumulation so long as additional labor power is indeed available for accumulating capitalists to purchase. However, there is no reason to presume that such ready-to-be-employed reserves of labor power are always plentiful. If the demand for additional labor power outpaced the available supply, economic cycles might emerge.

A greater demand for than supply of additional labor power will normally drive up the market price of that labor power—that is, will increase money wages. Given the length of the working day, rising wages will leave less surplus value for the capitalist employer. Thus, when capitalists appropriate surplus, accumulate a good portion of it, hire more workers, expand output and sales in a self-reinforcing spiral, they enter into a cyclical upswing. However, such growing accumulation may outpace the available supplies of additional labor power. Industrial capitalists may run out of qualified workers to hire. Since they will still need to accumulate surplus for competitive reasons, they may well secure additional workers by offering already employed people an incentive to move from their present positions. This incentive is higher wages. But by paying higher wages, competitive capitalists eat into their own surpluses.

In these circumstances, capitalists confront the question of how to react to rising wages and the resultant pinching of their surplus appropriation. They could stoically accept a lower rate of exploitation, but that is highly unlikely. Not all capitalists are equally hurt by rising wages; these increases cause the greatest damage to those who rely most heavily on labor (versus machines) in production. But fearful of falling behind their competitors all damaged capitalists will likely feel constrained to offset the impact of rising wages on their positions. They may decide to suspend some or all of their production activities until wages come back down and they can resume production at an acceptable rate of exploitation.

In this case, the capitalists who were most damaged by rising wages will take the lead. They will close operations, lay off workers, and cut back orders to their suppliers of equipment and raw materials. Their laid-off workers will in turn cut back purchases since their wages have disappeared. Their suppliers will lay off workers since they have lost sales, and they, too, will cut back orders to their suppliers, and so on. The result, in effect, will be a downward economic spiral characterized by falling incomes, employment levels, output, sales, and accumulation.

The internal contradiction of capitalism here is that a period of rising economic activity and well-being sets in motion its own opposite, an economic downswing of classic dimensions. The specific linkages between class processes, competition, accumulation, and the sale of labor power generate an economic cycle. Moreover, the mechanisms that transform an upswing into a downswing also generate the reverse movement. Thus, when unemployment spreads far enough and economic activity is constricted enough, desperate unemployed workers tend to accept lower wages, and bankrupt firms tend to offer their equipment and supplies at cheap prices. Lower wages and cheaper physical inputs then combine to lead some capitalists to anticipate profits if they resume production and if other capitalists do likewise. In this way an upswing of rising production, appropriation, accumulation, and so on, recommences.

This Marxian explanation of cycles as results of capitalist contradictions does not imply that cycles result necessarily from accumulation. Whether accumulation has such results depends on everything else that is occurring simultaneously—that is, all the conditions of the existence of a particular phase of accumulation. For example, if accumulation began to outrun available additional supplies of labor power, rising wages might not occur for years if immigration were to increase and replenish supplies. Alternatively, changes in family life might increase the supply of labor power by sending formerly home-bound wives and children out to seek jobs. Or laws diminishing social security benefits for the elderly might force millions of retired persons to return to the job market. A combination of such developments might make possible an indefinitely extended period of accumulation unmarred by labor shortages and rising wages.

Another possibility is that even if wages were driven up, capitalists might respond not by cutting back production but by automating their production lines. If labor-saving machines were available, they might now be purchased by capitalists faced with the even costlier option of paying higher wages. In this case, fewer workers would be laid off than would likely have been the case if production cutbacks had been the chosen capitalist reaction to higher wages. It is even possible that some of the laid-off workers would find new work in the industries making the machines that had displaced them from their former jobs. In this case, accumulation would lead to rising wages, but these would not last long, for automation would replenish the pool of available labor power and thereby permit accumulation to proceed indefinitely.

On the other hand, accumulation can generate a cycle in which the cyclical downswing is deeply disruptive of the capitalist society in question. In such a case, accumulation sets in motion disaccumulation on a scale that goes beyond negating the prior period of accumulation. The entire economy contracts, perhaps for many years, as in the depression of the 1930s in the United States and most other capitalist countries. In such an environment, movements for radical social change could grow and perhaps win power. The political turbulence of the 1930s across Western Europe and North America offers examples of this possibility.

When they speak of cycles as crises, Marxists mean that any downswing is a potential threat to capitalism. It is a threat because it confronts everyone with the severe economic, social, and personal costs of the capitalist system. Cycles are dramatic and concrete illustrations of certain critiques of capitalism. Finally, a downturn is a threat if the suffering it imposes drives people to active political movements for basic, anticapitalist social change. However, any particular cyclical downswing or crisis need not realize any of these potentialities; it can be minimized, postponed, or offset by other processes that are occurring simultaneously within the society.

This leads us back to the Keynesian idea of increased state management of aggregate effective demand to avoid the worst of the capitalist crises. However, the logic of overdetermination implies that the avoidance of a crisis is not reducible to any one cause such as Keynesian policy. Whether such a policy will succeed in any particular crisis situation will depend on the specific overdetermination of that crisis—that is, all the processes other than Keynesian policy which influence its specific qualities.

In Marxian theory, accumulation is not the sole mechanism that can engender cycles. Marx originally pointed also to developments impinging on capitalists' abilities to appropriate surplus value as possibly leading to cyclical downturns. Thus, for example, competition might well foster technological improvements in production which required capitalists to purchase ever more expensive pieces of machinery in order to survive. The constant capital (C) portion of total capital would rise in relation to both V and S. As a result, the ratio of S to $(C + V)$—sometimes called the value rate of profit—would fall. Capitalists confronting such falling value rates of profit might then hold back production, thereby setting in motion the cyclical pattern discussed earlier.

Still another potential cyclical mechanism, often mentioned by Marx, is the problem he called "realization." Industrial capitalists must find buyers for the commodities produced by their productive laborers. Only then will they realize, in money form, the surplus value appropriated from those workers. This money enables them to buy more raw materials, equipment, and labor power and thereby recommence the production process. Should any social development prevent capitalists from finding the necessary buyers, this too might set off production cutbacks, layoffs, and the cyclical downswing. Beyond climate, political upheavals, and other factors that might prevent capitalists from realizing their surplus value, Marxists are concerned to show how such a crisis mechanism might emerge out of the internal contradictions of the capitalist system.

In this case, a realization problem can be shown to be an ever-present possibility in capitalism. The reason for this is a contradiction within the relation between industrial capitalists and their employees. To survive competitively, the capitalists need to keep the wages and salaries they pay as low as possible. They must strive ceaselessly to achieve this goal. Yet they rely heavily on the same employees to purchase, out of their incomes, the consumer commodities that capitalists sell in the market. The more successfully they restrict their employees' incomes, the more likely they are to face a realization problem when it comes time to sell those commodities. If they cannot sell them, they may set in motion the cyclical pattern again. Then again, if foreign buyers can be found, realization problems may be postponed for a long time. Or perhaps a government spending program might intervene to absorb otherwise unsold commodities, and so on.

Cycles can thus emerge out of the peculiar contradictions of the capitalist system. That system is no smoothly functioning, unambiguous engine of growth and prosperity. Indeed, the empirical history of capitalist cycles supports the Marxian notion that capitalism's recurrent downswings produce significant negative economic and social effects. Nor does any adequate measure exist to suggest any sense in which capitalist upswings have had more positive effects than downswings have had negative effects. What is clear, from the Marxist perspective developed here, is that the capitalist class structure in which production occurs subjects its people to regular and massive economic and social disruptions of social life.

Other social processes may alter or offset a particular set of capitalist contradictions so that the potential for a cyclical downswing does not become actual. Likewise, a downswing can under certain historical circumstances function as the prelude to long and intense cyclical upswings. However, Marxian theory's class analysis of capitalism by means of its value equations explains why cycles recur periodically. Various internal contradictions (of which a few examples were presented above) tend toward cyclical movement. While that movement may be delayed or modified in this or that specific historical instance, there is no reason to suppose that the structural mechanisms engendering the cycles could be successfully offset in any regular way. Nor can Marxian theory envision a capitalism in which these mechanisms could be removed. The continuing resistance of cycles to the endlessly refined monetary and fiscal policies of capitalist governments attests to the fact that their roots lie in the basic features of the capitalist class structure.

Marxian theory's distinctive interpretation of cycles or crises does not locate them as effects primarily of natural phenomena (droughts, soil depletion, floods, heat, etc.) or political phenomena (government policies, wars, laws, etc.) or cultural phenomena (changes in uncertainty, popular philosophies, religions, tastes, etc.). Analysts friendly to capitalism have offered precisely such explanations over the last two hundred years. For example, in the United States today, conservatives often argue that the cycles in twentieth-century U.S. capitalism have been the result of too much government intervention, while liberals retort that the problem is precisely too little intervention. A variant of this debate concerns what kind of intervention could have avoided or minimized the cycles—the neoclassicals' monetarism and reliance on market adjustments or the Keynesians' state intervention.

From the Marxian perspective discussed here, all such debaters share the view that cycles could be eliminated or rendered minimally destructive if only the right political steps were taken in relation to the capitalist economy. Despite their differences with one another, the debaters still do not see the sorts of basic, structural contradictions emphasized in Marxian theory. Instead, they stress the fix-it approach to what is for them a desirable economic system that has some minor flaws to repair.

In contrast, Marxian analysis stresses the linkage of cycles to internal contradictions that can be "fixed" only by basically transforming the economic system that regularly reproduces those cycles. Marxian theory offers a distinctive interpretation of cycles which is tied to its broader critique of capitalism as a whole. That interpretation depends in turn on Marxian theory's concepts of class and value.

G. Capitalist Subsumed Classes

To this point, our discussion has emphasized mainly the capitalist fundamental class process. Our major protagonists have been productive laborers and industrial capitalists, the performers and appropriators of surplus value respectively. However, as we have noted, a capitalist class structure includes as well people who neither produce nor appropriate surplus value. Among these are the subsumed classes, people who distribute and/or obtain distributed shares of the surplus from the industrial capitalists who initially appropriated it. We can indicate the extended range and scope of Marxian economics by considering next some representative examples of capitalist subsumed classes and how they interact with capitalist fundamental classes.

G.1. Moneylenders and Subsumed Classes

The competitive struggles among industrial capitalists often compel them to turn to moneylenders to survive. The specific purposes of loans to industrial capitalists vary. In one case, the industrial capitalist may need a loan to be able to purchase some inputs that are temporarily cheaper than usual, lest a competitor do so. Or he or she may need a loan in order to install an expensive new technology before a competitor does. Another kind of loan is arranged when the industrial capitalist encounters temporary difficulties in selling his or her commodity outputs. Without revenues from the sale of outputs, the industrial capitalist would be without funds to pay employees or the suppliers of raw materials, who might then leave their jobs or orient their business elsewhere, to the industrial capitalist's competitive detriment. A loan to cover the time in which buyers are found will allow workers and suppliers to be paid.

In each case, borrowing money enhances the competitive survival of the industrial capitalist. The loan is arranged in hopes of securing the industrial capitalist's conditions of existence. From the standpoint of the moneylender, the ultimate use of the loan is of little or no concern. The lender's goal is to recover not only the money loaned but also a kind of fee for making the loan: interest. This fee is the income of the moneylender. The industrial capitalist borrower must repay the loan and pay the interest charge on the loan. One source of the interest payment may be the surplus value the industrial capitalist appropriates from his or her productive laborers. In that event, the moneylender is involved in the subsumed class process as the recipient of a distributed share of that surplus value. Such moneylenders constitute a capitalist subsumed class.

We can sketch the economic relationships involved here by slightly expanding our original value equation for capitalist commodity production. Thus we would rewrite our $C + V + S = W$ equation as

$$C + V + S_1 + S_r = W.$$

In this equation, S_1 is the portion of appropriated surplus distributed to moneylenders as interest payments, while S_r is the rest of the appropriated surplus value.

The relationship between industrial capitalist and moneylender includes, among the many other processes involved in any relationship among persons, two processes of special concern here. First, there is the

nonclass process of borrowing and lending. It is a nonclass process because it is precisely (and nothing more than) the act of temporarily passing funds from one person to another. Second, there is the subsumed
class process of distributing a portion of appropriated surplus value as
the interest payment accompanying the return of the borrowed funds.
The S_1 term in the equation locates the subsumed class process and the
two subsumed class positions it defines: that of the distributor of appropriated surplus value (the industrial capitalist) and the recipient of this
surplus value (the moneylender).

From the standpoint of the moneylender, the S_1 term represents the
interest income earned from lending funds. It is the subsumed class
payment received from the industrial capitalist. We can represent the
transaction from the moneylender's perspective as follows:

$$M \longrightarrow M + S_1.$$

The moneylender is a kind of capitalist too, since the lending process
accomplishes the self-expansion of his or her money. As we noted earlier, the moneylender is not an industrial capitalist, because the self-
expansion of value is not accomplished by the direct appropriation of
surplus value from any productive laborers. For that reason, we call
such moneylenders "nonproductive capitalists."

Moneylending is a process that can occur in a variety of modern institutional settings. Banks, insurance companies, industrial corporations,
individuals, governments, and others can and do lend money. Moreover, moneylenders need not and do not lend money only to industrial
capitalists. When money is lent to persons other than industrial capitalists, it follows that any interest payments involved are not distributions
of appropriated surplus value. This is because we have defined industrial capitalists as the only appropriators of surplus value in capitalist
class structures. Only when loans go to industrial capitalists and when
these capitalists pay interest out of the surplus value they appropriate
can we say that the relationship between lender and borrower includes
the subsumed class process as well as the moneylending process.

Loans to anyone other than an industrial capitalist can and do, in
American culture, typically carry interest charges. For example, one
worker can lend money to another worker and charge interest. A one-
month loan of $100 is repaid with interest, say, of $2. This $2 cannot be
considered a subsumed class payment, because the worker does not appropriate surplus value in the first place. It amounts to a nonclass interest payment precisely because no appropriation of surplus value or any
distribution of appropriated surplus by an appropriator is involved.

This raises the question of just which rates of interest will occur in a
capitalist society and what influences those rates. Our analysis sug-

gests that subsumed-class interest payments represent only one of many kinds of interest payments. Presumably, lenders will evaluate the credit-worthiness of industrial capitalist borrowers differently from that of the various other kinds of borrowers. We would thus expect a complex pattern of interest rates on borrowed funds depending on the various conditions confronting potential borrowers and lenders as they reach their loan agreements. One influence upon that pattern, one determinant of the structure of interest rates in a capitalist society, is the class structure. That is, the specific conditions of the production and appropriation of surplus value will participate in overdetermining both the demand for loans and the sources available to make interest payments. Given its focus on class and its general objective of teaching how class processes influence social life, the Marxian approach to the issue of interest rates will stress the shaping of those rates by class processes without, of course, making class into the sole or essential determinant of interest rates.

G.2. Managers and Subsumed Classes

Just as industrial capitalists often depend on the nonclass process of lending to secure their conditions of existence as appropriators of surplus value, they likewise depend on many other nonclass processes. One of these is the process of managing people, literally controlling certain behavior by persons designated as subordinates. Industrial capitalists typically rely on the nonclass process of managing subordinated productive laborers because of the class structure of capitalism, just as that structure often compels their reliance on the nonclass process of lending money.

Management is a necessary process for industrial capitalists because in its absence they might not be able to appropriate surplus value. The reason for this begins with the market for labor power. Industrial capitalists enter that market intent upon buying what productive laborers wish to sell—namely, their labor power. Presuming that the labor power is exchanged at its value, that alone does not guarantee the production of surplus value by the capitalists. Buying labor power means only that the industrial capitalists dispose of, control, and in a sense "consume" labor power by setting it to work with equipment and raw materials. While working, the laborers may produce more or fewer commodities. Having sold their labor power for a wage payment, they may or may not work hard to produce commodities for the industrial capitalists to sell.

If they do, well and good. The industrial capitalists can then focus attention on distributing surplus value elsewhere to survive competitively. However, suppose that workers, for any reason, cannot or perhaps do not wish to work hard. This worries the industrial capitalists, who know that if other industrial capitalists do have hard-working laborers and so obtain more output from them, they will be able to outcompete them. Managers may solve the problem by supervising laborers to ensure that they labor at maximum intensity. The process of managing thereby becomes a condition of existence of surplus labor appropriation; it participates in overdetermining the capitalist fundamental class process.

The management process has costs; it is necessary to pay for the unproductive labor power and other commodities needed to accomplish such management. To the extent that management becomes a condition of existence of the industrial capitalists' appropriation of surplus value, a portion of that surplus value will have to be distributed to a class of persons who perform the management process.

Managers would then be a subsumed class whose relationship to the industrial capitalists would include three processes of interest to us here. First, managers engage in the process of managing productive laborers. Second, they sell their labor power to the industrial capitalists. Third, they obtain in exchange a distributed share of the industrial capitalists' surplus value in the form of management salaries. The empirical record of capitalism suggests that this particular capitalist subsumed class of managers has expanded rapidly and globally during recent decades.

Of course, if somehow the management process could be accomplished without requiring any distribution of appropriated surplus, then no subsumed class process would be involved. For example, if workers' beliefs committed them to intense labor for employers without any supervision, then no management process would be necessary, and hence no subsumed class payments would be made to managers. To take another example, a successful political movement for worker self-management might accomplish the management process without requiring any surplus distribution.

Finally, we can show how the Marxian theorization of the subsumed class of managers parallels that of the subsumed class of moneylenders. We can rewrite the value equation in a form that has been further expanded to include a subsumed class distribution to managers for salaries plus commodities needed for managing:

$$C + V + S_1 + S_2 + S_r = W.$$

The surplus distribution, S_2, is the salary plus managing budget obtained by managers from the industrial capitalists who employ them.

There is, of course, no necessity that the process of managing people, including workers, must occur together with the capitalist subsumed class process. That will be the case only when the people being managed are productive laborers and when managers' salaries are defrayed out of surplus value distributed by an industrial capitalist appropriator. For example, if a worker hires a group of fellow-workers on a Sunday to paint the worker's home, and if a manager of those workers is hired as well, no subsumed class process is involved. The salary paid to this manager cannot come from surplus, since the worker doing the hiring does not appropriate any surplus. No subsumed class process is involved, although the managing process certainly is.

G.3. Merchants and Subsumed Classes

Yet another potential competitive disability can confront industrial capitalists and require another distribution of some portion of appropriated surplus. In this case, the problem is the time it takes industrial capitalists to find buyers for produced capitalist commodities. The faster industrial capitalists can exchange finished commodities for money, the sooner that money can in turn be exchanged for labor power and raw materials. The faster industrial capitalists literally turn over their capital from money to commodities and back to money, the more surplus value given starting sums of money can generate in a year's time. Competition between industrial capitalists can and does involve turnover times.

Imagine, to take a simple example, two industrial capitalists, each starting with the same initial stock of capital and each enjoying the same technology and same rate of exploitation. The only distinction between them is turnover time. Thus each capitalist takes, say, one month to go from the purchase of labor power and commodity inputs to finished commodity outputs. Thus each has finished commodities to sell at the end of each month. However, one capitalist takes one month from end of production to sale of commodities, while the other takes two months.

The first capitalist will sell commodities produced in January by the end of February. The revenues realized from that sale can then be spent on labor power and commodity inputs to renew the production cycle again in March. The next sale will occur at the end of April, and so on. The second capitalist will not sell January output until the end of March. Thus, this capitalist's production cycle can recommence only in April, and the products of that cycle can be sold only by the end of June.

Over a year's time the first capitalist will turn over capital six times, while the second will turn it over only four times. The first capitalist's capital will produce and realize surplus value six times per year, while the second capitalist's capital will realize surplus value only four times.

Thus, despite their identical technologies and rates of exploitation, the first capitalist will have more surplus to distribute by year's end than the second, and may thereby secure the conditions of his or her existence more successfully than the second.

It thus becomes quite literally a condition of the second capitalist's continued existence as a surplus-value appropriator that he or she find some way to reduce turnover time at least to parity with his or her competitors. Enter the merchant. The merchant is a person with a stock of money, in this regard rather like a moneylender. However, unlike moneylenders, merchants do not make loans. They use their stocks of money to buy commodities and thereafter to sell them. Buying is the nonclass economic process of commodity exchange. It is simply the exchange of money for commodities. As such it has nothing necessarily to do with the production, appropriation, or distribution of surplus value.

However, suppose that our second industrial capitalist, worried that his or her competitive survival is jeopardized by slow turnover time, approaches a merchant with a deal. The deal calls for the merchant to buy the industrial capitalist's commodity outputs as fast as they emerge from the production line. The merchant is to buy the commodities at their full values (W, as in $C + V + S = W$). This will greatly speed up our second industrial capitalist's turnover time and perhaps even permit him or her to outcompete the first capitalist. In short, the merchant performs a nonclass process—namely, the immediate *purchase* of commodities (which clearly is *not* their production). This purchase is a condition of the existence of the capitalist's appropriation of surplus value.

Merchants will not agree to this proposed deal unless they are paid to do so. If they buy an industrial capitalist's commodity outputs at their values and then resell them at their values (which competition among sellers will force them to do), they will obtain no income or gain from these transactions. Therefore, to obtain their assent to the proposed deal, each industrial capitalist must distribute to the merchants a fee for buying his or her commodity outputs as fast as they are produced. If the source of that fee is a distribution from the industrial capitalist's appropriated surplus value, the merchants are involved as recipients in a subsumed class process. Such merchants thus constitute a capitalist subsumed class. We may include this subsumed class process, the fee to merchants, as S_3 in our expanded enterprise equation:

$$C + V + S_1 + S_2 + S_3 = W.$$

The industrial capitalist's relationship to such a subsumed class merchant includes two processes of interest to us here. First, the relationship involves the nonclass process of commodity exchange: the industrial capitalist's products in exchange for the merchant's money.

Second, the industrial capitalist's distribution of a portion of appropriated surplus value to the merchant to secure the merchant's performance of the process of buying capitalist commodities and thereby to minimize turnover time.

In practice, industrial capitalists and subsumed merchants net these two opposite flows of money. That is, the industrial capitalist does not actually sell the merchant commodities at their full value and then send a check as the merchant's fee. Instead, the industrial capitalist subtracts the fee to the merchant from the money the merchant must pay for the commodities purchased. Only one transaction occurs. The merchant in effect acquires the capitalist's commodities at a discount from their value, a discount equal to the agreed fee. When the merchant then sells these commodities at their values, the merchant's income is precisely the difference between what the commodities cost and the revenue they brought when sold.

From the perspective of the merchant, the transaction might be condensed to look like this:

$$M \longrightarrow C \longrightarrow M + \Delta M.$$

Here ΔM represents the difference between what the merchant paid for the commodities and the revenues received from their sale. Marxian theory offers a distinctive interpretation of the economics of merchants by focusing on the relation of merchants to the production, appropriation, and distribution of surplus value. In our example, ΔM is a subsumed class payment by an industrial capitalist to secure the condition of existence known as minimization of turnover time: $\Delta M = S_3$.

Merchants are thus another kind of capitalist, although different from both industrial and moneylending capitalists. Merchants are capitalists because their activity as buyers and sellers typically accomplishes the self-expansion of their value—which is the definition of capital. However, they are unlike industrial capitalists because they neither appropriate surplus value nor produce commodities. They expand their capital through buying and selling, not through exploitation. Merchant capitalists are unlike moneylending capitalists because their self-expansion does not involve the nonclass process of lending; it rather involves the nonclass process of commodity exchange.

Merchant capitalists invest their capital in buying commodities to be resold for more than they cost; their goal is to increase their capital by ΔM. Moneylending capitalists invest their capital in making loans; their goal is to increase their capital by interest payments. Industrial capitalists invest their capital in producing commodities; their goal is to increase their capital by appropriating surplus labor as surplus value, S. Presumably, there is some mobility of capital between these different kinds of investment. An industrial capitalist who could obtain greater expansion of his or her capital in merchanting or moneylending might shift out of industrial capitalist investment into one of those processes, and vice versa. Hence we might expect to see some tendencies for rates of the self-expansion of capital in all three kinds of investment to follow one another, unless counteracting tendencies intervened.

Again, as noted in the previous cases of the subsumed classes of moneylenders and managers, the process of merchanting need not occur together with the subsumed class process. Whenever a merchant buys from someone other than an industrial capitalist, the process of buying occurs but no subsumed class distribution of surplus occurs. For example, if a manager sells a used car to a merchant who resells it for more, the merchant capitalist has indeed expanded his or her capital. However, the source of the expansion, ΔM in the merchant equation above, is *not* then surplus value appropriated by such a manager. Managers do not appropriate surplus value; only industrial capitalists do that. In this case, the gain in the merchant's capital is the loss of the buyer to whom the merchant sells. No new values are produced, because neither the production of commodities nor that of surplus labor is involved.

G.4. Other Capitalist Subsumed Classes

Moneylending, managing, and merchanting (buying and selling capitalist commodities) are only three of the many kinds of nonclass processes that may historically occur together with the capitalist subsumed class process. In other nonclass processes performers also receive distributed shares of surplus value from industrial capitalist appropriators. A brief discussion of some of these will further clarify the notion of subsumed classes and thereby illustrate how Marxian theory is extended to encompass the specific features of any particular capitalist economy.

Landowners typically occupy positions within the capitalist subsumed class structure. They do this because the particular nonclass process that they perform—the granting of access to their owned portions of the earth's surface—provides a necessary condition of existence for all industrial capitalists. If land is privately owned by individuals (which is of course a historically variable situation since many societies have not permitted private property in land), such individuals have legally sanctioned rights to withhold their land from productive use by anyone. Thus, any industrial capitalist seeking to appropriate surplus value must obtain access to the piece of land (or possibly water) on which that appropriation is to occur. Whether the capitalist commodities to be produced are agricultural or industrial or consist of services, their production cannot be accomplished under present technological conditions unless that production takes place on some portion of the earth's surface.

Industrial capitalists gain access to some portion of the earth's surface—access provided by its legal owners—because in return they distribute a share of appropriated surplus value to the owners. For historical reasons, payments for access to private property in land are called rents. Thus one kind of rent payment is a subsumed class distribution. Other kinds of rent are not subsumed class payments. Providing access to privately owned land to anyone who is not a surplus appropriator will typically fetch a rent payment in return, but that is clearly not a subsumed class payment since it is not a distributed share of surplus appropriated by the rent-payer.

Indeed, rent payments themselves may be altogether dispensed with. For example, if private property in land were abolished in a capitalist society and if instead the government allocated land to capitalist producers according to some ethical rules, no rental payments would occur. In this case, access to the earth's surface—which remains, of course, a condition of existence of the capitalist fundamental class process—would not require any distribution of surplus value. Hence, in this case, the nonclass process of providing access to the earth's surface would occur without being combined with the capitalist subsumed class process.

In most capitalist societies the state provides a set of conditions of existence for industrial capitalists and typically receives in return subsumed class payments. For example, certain high-tech industrial capitalists may require productive laborers with extensive university training in various skills. Those skills constitute conditions of existence for the appropriation of surplus value in the production of high-tech commodities such as computers. The state can build and operate schools that accomplish the requisite training. The state thereby performs a nonclass process—the cultural process of imparting knowledge—which secures a condition of existence for the capitalist fundamental class process in computer production. The state obtains in return a distributed share of the surplus appropriated by industrial capitalists. For historical reasons, these payments are usually called "taxes."

Taxes paid by industrial capitalists to finance the state's provision of conditions of existence for surplus value appropriation are capitalist subsumed class payments. The individuals occupying the specific state position of receivers of tax payments—in the United States these are members of the U.S. Senate and House of Representatives—are thus members of a subsumed class. In this example, the nonclass process of education occurs together in society with the subsumed class process. However, as noted above in regard to rents, tax payments and subsumed class payments need not occur together. For example, taxes paid by anyone other than an industrial capitalist are not subsumed class payments, because they are not portions of appropriated surplus value. The Internal Revenue Service of the United States makes the distinction between corporate and individual income taxes; this very roughly parallels the notion of the difference between taxes that are, and those that are not, subsumed class payments.

Moreover, a state might very well provide industrial capitalists with conditions of existence such as technical education and not obtain in return any subsumed class payment. In the United States, this could be accomplished if the Congress taxed individuals rather than industrial corporations to pay for technical education. Then, no subsumed class payment would be required to secure the performance of the nonclass process of technical education. Of course, if Congress shifted the burden of taxation onto individuals while using tax revenues so generated to provide conditions of existence to industrial capitalists, it might eventually confront mounting individual resistance and hostility. Then again, since states in capitalist societies have monopolies of military force, they might well be able to dissuade such individuals from taking concerted action to change the tax system or the class structure.

Indeed, the military force deployed by a state—a nonclass process— to protect the existing class structure provides another condition of existence of industrial capitalists. Providing security against the opponents (foreign and/or domestic) of a capitalist class system provides industrial capitalists with conditions without which they could not continue to appropriate surplus value. Of course, the taxes that must be levied to pay for the military might also fall upon individuals and thus similarly require no subsumed class type of tax.

Monopoly is still another nonclass process that can occur together with the capitalist subsumed class process. One kind of monopoly process is the control of buyers' access to the market for a commodity. A monopolist is then a person who controls such access, just as a landlord controls access to privately owned land. Usually such control requires that alternative markets or other sources of the commodity not be available to buyers for particular historical reasons. Then the monopolist's process of controlling access to a market in the commodity permits him or her to demand a fee for access to that market. Note again the parallel with the existence, for whatever historical reasons, of private property in land, which similarly permits the landlord to demand rental fees.

To illustrate this sort of monopoly, consider the example of a capitalist commodity producer who is also able to occupy a monopoly position in regard to the market for that commodity. This industrial capitalist produces, say, local telephone service. If laws permit no other firm to offer the service, this capitalist not only produces telephone service but also controls access to the market for telephone service. Such an industrial capitalist can then charge the buyer for access to the market as well as for the value of the commodity purchased. In effect, the monopolist-producer can combine both charges and thus gain a total price that is higher than the value of the commodity sold.

From the standpoint of the telephone service capitalist, the surplus appropriated from hired productive laborers is supplemented by the charge to the firm's customers for access to the monopolized market. The monopoly revenue over and above the commodity's value accrues to the telephone capitalist no matter to whom the telephone service commodity is sold: laborers, other industrial capitalists, merchant capitalists, and so on. Of course, the ability to obtain such monopoly revenue depends on how long the social conditions endure that deprive buyers of alternative sources of the commodity or of different commodities they might substitute for the monopolized one.

From the standpoint of Marxian class analysis, we will look more closely at the source of the monopoly payment made to gain access to the market for local telephone service. Suppose that one buyer of monopolized local telephone service is an industrial capitalist who purchases the service as part of the input commodities needed to produce some output commodity. In this circumstance, Marxian theory accounts for the value of the purchased local telephone service under the heading C in the buying capitalist's equation $C + V + S = W$. The monopoly fee that has to be paid (in addition to the value of the purchased telephone service) is considered a distribution of the buying capitalist's appropriated surplus value, which secures a condition of existence for the buyer's ability to appropriate surplus labor—namely, access to an input that is indispensable for producing some output commodity. Therefore, in this case, the nonclass process of controlling access occurs together with the capitalist subsumed class process. Such monopolists constitute a capitalist subsumed class.

It is worth noting one more time that when monopolists obtain their monopoly revenues from buyers who are not industrial capitalists, such revenues are not subsumed class payments, and such monopolists do not then constitute a capitalist subsumed class.

In all of the cases of subsumed classes considered above, the subsumed class process differs from nonclass processes such as moneylending, managing, merchanting, landowning, educating, and monopolizing. Only the processes of surplus labor appropriation and distribution refer to class, while "nonclass," by definition, encompasses all of the other processes of social life. Marxian theory inquires whether and under what specific historical circumstances some of these nonclass processes provide conditions of existence for the capitalist fundamental class process. It inquires further whether industrial capitalists distribute portions of the surplus value they appropriate to secure the performance of some of these nonclass processes. Individuals who perform those processes and receive such distributions are members of a subsumed class. Individuals who perform those processes (moneylenders, managers, merchants, landlords, state officials, monopolists) but do not receive distributions of surplus from industrial capitalists are not members of a subsumed class. Their incomes derive neither from appropriating anyone's surplus nor from receiving a distributed share of such surplus from an appropriator.

H. Class Positions and Individuals' Incomes

In Marxian theory, with its overriding concern to show how class processes matter in modern societies, considerable attention is directed to individuals' incomes. Other theories are interested largely in the relative sizes of different individual incomes or, as in neoclassical theory, in the connection between individual income and the productivity of the resources that each individual contributes to production. By contrast, the aim of Marxian theory is to show the role of class in determining the distribution of incomes among individuals in any society. The goal is to explore the interrelations between class processes and income distributions.

H.1. Class Processes and the Distribution of Income

In terms of Marxian class analysis, an individual in a capitalist society can obtain income in three ways. By "income" we mean a flow of values that can be exchanged for commodities. First, a person may obtain income by participating in the capitalist fundamental class process by appropriating surplus value. Such a person would be an industrial capitalist. Second, a person may occupy a subsumed class position as the recipient of a distributed share of appropriated surplus value. Bankers, managers hired by industrial capitalists, landlords, monopolists, senators, representatives, and merchants are examples of persons who earn incomes by participating in the capitalist subsumed class process. Third, a person may obtain income by participating in nonclass processes that generate inflows of value. For example, an individual might sell a collection of antique watches to another individual for money. This is an income-generating, nonclass process of commodity exchange. It is not a fundamental class process, since no surplus value is being produced or appropriated by either individual in the process. Nor is it a subsumed class process, since the absence of surplus appropriation means that neither individual is in a position to distribute surplus. It is simply a nonclass process that generates income without either the fundamental or the subsumed class process occurring together with it.

Other examples of nonclass income include receipts from participating in what we might call the process of gifting. One person gives another a gift. The recipient thereby obtains income, but clearly the gifting process is neither a fundamental nor a subsumed class process. It is an income-generating, nonclass process of considerable importance in many societies. Stealing is another example. Indeed, we have already touched upon other nonclass, income-generating processes in our discussion of individuals who sell labor power, merchants who buy from persons other than industrial capitalists, landlords who grant access to land to such others, monopolists who raise prices above values to such others, and so on. Such persons obtain their inflow of value by engaging in income-generating, nonclass processes exclusively (the selling of commodities, merchanting, granting access to privately owned land, granting access to commodity markets, and so on).

Marxian theory divides incomes into fundamental, subsumed, and nonclass kinds according to the processes that generate such incomes to any individual. It highlights the relationship between any individual's receipt of income and his or her participation in fundamental, subsumed, and nonclass processes respectively. This distinctive contribution permits Marxian analysis to specify how changing class processes in any society impact on income distributions and vice versa.

Let us summarize the Marxian general theory of income distribution symbolically as follows:

$$Y = Y_{fc} + Y_{sc} + Y_{nc}.$$

Here, Y still stands for the total income received by an individual (as in chapter 2). However, to specify the Marxian analysis of that income, we introduce the subscripts fc, sc, and nc to indicate its fundamental class, subsumed class, and nonclass sources respectively. Thus, Y_{fc} represents income obtained from participation in the capitalist fundamental class process: appropriating surplus value. Y_{sc} is the income from participation in the capitalist subsumed class process: receiving a distributed share of surplus value from the appropriators. Finally, Y_{nc} represents income from participation in a nonclass process that itself generates an inflow of value.

Every individual's income over any period of time can be analyzed into these class and nonclass terms. Some of the terms might be zero. An old grandparent's income might be dependent exclusively on gifts from children and grandchildren; hence that person's income equation would set $Y_{fc} = 0 = Y_{sc}$. Directors of a bank that lends money might divide their interest income into two kinds, Y_{sc} and Y_{nc}, if some of the interest they earned on loans came from industrial capitalists and the rest came from borrowers who were not industrial capitalists. A productive laborer whose income flowed exclusively from selling his or her labor power would show an equation in which $Y_{fc} = 0 = Y_{sc}$, since his or her income would flow solely from participation in the nonclass process of commodity exchange: labor power for money.

Not only can such an equation be used to construct a class analysis of any individual's income, it can likewise be employed for groups of individuals who share a specific class/nonclass distribution of income. Thus we can and will later write equations for the income of industrial capitalists grouped into, say, the board of directors of a modern corporation. We can also write equations for state officials such as members of Congress, who receive state income, or for clerics who receive the income of a religious institution, and so on. Equipped with such equations, Marxian theory explores the interrelations between class processes, on the one hand, and the institutional incomes of corporations, states, religious establishments, and so on, on the other. Such explorations constitute one part of specifically Marxian social analysis.

H.2. Occupying Multiple Class and Nonclass Positions

Any individual can occupy more than one class position and thereby receive multiple kinds of class incomes. The same is true for nonclass positions and the kinds of income they may generate. Consider, for example, a woman who sells her labor power to an industrial capitalist and obtains some money income in exchange. This woman's income equation would contain a term for this nonclass (exchange process) income:

$$Y = Y_{nc}.$$

However, this woman might also have loaned money to (e.g., by purchasing the bonds of) some industrial capitalist firm. She would then receive interest. This must be considered a subsumed class payment since it is a distribution of the surplus value appropriated by the borrowing industrial capitalist and serves to secure his or her continued access to the loaned money. Thus we must extend this woman's income equation to take account of her subsumed class position and the income it generates to her:

$$Y = Y_{nc} + Y_{sc}.$$

Finally, let us suppose that she also keeps a passbook account at her local savings bank, which provides her with interest income. This must be included in her income equation as a second kind of nonclass income, because the bank in question is purely a borrowing and lending institution; it produces no capitalist commodities. It neither employs productive laborers nor appropriates any surplus value; it obviously cannot then distribute any appropriated surplus value either. So its payment of interest on this woman's savings account is a nonclass income to her as a result of her participation in the nonclass process of lending money to someone other than an industrial capitalist. Her summary income equation must contain two terms for her two nonclass sources of income: Y_{nc1} for her participation in a commodity exchange process (selling her labor power), and Y_{nc2} for her participation in a lending process involving someone other than an industrial capitalist:

$$Y = Y_{nc1} + Y_{nc2} + Y_{sc}.$$

Consider a second example, a man who inherits land from his relatives and then signs a lease agreement with an industrial capitalist who rents part of the land for a commodity-producing factory. The rental payments received constitute a subsumed class income, Y_{sc}, to this man:

$$Y = Y_{sc}.$$

However, suppose that this man also hires two people to work on another portion of his land and to produce crops for sale. Upon their sale, the man realizes a fundamental class income—namely, the surplus value he appropriates from these workers. To take account of this, we must amend his total income equation to include the surplus value he appropriates, Y_{fc}:

$$Y = Y_{sc} + Y_{fc}.$$

If, finally, this man also takes a full-time job with—that is, sells his labor power to—an industrial capitalist, he will obtain nonclass income: the wages received in exchange for his labor power, Y_{nc}. His complete income equation would then be:

$$Y = Y_{sc} + Y_{fc} + Y_{nc}.$$

As these examples suggest, the Marxian analysis of income distribution implies the presumption that individuals often occupy multiple class and nonclass positions. They earn incomes via their participation in different processes, both class and nonclass in nature. There is good reason to suppose that different individuals will change their class/nonclass distributions of their respective incomes at various moments across their lifetimes. It follows that knowledge of the amount of any individual's income or even of one source of that income is insufficient for a Marxian analysis of that income or of that individual to take place. Such an analysis requires that we pinpoint the class components of the individual's income.

Marxian income analysis begins with the class/nonclass composition of anyone's income. The reason why class is so important here is that it returns us to the purposes of Marxian theory generally. Marxists want to know how individuals and groups relate to the class structure because of the Marxian objectives of changing that class structure. Hence, studying the size of a person's or group's income, or knowing merely one component of it, is inadequate from the Marxian point of view. Such knowledge is an abstraction from the class complexities of anyone's income, and these complexities are precisely what Marxian analysis aims to understand.

Analyzing income distribution in terms of class (fundamental and subsumed) and nonclass processes helps focus attention on the complex ways in which class structures influence social life. Marxian analysis stresses the possibility and indeed the probability that most individuals participate in multiple different income-generating processes. Thus, political strategists seeking to enlist people in movements to change a society's class structure need to understand the complex class involvements that individuals' incomes reflect. They need as well to project how class changes will likely impact on the incomes of various social groups. Marxian theory speaks to such needs.

This Marxian theory stands opposed to any theorization or categorization of incomes or of income distribution which divides people into "classes" according to the size of their incomes. That use and meaning of the term "class" is radically opposed to what we have found in Marxian theory. As we understand Marxian theory, it distinguishes clearly between income on the one hand and class processes on the other. As the above examples indicate, we cannot deduce an individual's class positions from the size of his or her income, nor can we deduce an individual's income from his or her class participations. In Marxian theory the relationship between income and class is far more complex than that.

I. The Complex Class Structure of Capitalist Firms

A central part of all modern economic theories concerns the causes and consequences of the behavior of capitalist firms. Of course, different theories generate different analyses of these firms. In neoclassical theory, the behavior of capitalist firms can be reduced ultimately to the desires and wishes of their resource suppliers, their technological possibilities, and the preferences of their customers. We can show the consequences and implications of Marxian theory by elaborating its particular way of approaching firms. Building on our introduction to the Marxian theory of the firm in section E.5 of this chapter, the following section will present a general class analysis of modern capitalist firms.

I.1. The Class Analysis of Capitalist Firms

A capitalist firm is always a particular institution located in a specific society. However, here we will analyze some of the class and nonclass processes that generally occur at the social location, or site, that is called a capitalist firm. Our emphasis will fall on the class and nonclass income-generating processes because that extends the Marxian theory developed in this chapter and because this book is about economics more than it is about other aspects of society.

By "capitalist firm" we mean simply an enterprise in which some initial sum of money is expanded quantitatively. That is, the money goes through certain processes by which its value is enhanced; in short, the money functions as capital. Because of this self-expansion of value, the firm that manages all of this is called a "capitalist enterprise." There are, as we noted earlier, different kinds of capitalist enterprises. The industrial capitalist enterprise expands value by appropriating surplus value generated by laborers in the course of commodity production. The merchant capitalist expands value by selling commodities for more than was paid for them. The moneylending capitalist accomplishes the expansion of capital by receiving principal plus interest in return for lending principal alone.

In the case of each such enterprise, Marxian theory summarizes its inflow and outflow of values in specifically class analytical terms. The equational form of that summary is as follows:

$$Y_{fc} + Y_{sc} + Y_{nc} = E_{sc} + E_{nc}.$$

The terms on the left-hand side of this equation have already been discussed in the section on the distribution of income. The terms on the right-hand side require brief explanation. E_{sc} refers to expenditures made by this enterprise from the surplus value it appropriates. These are subsumed class distributions expended by the firm to secure various conditions of existence for its appropriation of surplus value (the latter being the Y_{fc} to the left of the equal sign). E_{nc} refers to those expenditures by the firm whose source is not surplus value—namely, Y_{sc} and Y_{nc}. The expenditures under E_{nc} are intended to secure the conditions of existence for the firm's continued receipt of Y_{sc} and Y_{nc}. In this way, they parallel the role of E_{sc}, which secures continued surplus value appropriation.

Every capitalist firm can have such a Marxian class analytical equation written for it. Firms will differ from one another according to the differing values taken by the five terms in their respective equations. For example, an industrial capitalist firm exclusively engaged in commodity production can be represented simply as follows:

$$Y_{fc} = E_{sc}.$$

This is the archetypal industrial capitalist firm we have discussed throughout this chapter. Its capitalists appropriate surplus value, Y_{fc}, which they then distribute to subsumed classes, E_{sc}, in hopes of securing their conditions of existence.

By contrast, a purely merchant capitalist firm would be represented simply as follows:

$$Y_{sc} = E_{nc}.$$

This equation indicates that the merchant capitalist's income, Y_{sc}, is derived exclusively from his or her participation in the capitalist subsumed class process—that is, from buying commodity outputs from an industrial capitalist. The merchant capitalist then spends E_{nc} to secure the conditions of existence of his or her participation in the particular subsumed class process that generates the Y_{sc}. These merchant expenditures might include payments for the unproductive labor power of clerks, bookkeepers, and so on, as well as the rent for warehouses and other commodities needed to perform the merchanting.

Finally, consider how Marxian theory approaches a capitalist enterprise engaged exclusively in consumer lending. This firm expands its capital by lending to individuals for consumption purposes and obtaining interest payments for such loans. Its Marxian class analytical equation would be

$$Y_{nc} = E_{nc}.$$

This firm draws purely nonclass income. It earns no fundamental class income, because its performance of the nonclass process of lending money does not involve the appropriation of surplus value (no commodity is produced by productive laborers hired by the lending capitalist). It likewise earns no subsumed class income, because the consumer-borrowers it lends to are not themselves industrial capitalists. Therefore, they do not appropriate surplus labor, and so cannot pay interest out of appropriated surplus value.

None of the three kinds of capitalist firms described above need stay forever tied to its particular source of income. Capitalist firms can and do change historically. They variously add, change, and drop income-generating processes as they react to the opportunities they perceive in their environments. Industrial capitalists may find it advantageous to use revenues to make loans to employees, thereby adding a Y_{nc} to their Y_{fc}. Merchant capitalists may decide to stop depending solely on their suppliers for commodities and begin to hire productive laborers to produce the commodities they will then sell, thereby adding a Y_{fc} to their Y_{sc}.

In general, the terms on the left of the capitalist enterprise equation—Y_{fc}, Y_{sc}, and Y_{nc}—variously equal or exceed zero as the specific history of each firm unfolds. At various times, a particular enterprise can earn Y_{fc} and/or Y_{sc} and/or Y_{nc}. General Motors Corporation, for example, can make cars (earn Y_{fc}), charge interest for loans to other industrial capitalists (earn Y_{sc}), and charge interest for loans to car-buying consumers (earn Y_{nc} via the General Motors Acceptance Corporation). In any given year, Y_{fc} may be greater, equal to, or smaller than either Y_{sc} or Y_{nc}, according to the development of the economy and the strategies of GM's board of directors.

I.2. Capitalists and Corporate Boards of Directors

A capitalist can be an individual, or a group of individuals can share the social position of a capitalist. In modern capitalist enterprises, called "corporations" for historical reasons, the role of capitalist is played by a group numbering typically between 9 and 20 individuals: the board of directors. They appropriate surplus value and/or receive subsumed class distributions and/or obtain nonclass incomes. Their participation in one or more of these income-generating processes will determine the kinds and sizes of their incomes.

The early history of many capitalist enterprises reveals one person in the position of capitalist. A colorful and often mythical literature of tycoons, rugged individual entrepreneurs, and cutthroat competitors surrounds this early history. However, as capitalist enterprises survive competition and grow, a pronounced trend transforms most of them into corporations whose capitalists are no longer single individuals but rather boards of directors.

Everything Marxian theory says about capitalists holds whether it is a matter of one person in that position or a group of persons sharing that position. However, an important conclusion of Marxian theory can be illustrated by briefly examining the transition from individual capitalist to board of directors. Contrary to the literature, both popular and academic, "pure" capitalists are more likely to be found among boards of directors than among individual capitalist entrepreneurs.

Consider, for example, an individual industrial capitalist. In the early years of an enterprise, this person will likely do many things in and for the firm. He or she will rarely simply appropriate surplus value.

More than likely, he or she will also become involved in managing productive laborers, marketing the finished output, pouring personal funds into the firm (which makes capital available to the firm), and not infrequently doing some productive labor alongside the hired laborers. In other words, the early individual industrial capitalist usually does more than participate in the fundamental class process as an appropriator. He or she participates as well in the subsumed class process, not only as a distributor, but also as a recipient, of shares of surplus value. He or she performs a variety of nonclass processes that constitute the conditions of existence of the capitalist fundamental class process (in our example, managing, merchanting, and moneylending), and may well also sell his or her own labor power and so produce as well as appropriate surplus value.

The individual industrial capitalist occupies many different class and nonclass positions within one enterprise. Such an individual is not "purely" an industrial capitalist in the sense of being exclusively the appropriator of surplus value within the enterprise. By contrast, members of a modern industrial corporation's board of directors are more nearly "pure" capitalists. Many board members have no other relation to or function within the corporation besides appropriating surplus value and distributing it to subsumed classes. Such members gather every quarter of a year at the corporation's headquarters for a day of meetings. They literally receive the surplus value appropriated from the corporation's productive laborers during the previous three months, and then deliberate collectively to decide what subsumed classes are to get what portions of that surplus value.

Such board members actually display the classic outlines of the Marxian theory of industrial capitalists. They appropriate surplus value and distribute what they have appropriated. They may do nothing else within or for the corporation. They are pure capitalists in the Marxian sense of the term. It is quite true, of course, that many corporations include among the members of their board of directors individuals who are also top managers within the firm. Such "impure" capitalists do then occupy two class positions: the fundamental class position of a surplus value appropriator plus the subsumed class position of a hired manager. Still, this is a far less impure kind of capitalist than the individual entrepreneur who typically occupies many different class positions within the firm.

An individual who occupies multiple class positions within an enterprise—say, those of appropriator and manager discussed above—will then often be at both ends of a flow of value. The corporate president, who sits on the board of directors, will not only distribute surplus as a board member but will also receive such surplus distributions as a paid manager. Similarly, the early individual capitalist entrepreneur functioned both as lender and borrower in the process of loaning personal capital to the enterprise in which he or she appropriated surplus labor.

Marxian theory focuses on the multiple class positions occupied by individual capitalists at various points in an enterprise's history. The goal of this analysis is to produce a history and current assessment of the enterprise which stresses its changing relations with the class structure of the society in which it exists. From this standpoint, capitalists appear frequently to pass sums of value to themselves via the multiple class and nonclass positions they occupy. Indeed, it would be more precise to say, for example, that individuals as industrial capitalists pass sums of value to themselves as subsumed class managers. Moreover, a Marxian theoretical accounting system for enterprises must measure such flows alongside all others in order to ensure consistent arithmetic formulations of the theory.

This means that arithmetic measures in Marxian theory will likely differ from arithmetic measures in non-Marxian theory since the objects of those theories are understood very differently. We can illustrate this by presenting a Marxian analysis of the widespread term "profit," which figures prominently in nearly every kind of economic theory. Our class analysis and the resulting arithmetic measures and relations it suggests produce a new and distinctly Marxian interpretation of what industrial profit is and what meaning it can have for Marxian analysis.

I.3. A Marxian Theory of Industrial Profit

A capitalist enterprise's general income and expenditure equation can be investigated to understand, in Marxian class analytical terms, the meanings of "profit." We will begin by considering a firm that is engaged only in commodity production and whose sole source of income is appropriated surplus value:

$$Y_{fc} = E_{sc}.$$

We will extend this equation by disaggregating this firm's expenditures as follows:

$$Y_{fc} = E_{sc1} + E_{sc2} + E_{sc3} + E_{sc4} + E_{sc5} + E_{sc6} + E_{sc7},$$

where

E_{sc1} = subsumed class payments to landlords
E_{sc2} = subsumed class payments to moneylenders (bankers)

E_{sc3} = subsumed class payments to managers' salaries

E_{sc4} = subsumed class payments to managers for capital accumulation (buying more C and V)

E_{sc5} = subsumed class payments to merchants

E_{sc6} = subsumed class payments to the state (taxes)

E_{sc7} = subsumed class payments to shareholders (dividends).

Typically, modern U.S. corporations define their "profits" (sometimes labeled "net income") as the residual when "costs" of production are subtracted from "revenues" received as commodities are sold. To produce a class analysis of profit we must determine the class meaning of such "costs" and "revenues." The meaning of "revenue" is relatively straightforward. Revenue amounts to what we have earlier called W ($= C + V + S$). However, the concept of costs poses more problems for us.

Modern corporations do not accept or use class terms. Nor do the government statistical services that define, gather, organize, and publish the economic data relied upon by most analysts of capitalist economies. Thus, they do not see or measure costs in terms of, for example, $C + V$. If they did, their concept of costs would equal the Marxian concept of constant capital plus variable capital ($C + V$). Then their concept of profit would be the equivalent of the Marxian concept of surplus value. However, that is not the case.

Their concept of costs includes more than $C + V$. For example, their costs typically include also rents, interest payments, managerial salaries, and discounts to merchants. In Marxian theory, these payments by a capitalist are portions of the appropriated surplus value, portions distributed to subsumed classes. They are thus crucially different from C and V, which are commodities purchased prior to there being any surplus to distribute.

From the Marxian theoretical standpoint, then, what such a corporation calls its "profit" would be understood in Marxian terms as follows:

$$\text{Profit} = W - [C + V + E_{sc1} + E_{sc2} + E_{sc3} + E_{sc5}],$$

or since $W - [C + V] = S$,

$$\text{Profit} = S - [E_{sc1} + E_{sc2} + E_{sc3} + E_{sc5}],$$

where

E_{sc1} = subsumed class payment to landlords

E_{sc2} = subsumed class payment to moneylenders

E_{sc3} = subsumed class payment to managers

E_{sc5} = subsumed class payment to merchants.

Thus, in class analytical terms, what capitalist corporations and most government statistics in capitalist societies report as profits is definitely not the same as what Marxists mean by surplus value. Quite the contrary, these profits are merely one part of surplus value—namely, the sum of the subsumed class payments to managers for accumulating capital (E_{sc4}), plus the subsumed class payments to shareholders (E_{sc7}), plus the subsumed class payments to the state (E_{sc6}). The popular term of American corporations, "after-tax profits," would then be the sum of E_{sc4} plus E_{sc7}.

Marxian theory's basic distinction between surplus value and profit is possible only because of its class analytical foundation. It is the focus on class processes which leads Marxian theory to that distinction. Moreover, some central conclusions of Marxian economics depend on this distinction between surplus value and profit.

For example, Marxian theory recognizes that it can draw no inference about the fundamental class process from the fact, say, that capitalist corporations are reporting falling profits. This is because, as our equations above demonstrate, falling profits could result from *either* a reduced surplus appropriation in the fundamental class process (a smaller S) *or* increased subsumed class payments from the surplus (a larger E_{sc1}, E_{sc2}, E_{sc3}, or E_{sc5}). Industrial capitalists' profits could fall, not because less surplus value was appropriated from productive laborers, but rather because various subsumed classes were able to extract larger distributions of surplus. Both kinds of change could occur at once to produce falling profits. Indeed, profits would also fall if industrial capitalists appropriated additional surplus but at the same time the extra demands of subsumed classes siphoned off more than that addition.

Marxian theory can likewise draw no inference about "efficiency" from non-Marxian studies of relocations by capitalist enterprises from one region to another. Often, such moves are explained or justified on the grounds that the industrial capitalists were simply responding to differences in profit rates, moving from regions of lower rates to those of higher rates of profit. According to this argument, such moves are considered efficient because profits necessarily reflect the efficiency with which capitalist enterprises transform inputs and labor power into commodity outputs. In non-Marxian theories, efficiency is directly connected to profitability (e.g., the marginal productivity of capital); thus, inferring efficiency gains from relocations to regions of higher profits makes sense. But this argument does not make sense from the standpoint of Marxian theory.

In Marxian theory, an industrial corporation that moves from the northeastern part of the United States to the southwestern Sun Belt to achieve greater profits may well do so without that having anything to do with what Marxists define as "efficiency." Consider, for example, that a Marxian measure of efficiency is the total amount of labor input $(EL + LL)$ required per unit of commodity produced. The above industrial corporation's move might then be explained by the possibility that land rent, merchants' fees, and/or managers' salaries are lower in the Sun Belt than in the Northeast. Firms that relocated might actually suffer losses in efficiency in the Marxian sense. That is, they might produce fewer commodity outputs per unit of total labor input $(EL + LL)$. However, the reduced efficiency, which would diminish the amount of surplus value appropriated from productive laborers, would be more than offset by the reduced subsumed class payments to landlords, managers, and merchants. The results would be higher calculated profits, continued movement of capitalist enterprises from the Northeast to the Southwest, but a trend toward lower efficiency in Marxian terms.

The same reasoning requires Marxian theorists to recognize that a period of rising industrial capitalists' profits might well mask a deteriorating rate of surplus value. Class struggles between industrial capitalists and productive laborers over the rate of exploitation could diminish the quanta of surplus value appropriated by capitalists (falling S). However, this decline could be hidden statistically if subsumed class payments were falling even more rapidly, as, for example, when interest rates drop quickly because of central bank policies (falling E_{sc2}). In the absence of direct attention to the complex changes taking place in both the fundamental and the subsumed class process, Marxian theory rejects inferences about class structures and changes drawn from statistical movements in published corporate profits.

Marxian theorists do not deny, of course, that industrial capitalists can and often do make their decisions with the objective of maximizing their profits or profit rates. What Marxian theorists want to stress is that such decisions aimed at that objective are peculiar effects, in part, of a non-Marxian theory lodged in the capitalists' minds. To accept that objective and make decisions accordingly may well maximize profits. Non-Marxian theories may well draw a necessary equivalence between maximized profits and what they conceptualize as productive efficiency. However, from the Marxian standpoint, maximization of profit (as understood in class terms through the equations above) has no necessary relation to the appropriation of surplus value or its distribution to subsumed classes or the ratio of commodity outputs to commodity and labor inputs.

In Marxian theory, maximizing profits is perfectly consistent with both rising and falling rates of surplus value, rising or falling distributions of subsumed class payments, rising or falling efficiency ratios of outputs to total labor inputs in production. Marxian theory criticizes non-Marxian theories for seeking to justify capitalism by equating what is nothing but its peculiar rule for capitalist decision-making with some absolute standard of efficiency. The profit-maximizing rule of capitalist enterprises (making prices equal marginal costs in the neoclassical theory of the firm), hallowed in the texts of non-Marxian theorists, is then no magic path to the optimum efficiency of all possible worlds. Marxian theory shows that rule to be perfectly consistent with all kinds of inefficiency in class processes as well as the physical transformation of inputs into outputs.

One conclusion about corporate strategies which Marxian theory reaches is that the rule of profit maximizing, which does not make for efficiency, does serve another purpose. It does maximize those particular subsumed class payments which are *not* subtracted from S in the profit equations above—chiefly, E_{sc4} and E_{sc7}.

In terms of those equations, profit maximization becomes a means by which to deliver the maximum possible flow of value to shareholders (dividends) and the maximum possible flow of value to the discretionary control of boards of directors. Pursuing the rule of profit maximization has little to do with efficiency and much to do with favoring dividends, the retained earnings of corporations, and what boards of directors decide to do with those retained earnings (e.g., accumulate capital). Profit maximization turns out to be a rule for the maximization of a subset of subsumed class distributions of the surplus value, no more and no less.

Across the history of capitalist societies, the specific subset of subsumed class distributions included under the heading of "profit" has not always been the same. Sometimes, the distribution of surplus value for the personal consumption of the enterprise's capitalist(s) has been included. Modern commentators on large industrial corporations often suggest that dividends are largely excluded from the profit subset—that is, corporations aim to maximize after-dividend profits. Even at one historical moment, different capitalist enterprises may include different subsumed class distributions within what they maximize as profit. For example, private utility companies, which are subject to state regulations on their allowed profit rates, may maximize subsumed class distributions other than dividends and retained earnings, and so on.

Profit, then, is a category that fits into and belongs to non-Marxian theories. Marxian class analysis completely alters the concept by transforming it into a variable subset of subsumed class distributions. It goes even further by stressing that profit-maximizing rules—which amount to rules to maximize whatever happens to be the currently fashionable subset of subsumed class distributions—bear no necessary relation to what concerns Marxists: class processes and their interconnections with nonclass processes, including the technical efficiency of transforming inputs into outputs in commodity production. As in most other areas of economic analysis, here we can see again how Marxian and non-Marxian theories make very different sense of the performance and achievements of capitalist economies.

J. The Complex Class Structure of Other Social Sites

The unique analysis of industrial capitalist firms made possible by Marxian theory may be comparably applied to other major institutions in contemporary capitalist societies. Marxian theory prefers a term other than "institution," however, because of the connotation of permanence and fixity that often attaches to "institution." "Site" connotes merely a place in a society, a point where certain social processes and relationships occur; there is no need to suppose that they are in any sense fixed. Thus, "site" is more consistent with the Marxian theoretical view that all processes and relationships are overdetermined, contradictory, and hence constantly changing. In this spirit, we will examine Marxian theory's approach to three sites in capitalist social formations: households, states, and international economic relations.

J.1. Class Analysis and Households

Like enterprises, households are sites in society at which many social processes occur. In enterprises and households, for example, many of the same processes can occur: people speak, dream, eat, breathe, give orders, exchange commodities, do labor, pay taxes, and so on. Other processes may occur at one site but not the other. Sleeping occurs in households but is probably prevented in enterprises, while commodity manufacture is more likely to occur in enterprises than in households.

However, as even these few examples suggest, there is no hard-and-fast separation of sites in any society according to which particular processes occur in one rather than the other. At various times in human history, households were the important or even the main sites where commodities were produced for sale. In those times, the idea of distinguishing households from enterprises probably did not occur at all, or made little sense if it did. Consider, for example, the many peasant or farm households in rural areas. At other times, a rigid separation of sites was instituted: certain processes were proscribed at one site and thus strictly reserved for another. For example, sexual processes—from intercourse to speaking or sitting together—have often been strictly constrained to the household and nowhere else. Child-rearing was often treated similarly, although recently a movement has gained momentum which supports the presence at work sites of day-care and even schooling facilities.

While no fixed distinctions among sites exist, we can generally define them as loci of specific subsets of social processes. Thus enterprises differ from households according to the different subset of social processes each comprises.

We can say that households are where child-rearing, eating, sexual activity, and so on, usually (if not always) occur in modern capitalist societies such as the United States. We can contrast what is specifically different about enterprises by stressing that the processes of producing commodities (in the case of industrial capitalists), accumulating capital, buying labor power, and distributing dividends occur predominantly there and not in households.

Marxian theory asks two broad questions about every site in society which no other theory asks: Do class processes occur at any particular site chosen for theoretical scrutiny? If they do, which class processes occur there, and how do they interact with all the other processes of the society in which that site is located? In this section, we propose to ask and to sketch answers to these questions in regard to present-day households in capitalist societies such as the United States.

Fundamental and subsumed class processes can and typically do occur in such households. That conclusion of Marxian theory is reached through the following sort of analysis. Household labor produces goods and services: raw food materials are transformed into finished meals, cleaning equipment is utilized to transform disorderly and dirty rooms into clean and orderly ones, and clothing is repaired, to cite but a few examples. These production processes rarely result in commodities; households in the United States do not normally sell prepared meals, cleaning services, or clothing repair services. However, the absence of commodity production is not equivalent to the absence of class processes.

The production of these meals, cleaning services, and repair services involves not only the natural transformation of physical substances through labor but also the fundamental and subsumed class processes. To identify whether and how class processes occur in households, we must distinguish between necessary and surplus labor. Can we identify in households some people who are direct laborers, who not only perform labor that is needed to produce the goods and services they require to keep laboring in the household, but also do some surplus labor beyond their necessary labor? Marxian theory replies affirmatively.

Many housewives have traditionally performed the labor required to make meals, clean rooms, and repair clothing. Such women also perform surplus labor—that is, they produce a quantity of meals, cleaned rooms, and repaired clothing that exceeds their own personal requirements for or consumption of these products. Their husbands, cotenants of these households, typically appropriate the surplus labor embodied in these surplus products.

Thus we have identified the existence of a fundamental class process in such households as well as the corresponding fundamental class positions involved in it: wives performing surplus labor and husbands appropriating it. Of course, the sexual allocation of class positions need not always be the same. Husbands and wives could reverse class positions. Communes, tribal societies, cooperatives, and other household arrangements have displayed a remarkably varied array of distributions of men and women among class positions across history. However, the traditional household in the United States conforms rather well to our sketch of women as performers, and men as appropriators, of household surplus labor.

Marxian theory thus begins by affirming the existence of class processes inside the modern household. The next question is, Exactly which class processes occur there? Clearly no capitalist fundamental class process is involved. Husbands do not buy their wives' labor power, and no commodity production occurs (the wives' products are not typically sold). Hence neither value nor surplus value attaches to such products. The fundamental class process in these households must be noncapitalist. In trying to identify which noncapitalist form of the fundamental class process it might be, we look at the historical forms so far identified by Marx and Marxists. Marxian theory concludes that the traditional household in the United States today displays a class structure most nearly like European feudal class structures from the twelfth to the sixteenth century A.D. In short, part of a husband's "duty" is to protect wife and household, while a wife's duties concern "serving" and "obeying" the husband. The latter relationship resembles the serf's dependence on the feudal lord for protection. The wife is tied by many traditional and legal constraints to perform surplus labor for her husband rather in the manner that serfs labor for their lords. The wife believes it is the natural, moral, or religious order of the world for her to deliver surplus labor to her husband in a manner that is clearly reminiscent of feudal class arrangements. Surplus labor is typically embodied in physical goods and services rather than in value or money forms.

In this sense, many households in the United States in recent years have been sites of feudal class processes. By contrast, firms have chiefly been sites of capitalist class processes. The United States is thus understood in Marxian theory to be a complex society encompassing two very different class structures: homes and enterprises. Indeed, calling the

United States merely a capitalist society is an unacceptable oversimplification. It risks missing the specific differences between feudal households and capitalist enterprises and the problems people encounter in moving between these different and often clashing class structures. Marxian theory avoids such risks by directly confronting the different class structures of the two sites and posing questions about how they interact with one another and with the nonclass processes of the society.

The existence of the feudal fundamental class process in households implies the existence of the feudal subsumed class process. Husbands distribute portions of their feudal surplus product to secure their conditions of existence as feudal appropriators. Since the household of our example has only two people in it, one or the other must play the role of the subsumed class receiving distributed shares of the surplus. Thus, for example, some portion of the rooms cleaned by the wife will be set aside for paperwork connected with household management. If the wife does this work, the cleaned rooms will be surplus product which she produces, which her husband appropriates, and which he then allocates to her for use in her capacity as a member of the subsumed class, the household manager. If the husband does it, he will distribute the surplus product to himself as a member of the subsumed class (the manager), and so on.

This Marxian approach, which is only partially sketched here, proceeds to pose questions about the interactions between the two class structures, household and enterprise. Consider husbands who move daily from the class position of feudal appropriator to that of productive laborer in a capitalist factory. How will the occupancy of two so different class positions by the same individual affect his emotions, physical productivity, ideological persuasion, and political loyalties? Can any thinkers concerned with such individuals' actual or potential participation in movements for social change ignore the multiplicity of their class affiliations and instead lump them into one undifferentiated category of "proletarians"? In Marxian theory, the concept of husbands must encompass their specific and multiple class positions within and without households. Such an approach produces analyses of modern society that differ greatly from theories that abstract from and ignore class.

Similarly, consider wives in the role of feudal serfs. How might their attitudes toward household class structures change if they added a second class position—say, as productive laborers in a capitalist enterprise—to their feudal class positions? Or consider how the role of churches and synagogues would be distinctively approached by Marxian theory. Marxian theory would ask how religious processes such as preaching and rituals provided conditions of existence not only for the capitalist fundamental class process in enterprises but also for the feudal fundamental class process in households. Such a Marxian line of inquiry would produce a particular understanding of the persistently different attitudes of men and women toward religion. Marxian theory similarly raises distinctive questions about children, given its conception of feudal households and capitalist enterprises. For example, how are male and female children's attitudes toward class (conscious or unconscious) different because of the divergent multiclass role models provided by their mothers and fathers?

We cannot here do even minimal justice to the distinctive and new insights into family and household relationships opened up by Marxian class analysis. Subsection J.1 aims only to introduce the lines of inquiry fostered by Marxian theory when it is applied to households. Our major purpose in the remainder of section J is to elaborate the basic Marxian theory of class. Toward that end, we will consider next the role of the state in capitalist societies (which we now understand may include feudal and/or other noncapitalist class processes).

J.2. Class Analysis and the State

The state, another site in the capitalist social formation (it can of course also exist in other social formations), differs from the capitalist enterprise and household because of the precise subset of social processes that occur in the state. The processes that generally distinguish the modern capitalist state from other sites include the following:

- maintaining a standing military force
- designing and passing laws for the society
- adjudicating disputes over those laws
- enforcing compliance with those laws
- operating an educational system
- collecting taxes
- operating a postal system
- establishing and maintaining public parks

Again, past and present states have not been the exclusive sites of these processes. In some societies, the state does not maintain the only standing military force nor operate the only postal or public parks system. In those societies, these processes occur as well at other sites—for example, in enterprises that maintain armies, deliver mail, and sell access to parks. In parallel fashion, some societies exhibit a multiplicity of sites that design laws, enforce them, and adjudicate disputes over them. For example, alongside state legislative, executive, and judicial functions, religious assemblages may exist which enact religious laws, enforce them on coreligionists, and dispense religious judicial processes.

However, the history of modern capitalist societies suggests that the list presented above is fairly typical of processes that occur predominantly in the state. Note that the state comprises natural processes (e.g., wilderness preservation), cultural processes (e.g., education), economic processes (e.g., collecting taxes and buying commodities), and political processes (e.g., controlling group behavior via military and legal actions). While many analysts focus chiefly on the political processes in the state (the state is usually treated as an especially political institution), Marxian theorists identify all of the processes of which any state is composed, the nonpolitical as well as the political ones.

Marxian theory approaches the state with specific questions that reflect the particular contribution Marxists seek to make to movements for radical social change. Do class processes occur in the state? If so, which ones do, and how do they interact with the class and nonclass processes that occur at other sites in the society, such as enterprises and households? A Marxian theory of the state in any particular society focuses on the relationship, including its contradictions, between that state and the class structure of that society. Our brief introduction here concerns the kind of state that currently exists in the United States.

Marxists begin by inquiring whether the capitalist fundamental class process occurs in the state. Does the state, as such, hire productive laborers to produce commodities and thereby appropriate surplus value? The question might be rephrased as, Does the United States operate capitalist enterprises alongside those of private entrepreneurs and corporations? The answer is, Occasionally it does. The Tennessee Valley Authority, producer and seller of electricity as a capitalist commodity, is a frequently cited example. West European states operate such enterprises on a much greater scale than the United States does. In any case, the answer is yes, capitalist enterprises can be run by the state. In that event, one source of revenue to the state is the surplus value it appropriates via its own participation in the capitalist fundamental class process:

$$\text{State Revenues} = SY_{fc},$$

where SY_{fc} is the surplus value appropriated by the capitalist state in state enterprises and fed into state revenues.

The state may also be involved in the capitalist subsumed class process. The logic of Marxian theory implies that if the state is an appropriator of surplus, it must also then distribute that surplus to secure the conditions of existence for its participation in the capitalist fundamental class process. The state as industrial capitalist distributes surplus value just as private industrial capitalists do. We can represent the state's participation in this subsumed class process as follows:

$$SY_{fc} = SE_{sc},$$

where SE_{sc} is the distribution of SY_{fc} needed to secure the conditions of existence for the state's continued appropriation of surplus value.

The state can and usually does also participate in another subsumed class process as the recipient of shares of privately appropriated surplus value that are distributed to it in the form of taxes. Here the state performs various nonclass processes that secure conditions of existence for private industrial capitalists. These include legal guarantees of private property, laws constraining trade union challenges to private profitability, public health care to sustain productive laborers' productivity, and so on. To secure the state's performance of such processes, private industrial capitalists make subsumed class payments to the state—that is, pay corporate taxes out of their appropriated surplus values.

We can incorporate this second source of state revenues as follows:

$$SY_{fc} + SY_{sc} = SE_{sc} + SE_{nc},$$

where SY_{sc} = subsumed class state revenues, and SE_{nc} = the nonclass state expenditures needed to secure the conditions of existence for the state's receipt of subsumed class revenues. We must include SE_{nc} as well as SY_{sc} because the state must also make nonclass expenditures in order to secure the private industrial capitalists' conditions of existence. These expenditures are necessarily nonclass expenditures because they are *not* distributions of surplus value appropriated by the state (only the latter are counted in SE_{sc}): hence the term SE_{nc}. These include, for example, the wages and salaries of court clerks and officials, soldiers, and indeed most government workers, plus expenditures on the equipment and buildings used by them.

For Marxian purposes, the analysis of the flow of revenues to and expenditures by a state is not complete until account is also taken of possible nonclass revenues and then of the expenditures made by the state to secure them. State processes involve not only fundamental and subsumed class processes of the sort discussed above. To see only these processes would result in an inadmissible reduction of the state to only its direct relationships to class. States are also involved in nonclass processes that bear no direct relationship to class processes. Moreover, how the state participates in such nonclass processes can and does have implications for its involvement in class processes that are vitally important for Marxian analysis.

On the revenue side, the state can obtain nonclass revenues in a manner parallel to that of industrial capitalist firms. Any flow of value to the state which is neither surplus value appropriated from productive laborers hired by the state nor a subsumed class distribution to the state from private capitalists is, by definition, a nonclass state revenue. The examples are many: individual productive and unproductive workers who are required to pay personal taxes out of their wage and salary income, merchants and bankers who are required to pay taxes on the subsumed class revenues they obtain from industrial capitalists, and so on. All such taxpayers deliver nonclass revenues to the state. Nor can they be expected to do so for very long if the state does not provide them with goods and services that will keep them willing to be taxed.

States therefore hire people and equipment to provide goods and/or services to the people who provide the state with nonclass revenues. States build public swimming pools; stage elaborate pageants; subsidize medical care for elderly, indigent, or all people; provide military security; provide public education; and so on. States do not provide these goods and services as capitalist commodities sold in markets. If that were the case, government revenues from such commodity production would be appropriated surplus value (SY_{fc}). Rather, taxes in the form of nonclass revenues finance such services, which are then delivered to the public according to citizenship, age, need, location, or other non-market-price criteria.

The state's complete budget equation in class-value terms can thus be represented as follows:

$$SY_{fc} + SY_{sc} + SY_{nc} = SE_{sc} + SE_{nc1} + SE_{nc2},$$

where SY_{nc} refers to nonclass state revenues, SE_{nc1} refers to nonclass state expenditures made to secure the state's subsumed class revenues, and SE_{nc2} refers to nonclass state expenditures made to secure the state's nonclass revenues. This class analysis of the state in a modern capitalist society suggests a number of conclusions that distinguish Marxian state theory from alternative theories of the state. First, the state is a complex social site at which multiple class as well as nonclass processes occur. Second, the state has many different relationships with class and nonclass processes at other sites in society. Thus, it makes no sense to think of the state as being reducible to one process or one relationship.

The state is not "above society" in the sense of existing beyond the rough-and-tumble processes of everyday social life. It is not neutral in the face of those processes. Rather, the state is complexly dependent on all kinds of processes and sites in society for its revenues. In turn, other sites and processes depend on the state for their continued existence. The state, in Marxian theory, is no more above, beyond, or "neutral" vis-à-vis social life than are enterprises and households.

Marxian theory insists upon the multiplicity of the state's social roles. The state is not merely the tool of capitalists, providing them with the conditions they need to go on exploiting productive laborers. Nor is the state simply an institution of, by, and for all citizens, taxing them and using those revenues to provide public services for everyone's benefit. The former analysis is inadequate; it sees only the SY_{sc} and SE_{nc1} portions of the state equation. The latter analysis is similarly inadequate; it sees only the SY_{nc} and SE_{nc2} portions. Marxian theory rather combines all four of those terms plus the SY_{fc} and SE_{sc} terms into a properly complex class and nonclass conceptualization of the state.

A conclusion suggested by the Marxian approach concerns precisely the SY_{fc} and SE_{sc} components of the state equation. These represent the state's participation in the capitalist fundamental class process and then in the subsumed class process too as the distributor of surplus value. State capitalist enterprises do just that; they appropriate surplus value from productive laborers hired in the markets for labor power and they distribute subsumed class payments. There is no logical reason, in Marxian theory, to infer from the existence or growth of such state capitalist enterprises that the state or society is socialist or moving toward socialism.

For Marxian theory, socialism and communism represent societies built around a different, noncapitalist form of the fundamental class process. That is a very different thing from a society in which the state appropriates surplus value from the productive laborers it hires and exploits. The existence of the state as an industrial capitalist alongside or instead of individual private industrial capitalists is in no sense a realization of communism or socialism.

For Marxian theory, "communist" is the name for one form of the fundamental class process, a specifically noncapitalist form that displays the following general characteristics:

- productive labor is designed and performed collectively,
- surplus labor is appropriated collectively, not privately, and
- the collective appropriators of the productive laborers' surplus include two groups—the productive laborers and all the subsumed classes.

These characteristics imply that any person who participates in the communist fundamental class is both a performer and an appropriator of surplus labor. They likewise imply that any person who receives a subsumed class distribution also participates in distributing the surplus labor he or she receives.

Despite its cursory quality, this sketch of the communist fundamental class process suffices to show why, from the standpoint of Marxian class analytics, the decision of a state to operate capitalist industrial enterprises has no necessary relation to socialism or communism.

Historical evidence suggests a very different explanation for modern states' decisions to become industrial capitalists. Sometimes private capitalists want commodities to be available to them at prices that are too low for any surplus value to be realized by the private industrial capitalist who would produce them. Examples include telephone, telegraph, and postal services, rail and air transportation, electricity, gas, and steel—all of which are inputs to most capitalist enterprises. One solution would be for the government to establish capitalist industrial enterprises that could charge the desired low prices because of subsidies from other parts of the government's revenue. State postal, transportation, and communication enterprises in many capitalist societies offer ample illustrations, including the U.S. Postal Service, Amtrak, and Conrail. The establishment or growth of state capitalist enterprises may very well strengthen rather than threaten private capitalists. The historical record certainly supports such a Marxian interpretation. There is also historical evidence that occasionally citizens' movements pressure states to produce goods and services for mass consumption when private capitalists refuse to do so or charge prices that are unacceptable to the citizenry; the Tennessee Valley Authority was partly a product of this sort of pressure.

Another conclusion drawn from the Marxian theory of the state concerns the continuing social struggles over the United States' federal budget. The Marxian class equation for the state projects the logic of such struggles in terms of shifts among its six terms:

$$SY_{fc} + SY_{sc} + SY_{nc} = SE_{sc} + SE_{nc1} + SE_{nc2}.$$

We will begin by noting that private capitalist industrial enterprises have every interest in expanding SE_{nc1} *without* expanding SY_{sc}. They propose increased state provision of the conditions of existence for private exploitation while they demand reduced taxes on the surpluses they appropriate. This amounts to an effort to transfer the costs of the state onto individual taxpayers, or a shift from SY_{sc} to SY_{nc}.

This can be accomplished as well by cultural programs aimed at convincing individuals that an expenditure, which we here place in the category SE_{nc1}, should be understood differently and placed rather in category SE_{nc2}. For example, consider state military expenditures. From one perspective, they are considered to be processes that chiefly secure capitalists' abilities to continue exploiting productive laborers and hence SE_{nc1}-type expenditures. Suppose that private capitalists are suffering from the corporate taxes levied against their surpluses, SY_{sc}.

They might then mount a concerted media campaign to convince individual citizens that they and their personal property are immediately threatened by enemies abroad—for example, by "an evil empire." If the campaign is successful, individuals might well come to believe the message that they benefit directly and individually from government expenditures on the military. This amounts to shifting military expenditures from the SE_{nc1} to the SE_{nc2} category.

The point of such a shift would be to convince individuals that since military expenditures fall under the heading of SE_{nc2}, it follows that revenues to permit those expenditures ought to come from SY_{nc}—namely, from individual rather than corporate taxes. From a Marxian standpoint, the Reagan administration has displayed this sort of shifting process even more than other post-World War II U.S. administrations. Depending on all the other natural, political, cultural, and economic processes occurring in the society at any time, the relative powers of the industrial capitalist versus individual taxpayers can cause the shifting to go either way. The imposition of the U.S. federal income tax in the early years of this century has been followed by the steady shift of the tax burden back from corporations onto individuals again. In other capitalist countries, especially in Scandinavia, very different patterns of shifting have occurred over the last century.

Finally, a fully developed Marxian theory of the state in a capitalist society would take account of noncapitalist as well as capitalist fundamental class processes. To illustrate what this might mean, we must extend the state equation to incorporate a relationship between the state and the households in which the feudal fundamental class process occurs:

$$SY_{fc} + SY_{sc1} + SY_{sc2} + SY_{nc} = SE_{sc} + SE_{nc1} + SE_{nc2} + SE_{nc3},$$

where the newly introduced terms SY_{sc1}, SY_{sc2}, and SE_{nc3} reflect the inclusion of a relationship between the state and feudal households.

The newly introduced distinction between SY_{sc1}, the taxes levied on industrial capitalists, and SY_{sc2}, the taxes on feudal lords, indicates that the state must now be understood as subsumed to the feudal appropriators in the home as well as to the capitalist appropriators of surplus in industrial enterprises. That is, the state performs some nonclass processes that provide the conditions of existence for the feudal fundamental class process in households. Examples include instituting public education curricula that endorse feudal household class structures; passing and enforcing laws of property, inheritance, marriage, and divorce that support such structures; and administering tax regulations to subsidize such structures. At the same time, the state performs, as noted, various nonclass processes that secure the conditions of existence for industrial capitalist appropriators of surplus value. SY_{sc1} remains our term for the subsumed class tax payments made by industrial capitalists, while SY_{sc2} designates subsumed class tax payments by feudal household appropriators.

By the same logic, SE_{nc3} must be added to our state equation to take account of the state's spending on processes that provide the conditions of existence for feudal households' fundamental class processes. It is part of the value expended by the state for public education, legislation, judicial administration, and tax collection. These expenditures aim to secure the conditions of existence for household feudalism and thereby to secure the tax revenues derived from those feudal surpluses.

This extended state equation analyzes value flows to and from the state in terms of their multiple class and nonclass components. Such Marxian categories differ from those typically used in non-Marxian theories of the state. Non-Marxian categories govern the definition, collection, and organization of published data on states in modern capitalist societies. Therefore, such data categorize taxes in general or perhaps distinguish between business taxes and individual taxes. These distinctions are not germane to Marxian theory. A business tax can be SY_{sc1} or SY_{nc}, depending on whether the business in question is an industrial capitalist or a merchant capitalist. The category "business tax revenues" normally combines kinds of taxes that Marxian class analysis would separate. Similarly, state expenditures lumped together in the category "legislative activities," for instance, would be categorically distributed by Marxian theory among SE_{sc}, SE_{nc1}, SE_{nc2}, and SE_{nc3}. The pattern of distribution would depend on whether the legislation provided conditions of existence for the state's own appropriation of surplus value or for the state's other three sources of revenue. Indeed, most of the categories that appear in government data publications include more than one of our Marxian class analytical breakdowns.

Marxian analysis of the state in modern capitalist societies asks different questions, organizes its accounts of value flows by means of different categories, and generates different answers from those of non-Marxian theories. The Marxian theory of the state focuses attention on the variety of its class and nonclass component processes. It explores especially the complex linkages between state processes and the class and nonclass processes that occur at other sites in the society. The conclusions that Marxian theory strives to reach concern especially the relationship between the state as a social institution and the society's class structure.

J.3. Class Analysis and International Relations

As a theoretical and practical political tradition, Marxism has long been committed to what it calls "internationalism." Because, in the Marxian view, capitalism expanded from its West European base to organize the entire world economy, the transition to a new and better society necessarily involves an international movement. Such a society, in the Marxian view, depends in turn on a postcapitalist class structure, one whose egalitarian and collective forms of producing, appropriating, and distributing surplus labor label it as "socialist" or "communist."

The concern with internationalism has drawn Marxists' attention to analyses of international relationships. They have posed such questions as, How did capitalism generate a world economy? What class processes link nations together? How do these processes interact with the nonclass processes that do likewise? What connections exist between international class processes and domestic class structures? To answer such questions, Marxian theory must adopt a general approach to international relations that focuses on their class components and how these interact with domestic class structures. Sketching such an approach is our task here.

An expanding West European capitalism established a complex set of processes linking Europe and the rest of the world. At various times and in varying degrees many different processes composed such linkages. Pillage, theft, and crusading sometimes connected Europe to the rest of the world, as did religious missions, commodity exchange, distribution of motion pictures, and labor migrations, to name a few major international linking processes. The linking processes existing at any one time together constituted the international relations of that time.

What Marxian theory adds to the understanding of international relations is an understanding of class. That is, the Marxian approach focuses on class processes within international relations. The Marxian class approach in turn casts new light on the nonclass processes included within international relations. The result is a unique general theory of international relations. The Marxian theory of international relations parallels the Marxian theories of enterprise, household, and state discussed above.

Both fundamental and subsumed class processes can exist between and thereby link two different regions or nations. To take the example of a capitalist fundamental class process, we might consider a corporation in one country whose board of directors hired and appropriated the surplus labor of workers in a different country. The appropriation of such surplus labor would then occur across regional or national boundaries. The same applies to the capitalist subsumed class process. For example, industrial capitalists in one country who appropriated surplus labor from workers of identical nationality within their country, might then make interest or dividend payments to moneylenders or shareholders in another country. Such a subsumed class process of distributing portions of surplus value would then also occur across national boundaries and thereby become a component of international relations between the two countries. Recall, once again, that only the economic processes of surplus labor appropriation and distribution are class processes, while the lending of money is an economic nonclass process. Of course, noncapitalist as well as capitalist class processes can and do occur across national boundaries.

Some examples will suggest the implications of such a Marxian class analysis of international relations. A commercial bank on Wall Street lends money to a Latin American industrial capitalist in Brazil. The Brazilian industrial capitalist uses the borrowed funds to hire Brazilian productive laborers to produce computer components which it sells in Europe. These complex relationships include:

- the national capitalist fundamental class process that takes place inside Brazil;
- the international nonclass process in which a New York bank lends money to Brazil;
- the international subsumed class process in which a portion of the Brazilian surplus value is distributed to the New York bank as interest on the loan; and
- the international nonclass process of commodity exchange, in which Brazilian goods are exported to Europe in exchange for European funds imported into Brazil.

Of course, this list of economic processes, both class and nonclass, does not cover all of the processes involved in the international relations depicted in this example. Letters and telephone calls between New York and Brazil are international cultural processes; diplomatic maneuvers associated with the loan are international political processes; and climatic conditions affecting air travel between New York and Brazil are component international natural processes.

The specific processes chosen for the list reflect the focus of Marxian theory. They permit Marxian theory to reach some important conclusions about international relations. First, the particular international flows of funds in our example are not exploitative; that is, they are not appropriations of surplus value. The three international flows are a loan of money, a subsumed class distribution of interest, and payment for a commodity exchange. The only exploitation that occurs, occurs inside Brazil, as exploitation of Brazilians by Brazilians. Exploitation is not a part of these particular international relations among the New York bank, Brazil, and Europe.

By contrast, consider a situation in which a multinational industrial corporation in Dallas, Texas, establishes a branch office in Liberia to hire Liberian productive laborers to produce automobile components to be shipped to the United States. In this case, the Dallas corporation does appropriate surplus value in an international capitalist fundamental class process. At the same time, money also flows from the United States to Liberia in an international commodity exchange process as payment for the imported automobile components.

What Marxian theory highlights here are the differences that exist among the class and nonclass processes that constitute international flows of value. The flow of value from Brazil to the New York bank was a subsumed class process, while the flow of value from Liberia to the United States was a fundamental class process. The international relationships in the two cases differ because the social consequences of the two different kinds of class processes differ.

We can illustrate the differing social consequences by further elaborating our two examples. The New York–Brazil case involves Brazilian industrial capitalists, whose subsumed class payments back to New York depend on the conditions of their existence as appropriators of surplus value. Thus, if they could increase the rate of exploitation of their workers, they might appropriate enough surplus to reduce or eliminate their need for loans from the New York bank. In this circumstance, a rising rate of exploitation could reduce or erase the flow of international interest payments. This is nearly the opposite of the expected outcome of rising rates of exploitation in the Liberia–United States example. There, rising rates would likely mean larger flows of value from Liberia to the United States.

Clearly, from the Marxian standpoint, it makes no sense to apply the same name to all net flows of value into the United States from, say, countries in Asia, Africa, and Latin America. Such flows are not all instances of "imperialism" or "Third World exploitation." To organize them in these terms is to create a non-Marxian categorization that excludes the specific and different class contents and implications of each one. Other non-Marxian categorizations treat such flows as if they were uniformly commodity exchanges. In that case, the interest flows from Brazil to New York would be called payments for a service commodity—namely, the use of the loaned money. Similarly, the appropriation of surplus value from Liberia to the United States would be called payment for another service commodity—namely, the use of U.S. capital contributed to the Liberian production process. This approach also re-

moves class distinctions and indeed blocks out any notion of class altogether.

Both of these non-Marxian categorizations involve non-Marxian
conceptualizations of international relations. While they disagree with
each other, they both differ from Marxian theory in their *abstraction
from specific class processes and class differences.* What is centrally
emphasized in Marxian class analysis is absent from the non-Marxian
conceptualizations and categorizations of international relations.
Among the consequences of this basic theoretical difference is the non-
Marxian proposal of a single general political strategy for dealing with
international problems. Marxian theory, on the other hand, proposes
several different strategies because it sees very different class components in international relations and in the problems they present.

For example, consider the critics of international relations who define the patterns of net flows of value from Asia, Africa, and Latin
America to capitalist corporations in the national centers of the capitalist world economy as "imperialistic." The prevalence and growth of
such flows are linked to widening gaps of wealth and/or income between the imperial center nations and the peripheral, economically deprived hinterland nations. Critics of imperialistic international relations denounce the unjust and one-sided pattern of value flows,
proposing instead a new international order that would redirect the flow
so that values would move from rich lands to poor ones. Only when the
imperialistic world system is dismantled, they argue, will the poor nations of Asia, Africa, and Latin America finally be able to emerge from
their desperate and deteriorating social conditions.

Marxists react critically to such a line of reasoning, while sympathiz-
ing, of course, with the goal of aiding the poor nations. Marxists worry
that redirecting international value flows might have no affect at all on
what they see as a central issue for social progress in Asia, Africa, and
Latin America: the transformation of national class structures. Even if
Brazilian capitalists no longer paid interest to New York banks, Brazilian capitalists might still be able to secure their conditions of existence
in other ways, to go on exploiting Brazilian laborers, and to influence
Brazilian society in ways that Marxists and indeed many others would
oppose. Critiques of imperialism that abstract from class analysis in
terms of the production, appropriation, and distribution of surplus labor lead to political strategies and demands that also do not address the
central issue of class.

Similarly, non-Marxian theories of international relations which collapse all economic transactions into commodity exchanges will eventuate, for example, in programs for solving world poverty that abstract

from class. One popular program of this kind holds that poor nations around the world should immediately remove all legal, cultural, and political barriers to the maximum expansion of commodity trade. The expansion of trade is seen as the solution to poverty. According to this non-Marxian theory, drawing poor nations into a world commodity market would bring their people all the benefits of prosperity and growth enjoyed by the countries that first generated the world commodity market (the nations of Western Europe, the United States, Japan, and so on).

Marxian theory recoils from such a prescription because it fails to see what Marxists see in the expansion of European capitalism during the last centuries—namely, the establishment of a world capitalist class structure. For Marxists, that structure is the problem, not the solution. Extending that structure through greater commodity trade would only deepen the problem. What is needed in all countries, Marxian theorists argue, is a social transformation from capitalist to noncapitalist class structures.

Marxian theory contributes to critiques of international relations an emphasis on their class components and how those relations interact with domestic class structures. A Marxian critique of the relations between our New York bank and Brazil would first determine whether, and if so, what, class processes were included in those relations, and would then examine how those relations interacted with the domestic class structures in both Brazil and the United States. The same sort of investigation would apply to Liberia's relations with the United States. The critiques in both cases would aim to demonstrate how international relations provide conditions of existence for the class structures in all interacting nations.

Given Marxian theory's commitment to contradiction as the logical concomitant of overdetermination, a Marxian critique must also determine how international relations undermine the conditions of existence of domestic class structures. The ultimate point is to lend theoretical assistance to practical movements that are seeking to change both the class structures and general social conditions of nations. This, after all, is the point of Marxian analyses. In the case of international relations, Marxian critiques explain how current international relations strengthen domestic class structures in certain ways while also weakening them in other ways. Armed with such explanations, popular movements for social change can make strategies and demands regarding international relations consistent with class-conscious programs for domestic social change.

Thus, for example, a Marxian critique of Brazil's international relations will help a socialist party define its position on tariffs, exchange rate controls, capital exports, domestic tax changes, and so on. It can do this because it connects those issues to the domestic class structure the party aims to change. Other theories do not make, let alone stress, such connections. Marxian theory likewise assists a socialist party in determining the possibilities and limits of political alliances on international issues which might be made with other parties. It can do this because it connects those parties' international programs to the domestic class structure, and so on.

The Marxian critique of the modern capitalist world economy as "imperialist" takes on a powerful class dimension if and when it pinpoints the ways in which international relations are both overdetermined by class processes and participate in overdetermining them. Anti-imperialist theories—like nationally focused theories of social injustice and economic and political inequality—can abstract from class. Anti-imperialist theorists can explain the causes of the current world economy as greed, as drives to power, as removable imperfections in commodity markets, as effects of technological changes, and so on. Marxian theorists say to them, (1) we share your horror at the needless injustice and inequality of the world economy, but (2) we believe you will not change that economy without understanding and changing its component class processes. The specifically class analytical approach to international relations is Marxian theory's contribution to the broad movement to transform an imperialist world economy.

K. Suggested Readings

Fine, Ben. *Marx's "Capital."* London: Macmillan, 1975.

A short overview of Marxian economics based on lectures presented at the University of London.

Harvey, David. *The Limits to Capital.* Chicago: University of Chicago Press, 1982.

A comprehensive treatment of Marxian economics oriented toward current issues confronting especially U.S. capitalism.

Mandel, Ernest. *Marxist Economic Theory.* 2 vols. New York: Monthly Review Press, 1968.

This comprehensive survey covers developments in Marxian economics since Marx as well as Marx's work, with special emphasis on concrete examples drawn from contemporary sources.

Marx, Karl. *Capital.* 3 vols. New York: Vintage Books, 1977.

> The most recent and modern translation of the classic exposition of Marx's economic theory.

Resnick, Stephen A., and Wolff, Richard D. *Knowledge and Class.* Chicago: University of Chicago Press, 1987.

> An analysis of the Marxian tradition that incorporates recent developments in class analysis and the theory of knowledge.

Rosdolsky, Roman. *The Making of Marx's "Capital."* London: Pluto Press, 1977.

> A careful, thorough examination and critique of the entire structure of Marx's economic theories.

Sweezy, Paul M. *The Theory of Capitalist Development.* New York: Monthly Review Press, 1970.

> The single most widely used general introduction to Marxian economics by an American economist for an American audience.

Appendix 1. Why Does Marxian Theory Make Class Its Entry Point?

In this appendix we will consider a question often put to Marxists: Why do you make class your entry point rather than individual preferences or political power or race or sex or many other possible aspects of society? While we touched on this issue earlier in this book, a fuller statement may be useful here.

The answer now (as also in Marx's day) follows from what Marxists believe to be the social role of a theory. A theory invented and spread will have an impact on every other process in society. One form of this impact concerns the theory's entry point. Since it is so prominent, the entry point of a theory affects society by drawing attention to itself. To produce a new theory is, among other things, to focus interest on its entry point.

Marxian theory has always been self-conscious about seeking to draw attention and interest to the class process. As we noted earlier in this chapter, Marx believed that his fellow-revolutionists did not understand class and its roles either in the societies they sought to change or in those they dreamed of establishing. His theory aimed to rectify this situation: to focus attention on class and its relations to all the other, nonclass aspects of society and social change.

The point was not to claim that class was any more important a part of society than power or individual preferences or race or sex. Rather, Marx emphasized class by making it his entry point into social analyses for a specific, concrete purpose: to remedy the ignorance and underestimation of class which, in his view, undercut the revolutionary projects he supported. In this way he added the issue of class to the agendas and strategies for change of many of his contemporaries.

However, the class issue has once again receded among the many issues involved in movements for social change over recent decades. Americans in particular have stressed instead issues of the democratic distribution of power and of racial and sexual inequalities. Movements for broad social democracy and racial and sexual equality have generated new social theories whose entry points have been power, race, and sex. These theories have served to focus attention on those particular aspects of society, especially among people favoring social change. While some of these theories have been influenced by Marxian theory, they have tended to substitute nonclass processes for the class process as their entry points.

This situation has now provoked a pendulum swing back toward a concern with class, lest Marx's insights be lost to the movements for social change. Especially in the United States, people have become increasingly interested in Marxian theory for reasons quite similar to Marx's original motivation in producing his theory: to put class on the agenda for social change. The growing interest in Marxian theory among Americans has in turn stimulated the study of the Marxian tradition as it has evolved and diversified outside the United States over the last fifty years.

One result of the renewed attention to the Marxian tradition is the formulation of Marxian theory presented here. It addresses the question of why class is Marxian theory's entry point by stressing the current need for those interested in social change to confront the issue of class and to incorporate it into their strategies. One set of social conditions produced Marx and the revolutionary movements of his time. Current conditions have produced a revival of interest and work in Marxian theory, and for similar basic reasons. That is why class remains Marxian theory's entry point.

Appendix 2. Rising Exploitation with Rising Real Wages

Recall the earlier equation for the value of labor power:

$$V = e \cdot q.$$

Let us now calculate what portion of the change in V is accounted for by changes in each of the two factors on the right-hand side of this equation. First, there is the change in the per-unit value of wage commodities multiplied by the initial standard of living: $\Delta e \cdot q$. Second, there is the change in the standard of living multiplied by the initial per-unit value of the wage commodities: $\Delta q \cdot e$. Adding both changes, we derive the change in V:

$$\Delta V = \Delta e \cdot q + \Delta q \cdot e.$$

We may rewrite this equation in terms of percentage rates of change:

$$\frac{\Delta V}{V} = \frac{\Delta e}{e} + \frac{\Delta q}{q}.$$

It follows that a 10 percent decline in the value of labor power ($\Delta V/V$) and a simultaneous 20 percent decline in unit values of wage goods ($\Delta e/e$) would equal a 10 percent *rise* in real wages ($\Delta q/q$).

4 The Importance of Theoretical Differences

A. Marxism versus Neoclassical Theory

This book has presented an in-depth discussion of the two most important economic theories to appear in the last hundred years. In chapters 2 and 3, we described the structure of each theory and suggested some of the different consequences that flow from each. In this concluding chapter we have two purposes. The first is to compare and contrast the two theories systematically. The second is to explain carefully how they impact upon our lives in very different ways. We aim to show how alternative ways of thinking in general, and two economic theories in particular, shape social relationships in very different ways.

Let us recall that each theory has a unique structure. The individuality of each theory lies in the different concepts or sentences it uses to make sense of the world, to construct its particular knowledge of social life. This individuality raises two questions. First, where does each theory begin? What are the entry points of each theory? Second, what is the method or logic used by each to produce its other concepts—that is, to move from entry points to a developed understanding or knowledge? Marxian and neoclassical theories differ radically in their answers to these questions.

A.1. Different Points of Entry

Marxian theory begins with the concept of class. This is the initial concept or idea with which it organizes its understanding of all the objects (topics) with which it may be confronted. It thus always connects prices, wages, and profits, as particular objects of interest, to its organizing concept of class. Put simply, it produces a class knowledge of them. We can say, therefore, that Marxian theory is a class theory of the meaning of these objects.

Neoclassical theory, by contrast, begins with (1) the concept of self-interested, utility-maximizing individuals who are (2) endowed with initial productive resources and (3) an inherent ability to use the available technology to transform nature by means of the initial resources. Seen as aspects of human nature, these three initial concepts are used by neoclassical theory to produce the meaning of all objects with which it may be confronted. It thus always connects prices, wages, and profits to its organizing concepts of individual preferences, resource endowments, and technology. We might say, therefore, that neoclassical theory is an individual human nature theory of the meaning of these objects.

Comparing Marxian and neoclassical theories, we can now see clearly that they differ sharply in their ideas of how to begin to structure an understanding of social life. Added to this we have the results of chapters 2 and 3: different points of entry contribute to different understandings of (explanations for) economic relationships and events. Indeed, neoclassicals and Marxists see and participate in social life differently in part because of the different organizing concepts of their theories.

It follows that practitioners of the two theories may take very different actions in their lives because of the complex conscious and unconscious effects of such different ideas of where to begin in thinking about economy and society. To underscore the importance and power of entry points, we will provide several concrete examples later in this chapter.

A.2. Different Logics

Each theory not only has different entry points but also goes about constructing its sentences differently. The constructed sentences in each theory—its propositions and arguments—connect to that theory's particular points of entry in different ways. In short, there are two distinct logics at work in the two theories.

Neoclassical theory employs a logic known in philosophy as "deduction." This means that its new concepts or sentences are carefully deduced from prior ones—or, to use the mathematical term, are "derived" from them. From its entry points of human preferences, technology, and resource endowments, the concept of supply and demand for all commodities and resources is logically deduced or derived. In turn, from this concept of supply and demand, the prices of all commodities and resources are derived, and so on.

We could just as well read this last sentence in reverse. Then "derived" would be replaced by its opposite, "reduced." We could say that in neoclassical theory, price is first reduced to what determines it, supply and demand. Then supply and demand are reduced to what ultimately determines them: the entry-point concepts of individual preferences, technology, and resource endowments. These three aspects of human nature form the basic concepts, the essences, to which all other concepts in neoclassical theory are logically reduced.

In philosophical language these essentialized concepts are sometimes referred to as the origins (ultimate causes) of everything else that is to be thought about. We may think of them simply as together forming an anchor that determines and firmly holds together all of the concepts of the theory. The deductive logic of neoclassical theory is thus a form of essentialism.

Marxian theory develops quite differently. It employs as its connecting logic the antiessentialist method called "overdetermination." In this approach, each concept of the theory is complexly linked, as both cause and effect, to all the other concepts of the theory. Thus, no concept of the theory can be reduced from or reduced to any other; no concept functions as an essence.

To contrast the Marxian logic of overdetermination with neoclassical theory's essentialist logic, let us consider Marxian theory's entry-point concept: class. First of all, in Marxian theory class is not understood as an essence; class is not the ultimate cause of all that happens in the economy and society in which class occurs. Starting with its entry point of class, Marxian theory proceeds to consider other aspects of social life, such as commodity prices and enterprise profits. These are explored as simultaneously the causes and effects of class; they are not explored as ultimately caused by or explained in terms of class. Class is not their ultimate cause any more than they are the ultimate causes of class in society. The goal of Marxian analysis cannot then be to demonstrate how class is the ultimate determinant of, say, prices and profits. It is rather to explore the specific interrelations and interdependence of class on the one hand, and prices and profits on the other.

Marxian theory is thus a never-ending process in which its entry-point concept—the central focus of Marxists for specific historical reasons—is linked to an ever-growing range of other concepts, other aspects of social life. The link is one of overdetermination: class and nonclass aspects of life are woven together as mutual causes and effects of one another. The goal is to understand the precise ways in which each aspect is simultaneously the cause and the effect of all others, or, in philosophical language, how each aspect participates in the overdetermination of all of the others. Marxists can and do disagree in their analyses of the precise overdeterminations connecting class and nonclass processes.

Neoclassical theory is likewise a never-ending process in which its entry-point concepts of individual preferences, technology, and endowments are linked to an ever-growing range of other aspects of social life. However, in neoclassical theory the linkage is one of cause and effect, determination, or essentialism. These synonyms all refer to the notion that some parts of social life are the causes of others (the effects) without themselves being caused by those others. The goal of neoclassical theory is then to demonstrate exhaustively how more and more of society is the effect of essentialized human preferences, technology, and endowments. Neoclassical economists can and do disagree about the precise essentialist linkages between their agreed-upon entry points and everything else.

It follows that very different understandings will be produced from these two theories as each generates its particular analyses of economic structures and changes. Indeed, these different understandings raise the issue of whether we can really say that they are analyzing the same things. With different entry points and different logics, must they not mean different things when they use words like "labor," "value," "profit," "class," and so on? Yet many of the same words appear in the statements of both theories.

A.3. Different Objects of Analysis

Proceeding from their entry points, the two theories utilize their logics to construct explanations of whatever they take as interesting objects to analyze. To be consistent in our language, we might refer to the theoretical explanation of some topic as the exit point of a theory: the place to which we go in thinking from our entry point by way of our logic. Starting from different entry points and proceeding by way of different logics, we reach different exit points.

This means that we are typically confronted in the world with objects of analysis which, despite carrying the same label, mean very different things. For example, Marxists and non-Marxists produce different explanations of the concept "capitalism." They do likewise when they explain how an economy does and should operate. Although both groups of theorists often use the same words, these words take on their unique meanings according to the particular theories that use and thereby define them.

If, then, Marxian and neoclassical theories have objects of analysis, or exit points toward which they target their efforts, these too are different. Both theories may refer to their objects of analysis as "capitalism" or "the economy," but these words represent different conceptualizations of such objects. At times, theorists try to produce new labels, ones that have no place in contending theories, in order to distinguish their particularly theorized meanings. Marx, for example, invented "surplus value" to distinguish his notion of class from other notions; neoclassical theorists invented "marginal utility" to distinguish their concept of human choice from others'.

The question that now arises is, If the same term represents radically different meanings in two different theories, which one is correct? Is it

Marxism's "capitalism" or neoclassical theory's "capitalism"? There is an old tradition in human thought which argues that one of these two conceptualizations of the object "capitalism" must be truer, must be the closer approximation of what exists in the real world. We will return to this issue at the end of the chapter. At this point, we need only mention that this argument itself involves theories about what reality, knowledge, and truth are. Different theories of reality and knowledge can and do connect objects differently and so answer the question about the "correctness" of theories in very different ways.

A.4. Different Theories of Value

Table 4.1 summarizes the two theories of value presented in chapters 2 and 3. It connects concisely the three indices of difference between the neoclassical and Marxian theories. Reading the entry-point column of the table, we find the theories' different organizing concepts. Under the object column, we observe their differently produced explanations of what they both choose to call "prices" and "incomes." The different logics used are denoted respectively by the unidirectional arrow in the neoclassical row and the bidirectional arrow in the Marxian row. In the former, we see that the entry point determines the object, while in the latter, overdetermination links the entry and exit points to each other.

Each of these theories produces a logical explanation of price and income behavior. Table 4.1 illustrates the stark differences between these explanations. Neoclassical theory specifies how wants (utility) and scarcity (given technical production functions and resource endowments) combine to *determine* prices and incomes. Marxian theory views these as only two of the many nonclass processes that interact with the class process (S/V) to *overdetermine* prices and incomes.

The meanings of "price" and "income" as objects of analysis depend upon which sets of concepts are used to make sense of them. This is true as well for every other concept. The concepts of "need" and "scarcity" found in neoclassical theory take on very different meanings in Marxian theory. They too are conceived in that approach to be overdetermined

Table 4.1. Theories of Value

Theory	Entry Point	Logic	Object
Marxian	class (S/V)	←——→	prices and incomes
Neoclassical	wants (U)		
	scarcity (technology and endowments)	——→	prices and incomes

by still other nonclass and class processes. In neoclassical theory, "need" and "scarcity" have specific, fixed meanings, while in Marxian theory, "overdetermination" means that individuals constantly change what they understand those terms to be and therefore how they act in relation to what they understand to be "need" and "scarcity."

We have now come full circle to the beginning of this chapter. We have answered our two questions by showing how the entry points and logics of analysis of the neoclassical and Marxian theories differ. That has permitted us to see that these theories' objects of analysis necessarily differ as well. We may now confront the other major issue of this chapter: How and why do these theoretical differences matter in our lives?

B. Analytical Consequences of Contending Theories

Neoclassical and Marxian theories coexist in our society. Individuals and groups use one or the other or varying mixtures of both to try to make sense of the world. How people think about the world shapes their sense of the problems they face and the solutions they can and ought to pursue. Therefore, the theories people use influence the actions they take in solving the problems they think they have. Different theories contribute to different actions.

In this section we will explore the different consequences of the two theories for the various kinds of actions people take in American society. Our goal will be to demonstrate that the two theories' different analyses of economic objects influence people to take different kinds of action. The behavior of individuals and groups is shaped in part by which theory each endorses and uses. Since our lives are impacted in every possible way by the actions of those around us, we study different theories to help us understand and cope with those actions. Quite literally, the lives we lead are themselves among the social consequences of the different theories that are alive and working in American society. That is why we need to study the theories and their social consequences. Since what we think and do will in turn affect those theories, we need to know how they impact on society so that we may shape our attitudes and behaviors toward them.

B.1. Income Distribution: The Neoclassical View

For the past hundred years Marxists and neoclassicals have gone at each other over one of the most important questions ever to confront economics: Why are some people relatively poor and others relatively rich? In other words, what explains income and its distribution in societies?

Different answers to this question help shape citizens' conscious and unconscious attitudes toward poverty and affluence in America and in other societies. These attitudes in turn influence government expenditure and tax programs such as aid to the relatively less well-off and the structure of the U.S. federal income tax system. Our attitudes toward rich and poor figure prominently in America's books, plays, films, and television programs. These cultural vehicles create the voices of the characters we come to love, hate, and respect. Often these are the only voices we hear; thus their views on these matters cannot be taken lightly.

Different explanations for the causes of income and its distribution also influence politics: the people we elect, the laws they pass, the manner in which judges and juries interpret those laws, and the patterns in which the laws are enforced. These explanations inform our feelings toward the sexes, races, political parties, and nations of the world. Theories of poverty and affluence have a long history of affecting peoples' lives on a day-to-day basis, whether they are explicitly aware of the theories or not. Indeed, one purpose of this book is precisely to increase your awareness of the influences of different theories on your life and your society.

Let us now compare directly the neoclassical and Marxian explanations of income distribution and see where their different explanations lead. Neoclassical theory argues that the wealth of individuals, groups, and nations is explained by the choices each makes, combined with the technology and productive resources that are available to each to transform nature into useful goods and services. Wealth and poverty are thus understood to be the doing, the responsibility, of each individual, group, and nation.

Neoclassical explanations proceed by examining how choices are made and how they interact with available production possibilities. Individuals (groups and nations) *decide* to save a part of their income and devote the resources thereby saved from consumption to the production of still more goods and services. In economic jargon, individuals decide to save and then provide their savings as capital made available to the production process. Meanwhile, these and/or other individuals also *decide* to supply their labor to this same production process rather than consume their time in leisure activities.

In neoclassical theory, individuals are thought to exercise free will in making the decision to sacrifice the present consumption of their income and/or to sacrifice their leisure time. The incentive for individuals to make such sacrifices is the reward they expect and deserve in return for either or both sacrifices. To reverse a common adage from the sports world: "no gain, no pain (of sacrifice)." Neoclassical theory concludes by deducing each individual's income from the quantity of sacrifice each has voluntarily made. The theory insists that each individual's share of output (his or her income) is directly related to what each has contributed to that production by sacrificing consumption and/or leisure.

Sacrificing present consumption releases resources from use in the production of consumer goods and services. These resources can then be devoted to producing capital goods—that is, means of production such as tools, equipment, factories, and offices. These capital goods in turn can be combined with the labor provided by individuals who have willingly sacrificed their leisure. The result is the wealth of goods and services produced and made available for distribution. The quantity of extra goods and services produced in this way depends, as noted in chapter 2, on technology and on each individuals' initial endowment of resources, over whose disposition each makes a choice.

Neoclassical theory claims that the incomes of individuals are determined by those individuals' preferences (hence their choices for current versus later consumption and for leisure versus income from their labor), their endowments of resources, and the technology that is available to them. Neoclassical theory reduces each individual's income to its conceptual entry points: individual preferences or choices interacting with a given scarce resource and with known techniques of production. We all receive income in direct relation to how we choose to use our time and our initial endowments of productive resources. The more we sacrifice, the more we can contribute to production and the more we can and should obtain of the fruits of that production. We should therefore look at our own choices, our own self-interested behavior, to find the explanation for our high or low incomes.

It follows in neoclassical theory that for any given technology, the relatively affluent do not and cannot earn their income at the expense of the poor. The decision of the former to be thrifty and/or work hard is completely independent of the latter's opposite decision. In terms of profits and wages, neoclassical theory states quite clearly that those who receive profit income do not obtain it at the expense of those who choose to receive wage income. Rather, the source of profit income lies in an individual's choice to be thrifty and in the technically determined marginal productivity of his or her capital. In parallel fashion, the source of wage income lies in the choice to forgo leisure, to supply labor, and to obtain thereby the technically determined marginal productivity of the labor supplied.

Each individual is thought to choose independently to make sacrifices and/or supply resources to the production process. Each gets his or her just deserts. No one's wealth is the result of another's poverty.

Thus the questions of who gets what, and how much, are explained in terms of our choices, which reflect the preferences rooted in our human nature. They are as immutable as our genes. Individuals, groups, and nations are rich or poor in proportion to their natural endowments and their correspondingly natural choices. The poverty of some is independent of the wealth of others. If they are dissatisfied with their poverty, the poor must change their ways and become more like the rich; that is the only road to riches.

B.2. Capitalism: The Neoclassical View

Neoclassical theory elaborates this powerful conclusion to produce one of the most significant messages found anywhere in social theory. A society that establishes capitalism will achieve the maximum wealth—a point on its production possibilities frontier—for its citizens. By establishing capitalism, neoclassical theory means establishing two social institutions. The first is a free and fully competitive market for all resources and produced goods, a market in which no individual can control prices. The second is legally enforced private property, including the right of owners of resources and produced goods to dispose of them in a manner of their own choosing. For neoclassical theory, the existence of these two institutions in any society ensures the production of the maximum wealth of which that society is physically capable, given the free choices of its citizens and their presumed natural want for maximum wealth.

Capitalism conforms, then, to what neoclassical theory assumes to be the wealth-accumulating nature of human beings. The theory understands capitalism to be the optimum social system because it best facilitates what we all want to do: accumulate wealth for ourselves. It prompts and encourages each citizen to make decisions based on individual self-interest—that is, maximum wealth for each consumer and producer. As shown in chapter 2, the basic institutions of capitalist society guarantee the simultaneity of maximum producer profits and maximum consumer satisfactions.

This conclusion was first reached by Adam Smith, was later presented in mathematical terms by Pareto, and has most recently been given formal "proof" by Gerard Debreu (for which he was awarded the 1984 Nobel Prize in economics). It implies that capitalism is an intrinsically harmonious economic system. Producers and consumers seeking their own self-interest will thereby promote one another's interests automatically. Everyone ends up in the best possible economic position, such that no one could become better off (acquire more wealth) unless someone else became worse off.

One implication of this neoclassical argument is that the institutions of capitalism should be established everywhere as soon as possible since they are what all rational individuals and nations want for themselves. Where capitalism exists, it must be protected from the irrational persons or nations who would destroy it and establish irrational economic and social institutions—for example, collectivized property and centralized economic planning. The latter, because they are not capitalist, would impose all manner of production inefficiencies and consumption dissatisfactions. Where capitalism does not exist, the clear and obvious interest of all rational, self-concerned people must lie in establishing it. In particular, poor nations must recognize that capitalism is *the* way to become rich.

A second implication of this neoclassical conclusion is that capitalism rewards hard work and personal saving. Since individual incomes flow from the contributions individuals make to production, the more labor individuals contribute, the higher their wage income will be. The greater the portion of their income they save and contribute to (invest in) production, the more their profit income will be. Hard work and frugality are the twin virtues which, if practiced by poor persons in a capitalist system, will enable them to escape poverty.

A third implication is that, given individual wants and capitalist institutions, wealth can be gained by raising the productivity of resources. Technological changes can and do increase the incomes of those who supply the resources whose productivity is raised by those changes. Capitalism is thus a technically dynamic system since every citizen of a capitalist society has an interest in gaining more income by enhancing the productivity of whatever resources he or she contributes to production. Notice again the universally harmonious, mutually reinforcing interaction of capitalist institutions, technical changes, and rising incomes.

B.3. Poverty: The Neoclassical View

It follows directly from the neoclassical conception of income distribution in capitalist economies that the poor (both individuals and nations) are in that condition for one or more of three basic reasons. First, there are barriers that block individuals in a society from exercising their choices in a rational way. Such barriers impede capitalist institutions by interfering with the workings of free markets and/or constraining owners from freely disposing of their private property. Such barriers distort individual decisions and thus prevent the harmonious optimization of production efficiency and consumption satisfaction discussed above.

Neoclassical literature recognizes and discusses three kinds of barrier. The first kind derives from human weaknesses—for example, the desire of individuals to gain market control, monopolize resources or goods, and change buyers' choices by charging monopoly prices. The second kind involves certain natural imperfections in the human species—for instance, the inability of human beings to predict the future. Uncertainty in making choices that will affect future production and consumption can block the optimization of productive efficiency and consumer satisfaction. The third kind of barrier, which is nonhuman in nature, concerns the properties of some production technologies—for example, economies of scale. All three kinds of barrier are capable of causing the wealth of individuals and nations to fall below what it could be without them. All three can create poverty.

The second explanation given by neoclassical theorists for poverty in capitalist societies is that some individuals choose it. Some people prefer to live in relative poverty. They choose leisure rather than wage income from labor. They prefer to consume now rather than save and invest for future profit, rent, interest, etc. Nations, like individuals, are poor because of their particular preferences and the resulting choices they make.

The third neoclassical reason for poverty concerns neither barriers to markets and private property nor choices. It concerns productivity. If the resources an individual contributes to production are of little use, then that individual will in turn obtain little reward. Individuals who contribute low-productivity resources (unskilled labor, low-fertility land, etc.) will be rewarded with correspondingly small portions of output. Their incomes will be low in proportion to the low productivity they bring to production. The poverty of individuals and nations can thus be explained in terms of their low-productivity resource endowments.

To counter these three causes of poverty in capitalist societies, neoclassical theory generated a broad policy prescription. A rational society must identify and eliminate barriers to free-market decisions made by private property owners, whatever their source. The goal must be to create perfect capitalist market institutions in which each citizen has an equal chance to be rich or poor depending on his or her personal preferences and the given technological productivity of his or her privately owned resources. On this basic issue of removing market imperfections, both the liberal and the conservative side of the neoclassical approach agree. Their disagreements concern rather the sources of and specific mechanisms for removing such imperfections.

B.4. Income Distribution: The Marxian View

Marxian theory rejects the neoclassical reduction of income distribution in capitalist economies to the possession of certain essential attributes of human nature. It thus also rejects the idea that incomes can be constrained by barriers that effectively prevent those essential attributes from generating some "optimum" output and distribution of wealth.

Instead, Marxian theory approaches the issue of income distribution by inquiring about individuals' participation in class and nonclass processes. In particular, the focus of Marxian theory is upon class and nonclass processes that involve individuals receiving flows of value (in the form of money or commodities). These flows are what Marxian theory calls "incomes." Every individual who obtains any income does so, in Marxian theory, because he or she participates in class and/or nonclass processes that generate income. By contrast, neoclassical theory disregards the Marxian concept of class altogether; class plays no role in its theory of income distribution.

To summarize the Marxian theory of income distribution, we will consider examples of class and nonclass processes that generate incomes to individuals. The nonclass process of commodity exchange generates income. John sells his shirt to Mary, who pays for it with money. John obtains money income for participating in this nonclass process of commodity exchange. So does Mary, although her income is a flow of value in the form of a shirt, while John's is in the form of money. More important from the standpoint of Marxian theory is another commodity exchange process. Mary sells her labor power to an employer for payment in money wages. These wages are an income she obtains by virtue of her participation in this particular commodity exchange process.

Seeking to understand income distribution, Marxian theory asks how the relative size of such a money-wage income is determined in capitalist societies. It begins with a simple definition: the value of the labor power sold is equal to the value of the bundle of commodities required by the sellers of labor power to reproduce their ability to sell it. This means that the value of labor power (the income gained from selling it) is determined by two factors: (1) the bundle of specific commodities that sellers consume in order to reproduce their ability to sell their labor power, and (2) the value of each commodity in that bundle.

Marxian theory proceeds to explain the many diverse social forces that combine to overdetermine both factors. The specific commodities (factor 1) that sellers of labor power require are influenced by cultural, natural, political, and economic factors of all kinds. Moreover, since these are constantly changing, so too must the bundles change. The value of each commodity in the bundle (factor 2) is likewise overdetermined by all the other processes of society—all of which influence the amount of labor necessary to produce each commodity. Thus, Marxian theory claims that the incomes people obtain from selling their labor power are complexly overdetermined by all of the processes of society.

Marxian theory cannot and does not explain wage income by looking at only two of its determinants: the individual laborer's choice between income and leisure and the marginal productivity of his or her labor. That is the neoclassical approach. Marxian theory recognizes that individual choice and marginal productivity help determine wage income, but it does not ignore all the other determinants. The Marxian approach emphasizes the overdetermination of wages, while neoclassical theory focuses on only two of the many determinants of this kind of income.

To illustrate the breadth of the Marxian theory of income distribution, we will consider next the capitalist fundamental class process. As shown in chapter 3, this process involves the production and appropriation of surplus value. This appropriation by industrial capitalists constitutes a flow of value to them; it is an income for them. They sell the commodities produced by the productive laborers they employ; they buy productive labor power and means of production. The difference between the value of the commodities produced and sold and the value of the labor power and means of production purchased is the industrial capitalist's surplus-value income. It is a flow of value for which the capitalist makes no return flow. It is that "something for nothing" which outraged Marx and led him to call its occurrence "exploitation."

By including this fundamental class process in its analysis of capitalist economies, Marxian theory broadens its analysis of the distributions of income found in capitalist societies. Marxian theory stresses that in addition to obtaining income through participation in the commodity exchange process, it is possible to obtain income via participation in the fundamental class process as an appropriator of surplus labor. Many different social forces determine whether any particular individual will be able to participate in the class or nonclass income-generating processes discussed here.

Marxian theory recognizes that still other class and nonclass income-generating processes may exist in a society. Individuals participating in any of these obtain incomes too. Thus, the distribution of income among the citizens of a society depends on which class and nonclass income-generating processes exist in it and upon how different individuals participate in those processes. A Marxian analysis of income distribution is then necessarily a study of all of the social processes—cultural, natural, political, and economic (including class)—that determine the participation of citizens in the different income-generating processes of a society. There is no way to reduce this complexity to the neoclassical proposition that income distribution depends only on choices, techniques, and resource endowments.

B.5. Different Explanations of Profit

Table 4.2 summarizes the neoclassical and Marxian explanations of the source of profit (or what Marxists call "surplus value") in a society. In the table, $MP(K)$ represents the marginal product of the capital resource. MRS refers to the marginal rate of substitution between present and future consumption: the psychological propensity of individuals to postpone present consumption and supply the resultant savings in the form of capital to the production process. According to neoclassical theory, then, the origin of profit in a society is explained in terms of two essences: (1) the inherent productivity of "things" (machines, tools, etc.) as measured by $MP(K)$; and (2) the willingness of individuals to sacrifice gratification now for more later as measured by MRS. In short, profit is a just reward for individuals' personal sacrifices and their contributions to production.

According to Marxian theory, the origin of profit (surplus value) is the surplus labor produced by productive laborers and appropriated by industrial capitalists. Profit is a fruit of the exploitation that takes place in the capitalist fundamental class process (FCP). Whereas in neoclassical theory an individual obtains income only by contributing some resource to production, in Marxian theory no such mechanism exists. The marginal productivity of "things" and individual choices about labor, leisure, and consumption are not the essential causes or explanations of anything in Marxian theory. Rather, profit-receivers in Marxian theory obtain a portion of the income of society without making any productive contribution to generating that income.

The contrast here is striking. Neoclassical theory makes income a just reward of individual choice and effort. Marxian theory makes it a fruit of exploitation. Different theories lead to different analyses and different conclusions.

Individual choice and productivity matter in Marxian theory, but not as essences that determine everything about the economy. Rather they are merely two of the many factors that overdetermine all the aspects of any economy, such as income and its distribution among individuals. In Marxian theory, the labor power supplied by an individual may be very productive, but the wages received need bear little relationship to that

Table 4.2.   The Origin of Profit

Theory	Entry Point	Logic	Object
Neoclassical	$MP(K)$ and MRS	⟶	profit
Marxian	FCP	⟷	surplus value

high productivity. By contrast, industrial capitalists, who by definition have zero productivity in their class position as surplus appropriators, receive typically large profit incomes.

Marxian theory emphasizes and focuses upon the class process in society. Therefore, when the issue to be explained is income and its social distribution, the theory connects class to individual incomes. Individuals who occupy the fundamental class position of surplus appropriator receive a portion of the goods and services produced by others.

The clear implication is that industrial capitalists' incomes rightfully belong to those whose efforts made them possible. The notion of an income obtained without productive effort depends on the concept of class, which Marxian theory emphasizes and neoclassical theory denies. The class concept thus provides the cutting edge between Marxian and neoclassical theories generally and their approaches to income distribution in particular.

C. Political Consequences of Contending Theories

The two radically different theories clash in the modern world. A major point and purpose of neoclassical theory is to deny precisely what Marxian theory affirms: that class exploitation is a determinant of income distribution. A major point and purpose of Marxian theory is to deny what neoclassical theory affirms: that human choice and technology determine the social distribution of income. Different political goals and orientations are both the causes and the effects of these two theories.

Neoclassical theory informs the political agendas of most liberals and conservatives in the United States. It underlies their concern to remove all market imperfections that prevent individuals from making those decisions which would bring each one the income he or she wants and deserves: an income distribution that conforms to the human nature of all citizens. Marxian theory informs the political agendas of Marxists. For them, a major political objective is basic change toward a more just society: change that would remove class exploitation from modern society. They seek the redistribution of income which would follow from a changed class structure rather than the redistribution which a removal of market imperfections would entail.

The theoretical differences carry far-reaching implications. For Marxists, even if market imperfections were radically removed according to neoclassical prescriptions, class exploitation would not be eliminated. Even if the neoclassical vision of full employment, eradication of monopolies, perfectly disseminated information, and an end to market discrimination on grounds of race or gender were achieved, class exploitation could continue or grow.

Marxists might agree that certain institutional changes proposed in the neoclassical program of removing market imperfections are desirable: they might agree with certain stated objectives of that program. Historically, Marxists have often joined political forces with neoclassically inspired groups seeking such institutional changes. However, the divergent political consequences of the two theories emerge clearly in the fact that the Marxists' program would find even the achievement of the neoclassical program unacceptable. For Marxists, the neoclassical program, even if achieved, would leave intact the capitalist class structure and hence the social injustice, widespread misery, and social tensions associated with it.

Marxists must contend with the basic questions that are addressed to them about their political approach. How could a society that achieved full employment still produce misery and deepening social conflicts? What explains the Marxists' insistence that even an ending of racial and sex discrimination could open the way for greater capitalist exploitation and the social injustice it entails? How could the maximization of output for producers and consumers in a society coexist with a maximization of exploitation? How do Marxists explain such contradictions?

The Marxian theoretical answer has already been presented in this book. The class process is different from other processes—that is, from income distribution, commodity production, market discrimination, and so on. Changes in these processes as outlined in the neoclassical political program leave open the question of changes in the class process, which the neoclassical program denies and ignores. Marxists insist that changes in the nonclass processes that neoclassical theory stresses may well increase the level of exploitation (S/V) that occurs within the capitalist fundamental class process.

The Marxists' political answer begins by stressing that the continuation or intensification of capitalist exploitation has its own socially destructive effects. As indicated in chapter 3, the capitalist fundamental and subsumed class processes have all manner of undesirable social effects, ranging from deepening the inequalities of income among people, to generating debilitating economic crises, to provoking dangerous international expansions and confrontations. Marxists cannot limit themselves to the neoclassical political program, because that program does not directly transform the class process. In the absence of such a transformation, the door to exploitation's continued oppression of social life remains open.

The political consequences of the two theories are stark. The neoclassical political program celebrates the unambiguous good of the greater social wealth they expect will flow from the removal of market imperfections. More wealth is tantamount to political success. Therefore, specific proposals are evaluated in terms of whether and how they contribute to producing more wealth. In contrast, Marxian political programs stress relationships among people—for example, the relative poverty that can and will accompany the production of more wealth as long as exploitation continues in the society. By relative poverty they mean the gap between the value of labor power workers receive (V) and the surplus value they produce for capitalists (S).

Marxists argue that the neoclassical program's denial of the issue of class makes its goal of greater wealth through the removal of market imperfections consistent with no change in the class relations of society. By focusing on the mass of goods and services produced, neoclassical theory draws attention away from what Marxian theory stresses: the relational gap between producers and appropriators of surplus value. That gap, and the probability in the Marxian view that it will widen as a result of the neoclassical program, animate Marxists to build their different program. Marxian theory is a critical theory; it criticizes not only the social conditions of capitalist societies but also the neoclassical program to reform those conditions.

At particular historical moments, Marxists may well advocate various social reforms that are similar to those favored by the neoclassicals. Marxists sometimes argue that capitalist exploitation relies upon and promotes unemployment, monopoly powers, racism, sexism, and so on. However, that position is not equivalent to the belief that removing those conditions will necessarily make capitalist exploitation disappear. A basic difference between the Marxian and neoclassical political agendas remains the concern with the class process in the former and its absence in the latter.

Marxian political struggles against poverty, unemployment, monopoly abuses, racism, and sexism necessarily emphasize the overdetermined interrelationships between these undesirable conditions and the society's class processes. They differ from neoclassical campaigns against such conditions (when they occur at all) because the neoclassicals pointedly abstract from thinking about or acting against the class structure. Whereas Marxists link their politics on all specific issues to the broad social goal of class transformation, neoclassicals never do. Indeed, the modern histories of many capitalist societies include episodes in which neoclassically inspired political groups split from Marxian groups on the issue of class despite the agreed-upon hostility of the two sides toward certain specific social ills.

Interactions between neoclassical and Marxian theorists have varied from polite but friendly disagreements all the way to intensely hostile confrontations. Between political groups (social movements, political parties, labor unions, etc.) influenced by one or the other theory, relations have gone back and forth from alliances to persecution and occasionally to outright physical destruction. What kinds of relations existed between the two groups depended of course on the complex social conditions of each particular time and place.

The enduring issue, however, has been and remains the issue of class. Marxian objectives always include the transformation of class structures, the radical alteration of social relations whereby some people produce, while others appropriate and distribute, surplus labor. Neoclassical objectives never include such a transformation, although the social reforms advocated by neoclassicals may and often do overlap at least partially those endorsed by Marxists.

Marxian political movements demand the abolition of capitalism and its replacement by a class structure in which the producers of surplus labor also participate in the appropriation of their surplus labor and its distribution. They see such a class change as an indispensable part of the whole pattern of social changes they support to produce a more just and peaceful world. Neoclassical theorists believe that capitalism is the best possible social system, and that if certain imperfections are removed, it can and will provide the greatest good to the greatest number. They also believe that capitalism is most in tune with what they see as the basic nature of human beings.

The two theories and the politics they inspire have been involved in a historically epic debate for over a hundred years. They are engaged in that debate across the globe today. The history of our world in the coming decades will have much to do with that debate and its development in the immediate future. People concerned to understand the world and thereby gain some control over the flow of events and over their own lives need to confront the claims and counterclaims of these two great economic theories.

D. Which Theory Do We Choose?

We face two different theories, each of which has different objects of analysis, different standards for what is true, and different consequences for our lives. Neoclassical theory produces a knowledge of the society in which we live which it calls "capitalism." Marxian theory does likewise. However, the two knowledges produced—the two different senses of what capitalism is—have little in common. Neoclassical theory sees a privately owned and privately run economy in which competitive markets link optimizing producers and consumers. Marxian theory sees a particular kind of class structure in which exploitation is reproduced, with disastrous social consequences. Choosing between the theories amounts to choosing between alternative conceptualizations of the capitalist world we live in.

The different conceptualizations make a difference in our world. They matter in very practical ways. Suppose that a particular citizen believed that certain social conditions in the United States were abhorrent: for example, certain kinds of discrimination. If that individual believed and thought in terms of neoclassical theory, he or she would embrace political strategies aimed at eliminating certain perceived market imperfections. If that individual rather used Marxian theory to make sense of capitalism, he or she would doubt the efficacy of changing only market conditions. He or she would more likely support political strategies favoring radical changes away from the capitalist class structure.

Similarly, practitioners of the two theories would reach different conclusions about how to understand and respond to inflation, recession, war, domestic violence, and most other urgent social issues. Given the contradictions between the theories, between the divergent analyses they produce, and between the political solutions they support, how are we to choose between them?

We are actually familiar with this dilemma of choice in many other parts of our lives. Different religions present us with alternative concepts of God, morality, and the meaning of our lives. Different medical practitioners offer us different diagnoses of illnesses and different remedies for what they diagnose. Different traditions of cuisine, hair style, dress, and interpersonal relationships likewise show us a range of alternatives from which to choose in making still other commitments in our lives.

It is a peculiarity of American culture that while we generally favor tolerance toward or even encouragement of differences in religion, medical practice, life styles, and artistic judgments, we have a very narrow attitude toward the differences in theories of how society works. There it seems that we expect differences of opinion to give way to one absolutely right social theory. While we tend to believe that alternative concepts of God should coexist and interact with one another, we tend to ask of different social theories, Which one is correct? Which one "fits the facts"? Which one is to be embraced while the others are banished to the realm of falsehood?

It is the authors' view that America's maturity as a society requires that we accept the fact that social theories are irreducibly different. Just as we reject intolerance in religious, cultural, medical, and other areas of social life, we can and should reject it in the realm of social theories like neoclassical and Marxian economics. The cross-fertilizations and general enrichment of our society that result from religious, medical, and artistic tolerance would also emerge from our being tolerant in regard to these two theories.

In any case, the differences between neoclassical and Marxian economics have existed and conflicted for over a hundred years, and the debate continues in the United States today. We are left then with the question, How do we choose between these two theories?

D.1. Choosing Theories Because of Their Consequences

We might base our choices on the different effects produced in our lives by each theory. Consider some of these effects. One is the awareness of exploitation in society. Marxian theory literally teaches people to see something in human relationships which is not acknowledged by other theories. Becoming aware of class via Marxian theory often leads individuals to try to alter or eliminate exploitation. Another effect of a Marxian awareness of exploitation would likely be a unique attitude toward nonclass processes in society such as inequalities of power between men and women, whites and blacks, capitalists and workers, property owners and the propertyless. According to that attitude, these nonclass processes would be seen as both distinct from class processes and also in a relation of mutual overdetermination with them.

Other effects of embracing Marxian theory include a commitment to overdetermination rather than essentialism, given the theory's overdeterminist logic. Such a commitment requires that individuals utilizing Marxian theory cease looking for final, ultimate, essential causes or truths. Instead, they presume that different theories or explanations are born from the complex social conditions—natural, political, economic, and cultural—that combine to overdetermine them. Each theory differs not only in its specific propositions but also in the standards of truth, logic, and consistency it erects for its propositions. Such a commitment to antiessentialist ways of thinking carries the implication that no explanation is ever finished, or true beyond revision, or is anything other than one among several alternative explanations.

The effect of Marxian theory's consistent commitment to overdetermination is that subscribers to such a theory view their own position too as but one of several alternatives. They recognize that Marxian theory is no more a final truth than is any other theory. That admission, in turn, may open up a democracy of difference, an attitude toward social theories which celebrates them as richly different reflections of the complex currents shaping any modern society.

If this partial list of effects flowing from adherence to Marxian theory strikes you as attractive, you might then choose to adopt and use

Marxian rather than neoclassical theory. Yet you might also throw up your hands in frustration at the seeming chaos of accepting that the different theories that swirl around you cannot be ranked according to their truths, that they are just there, all different and all clamoring for your allegiance. You might also fear that if theories are different, without one being essentially right and thus the others finally wrong, might not some horrid, evil theory gain sway over most people's minds and actions? For individuals who are attracted to Marxian theory because they approve of the effects of its use, these are perfectly reasonable worries. But before we discuss these worries, we should consider the different effects of adopting neoclassical theory.

One of neoclassical theory's profound effects is its recognition and celebration of something that was repressed by the dominant religious theories prior to capitalism. That "something" is neoclassical theory's entry point, which it makes the essence of economy and society: the individual human being. This key idea is connected historically to the rise of a philosophy called "humanism." Developed initially during the long European transition from feudalism to capitalism, this philosophy attracted massive numbers of people who switched their allegiance from social and economic theories that focused on God as the cause, essence, and purpose of life, to theories that focused instead on individual human beings as the creators of their own world and on individual happiness as the goal of life.

Humanism is a broad, general theory—perhaps we should call it a philosophy—that explains the nature and development of society as the heroic struggle of each and every human being to discover and develop his or her given potential in the face of societal constraints. This central idea is likewise the entry point and essence for neoclassical economic theory. The latter is a particular form of humanism.

It follows that an individual might choose neoclassical theory because its consequences or effects include steps aimed at making social institutions permit and indeed facilitate the essential human struggle to realize individual potentialities. Such an individual would then choose neoclassical theory because it applauds and leads logically toward capitalist institutions, which are understood to be optimally appropriate to our human nature. Neoclassical theory implies capitalism which implies the maximum freedom of individuals to accumulate wealth and thereby achieve happiness and the realization of their potential. Neoclassical theory leads to a political program of social changes which promises to bring an end to market imperfections. For all these reasons, you might well choose to view the world through the neoclassical lens rather than the Marxian lens.

Actually, a moment's reflection should suggest to you that every per-

son's preference for one theory over another is influenced by a long list
of personal and social factors. More than just the effects of alternative
theories shape an individual's choices among them. Other influences on
theoretical preference include family background, schooling, religious
beliefs, age, sex, current family situation, employment conditions, political attitudes, and so forth. Moreover, since these influences change
across lifetimes, theoretical preferences change too.

For example, at one time a person might prefer neoclassical theory
partly because its political implications seem less dramatic and less
threatening than do those of Marxian theory. This preference might
also stem in part from where that person stands in the class structure. If
the individual is a receiver of surplus value from productive laborers, he
or she might prefer neoclassical theory because it denies the whole idea
of surplus and asserts instead that all incomes are rewards to individuals for what each contributes to production. High-income recipients
might understandably become deeply committed to neoclassical theory,
even to the point of thinking that no other reasonable or logical theory
existed.

Marxian theory often changes people's thinking about what capitalism is and how it works. Thus it presents dangers to those who benefit
not only from capitalist class processes but also from the broader population's belief in humanist philosophy and neoclassical economics. Societies in which a capitalist class structure is prevalent usually include
many people who are deeply distressed by the messages of Marxian theory. Marxists argue that in these societies the individual freedoms celebrated by neoclassical theory, schoolbooks, and politicians' speeches
are actually conditions for and facilitators of the exploitation of the nation's productive citizens. Some people in these societies will react by
preferring neoclassical theory rather than coping with all of the disruptive consequences in their personal lives that would flow from taking
Marxian arguments seriously. On the other hand, individuals who have
suffered from various kinds of discrimination, injustice, or oppression
within capitalist societies might be more willing to think in terms of a
theory that is fundamentally critical of capitalism.

Choosing between the two theories in terms of the varied consequences they entail is a complex matter involving all of the varied influences that shape our attitudes and preferences. The choice we make
among theories is as complex as most other important choices we make
in our lives. All of our choices are partly conscious and partly unconscious. We are aware of some of our reasons for choosing as we do, but
there are reasons we do not recognize until long after the choice has
been made, and there are still other reasons we never become aware of.
When we choose between two theories because of their consequences,

we are actually choosing for many other reasons as well, although we are aware of only some of them.

In the language of this book, all choices are overdetermined and contradictory. Every aspect of our lives plays a different role in shaping our choices and our partial awareness of the reasons for them. Our choices are contradictory because the infinite, varied influences on them and on our awareness push and pull them in different and often conflicting directions. We become acutely sensitive to this when we find choices difficult to make, when we struggle with the pros and cons we must contend with.

In Marxian theory, all preferences are overdetermined by all of the class and nonclass processes of society, whether or not an individual is aware of all of the overdetermining influences. The choice between theories can be based only in part on their different social consequences. The logic of overdetermination requires Marxists to reject the idea that any one basis—such as consequences—can determine theoretical choices. Marxian logic compels the view that just as class processes themselves are overdetermined, so too are the theories that exist in any society as well as the choices individuals make among them.

D.2. Choosing Theories Based on an Absolute Standard

There is a very different way to think about how to choose between neoclassical and Marxian theories. We might choose one on the basis that it is closer to the truth than the other. Despite both theories' logical arguments about capitalism, one of them might be thought to be closer to really existing capitalism. Our goal would then be to determine which one is closer or truer in that sense.

However, it turns out that choosing on this basis is every bit as complex as basing one's choice on the consequences of theories. There are different ways of choosing just as there are different theories to choose among. As economists debate alternative economic theories, so philosophers debate alternative ways of choosing among theories. Indeed, such philosophic debates are part of an entire branch of philosophy called epistemology: the study of thinking and truth and the relationship between them.

Just as there are alternative economic theories of what capitalism is, there are also different epistemological theories of what thinking and truth are. To believe that "truth" is a simple, straightforward essence that everyone understands in the same way is to ignore the different ideas and definitions of truth that have provoked debates and controversy in the past and continue to do so in the present. Thus we are all confronted not only with the question, How do we choose between economic theories? but also with the immediately following question, How do we choose between epistemological theories about what truth is? We face this problem if we propose to choose between neoclassical and Marxian theories on the basis of their approximation to "the truth."

Empiricism. One theory of truth (one epistemological theory) defines it as the correspondence of an idea with reality. The argument runs as follows: There is a real world out there which we as people can know by means of our five senses. Sight, smell, touch, hearing, and taste serve as channels through which the facts of "the real world out there" imprint themselves on our brains. When we think, we concoct ideas about how the world works. To determine which, if any, of these concocted ideas are "true," we compare the ideas to the "facts" of the world that our senses have gathered. The ideas that best "fit the facts," that correspond most closely to what our senses reveal about the real world, are then acclaimed as true.

This epistemological theory is called "empiricism." It is widely influential today; many people prefer it to the alternative theories of what truth is. For individuals who believe in empiricism, the choice between neoclassical and Marxian economic theories is properly to be based on an absolute standard of truth. The standard is "correspondence to the facts." Empiricists take both economic theories (as they do with alternative political, biological, chemical, and other theories) and compare the correspondence of each to the facts of the real world. The choice between them is then decided according to which theory corresponds most closely.

This standard is absolute because it does not recognize the possibility of multiple, alternative truths. It confers the positive title of "true" on one theory while negatively dismissing alternative theories as "false." Empiricism insists that we all sense the facts of reality in the same way, that we all see, hear, smell, taste, and touch "reality" in a uniform way. Our senses provide an absolutely accurate and reliable means of knowing the real and thereby of assessing theories about the real as to whether they are true (correspond to the real) or not.

Most neoclassical economists believe in such an epistemology. They defend their preference for neoclassical theory on the grounds of its greater realism, its closer correspondence to reality as against Marxian theory. They reject Marxian theory because it is, in their view, not capable of explaining the facts of real world economies or of guiding economic decision-makers. Most Marxian economists hold to the same epistemology. They too believe that one theory is true while the alternatives are not, and they too measure truth as a theory's correspondence to factual reality. However, when they test neoclassical theory against the facts, they conclude that Marxian theory makes the better fit, so they defend it against neoclassical economics. It is therefore no surprise that debates between the two economic theories often involve massive confrontations of data and statistical measurements that hammer home each side's claim that it best fits the facts.

The shared epistemology of both sides guarantees a great absolutist battle. Neither side can accord the other any status other than error. Moreover, each side has to ask itself why the other side persists in the absolute falseness of its position, why it turns away from the absolute truth to embrace falsehood. The answer reached by most theorists on both sides is that the other side has evil, ulterior motives that make it cling to what is "factually" untrue. Such debates over different economic theories frequently degenerate into mutual accusations of dogmatic adherence to false ideas, bias, distortion, and the lack of scientific honesty. They can turn very ugly. The two sides charge each other with purposely encouraging wrong ideas in order to further or prevent radical social changes.

In any case, for the empiricists on both sides the choice between neoclassical and Marxian theories is based on what they take to be the absolute standard of truth: the degree of correspondence of each theory to the real world as measured by human sense perceptions. This basis for choice is clearly different from that considered in the previous section, where the different theoretical and political consequences flowing from the two theories were used as a basis for choosing between them.

Rationalism.   Still another theory of truth claims that there is a real world out there which human beings can know by means of thought—that is, by means of logical reasoning. The assumption here is that the world has an underlying logic or order that can be captured only in and by human rationality. Human thought thus becomes the standard for truth, the absolute measure of the truth of all statements made about the world.

This epistemological theory is called "rationalism." When used in economics, this approach insists that the causal relationships in the economy are not revealed to us via our sensory observations, because our senses receive an infinite chaos of impressions, a mass of data. Our brains can focus on only *some* of the infinite impressions gathered by our senses. When, for example, we look at a person, our eyes literally see an infinity of facts, but our brains select out a few to register, to "think about." In the rationalist view, people *select* from among all the data gathered by the senses those which they think to be important or significant.

Rationalists insist that all people select according to some theory that guides each individual's sensory interaction with his or her environment. The "empirical facts" that appear to each individual depend, in the last instance, on the theory that guides that individual's receptivity to (selection among) sense impressions. Rationalists focus, then, on what they see as the core of any theory—namely, its logic or rationality, not the particular "facts" that its proponents selectively gather and present. Rationalists argue over which theory has a logical structure that most exactly matches the presumed logical order of economic reality. Rationalists are confident that the best theory, whose logic mirrors the inherent logic of reality itself, will best select the facts that are relevant to an explanation of actual economic events.

Some neoclassical and Marxian economists endorse the rationalist approach, either consciously or without any awareness that they are taking a partisan epistemological position. Both neoclassical and Marxian rationalists claim that theirs is the one theory whose logic matches the truth of economic reality. Each claims that its theory is the highest stage of human thought about economics and is therefore the closest approximation yet to knowing how economic reality works. Each sees its theory as the absolute standard against which to measure any statement made by anyone about economics. Consequently, each tends to dismiss the other (and indeed all other theories) as simply an inadequate understanding of reality. Each attacks all the others as erroneous and false.

Empiricists among neoclassicals and Marxists struggle over which theory best fits "the facts." Rationalists on both sides argue over which theory best captures the underlying logic of economic events. Rationalists as well as empiricists in the two camps charge each other with ignorance of "the facts" or ignorance of "correct theory" or of ignorantly clinging to outdated ideas for ulterior and intellectually dishonest purposes. There is rarely room among rationalists or empiricists for the notion of alternative theories' offering different ways to make sense of the world and of truth itself.

D.3. Choosing Economic Theories and Choosing Epistemologies

Disagreements over the definition of "truth" affect our choices among alternative economic as well as other theories. The empiricist and rationalist notions of a single, absolute truth grounded in factual reality or in the logic of thought are not the only epistemological notions available to us. There are others to consider as we discover that choosing among economic theories plunges us into the related choice among alternative epistemologies.

Consider an epistemological theory that disagrees both with empiricism and with rationalism. It asserts that our senses influence and are influenced by the theories we believe. It also asserts that both thinking and sensing are shaped by all the other aspects of our lives. In other words, our senses and our thoughts are overdetermined. How they work is shaped by everything else in our history and environment. This epistemological theory of truth argues that measuring different theories against "the facts," as in empiricism, or against "one true logic," as in rationalism, produces no absolute truth whatsoever. The reason for this is that these "facts" and these "logics" are not independent entities. They mutually codetermine each other. Thus, neither one can serve as an independent or absolute standard of truth for the other, as empiricists and rationalists claim.

For example, pessimists and optimists see very different things when they watch the evening TV news. Vegetarians and nonvegetarians experience different taste sensations when they eat various foods. Religious people feel something quite different from those who are uninterested in religion when they touch a holy relic. Two students with opposing political views hear a teacher's lecture in very different ways. In each of these examples it would not be surprising to find one party insisting that he or she never saw, tasted, felt, or heard what the other party insists were his or her sensations. In parallel fashion, individuals reason differently if they occupy different class and nonclass positions in society. For example, sellers and buyers of labor power think about life differently because of the diverse experiences linked to those different positions. Thoughts that occur to some individuals never occur to others.

From the standpoint of this nonabsolute epistemology, people can and do disagree over their sensations as well as over their conceptualizations. It follows that a theory that fits the facts for one person—as he or she senses those facts—may not do so for another person. A theory that captures the underlying logic of reality for one person—as she or he produces that theory—may not do so for another person. In the spirit of such an epistemological position, then, different theories are true for different people. There is no need to imagine or look for one theory that alone will fit "the" facts, as the empiricists claim, because there is no one set of facts which everyone recognizes as "the" standard of truth. There is likewise no need to look for one theory that alone captures the logical order of reality, as the rationalists claim, because there is no theory that captures everyone's differently apprehended realities equally. Instead there are theories and truths, both plural, which reflect and shape the different ways people sense, think about, and live in the world.

In terms of economic theory, there are clear differences among the three epistemologies just described. Empiricists would resolve the debate between neoclassical and Marxian economics by testing both against what they sensed to be "the" facts. In their view, the facts they perceive must likewise be the facts for everyone and therefore the absolute standard of truth for everyone. Rationalists would resolve the debate between neoclassical and Marxian economics by testing both against what each considered to be the true theory. In their view, the theory they discover via their reasoning must be the truth for everyone and therefore the absolute standard for everyone. By contrast, the alternative epistemological approach understands that thinking and sensing are overdetermined by each other and by everything else in society. Therefore, different theories will occur and appeal to people who sense, think about, and live in the world differently. People will reach different conclusions about the truths of alternative theories.

The world, then, is full of people who believe different theories are true because they have different ways of establishing what truth is. There are different standards of truth just as there are different theories of society, economy, nature, and so on. This is a nonabsolutist epistemology; it recognizes no single standard of truth and hence no one true theory standing above false theories. In this view, different ways of thinking about the world stand alongside different ways of sensing it. Theories are differently true; truths are irreducibly plural.

We have thus come full circle. Confronting the problem of choosing between two economic theories, we worked our way to the parallel problem of choosing among epistemologies (or theories of truth). Just as it turned out that truth could not be an unambiguous arbiter of our choice between economic theories, so we are now wise enough not to search for yet another absolute standard to solve our problem in confronting alternative epistemologies.

Our world is full of different, contesting theories about everything. While we may not be aware of them, alternatives exist to the way we think about everything. Nothing is thought about in the same way by everyone. There are also good reasons to believe that we become wiser the more we understand the alternatives, whether we choose them or not. Freedom of choice, as a moral value, presumably extends beyond the array of toothpastes in a drugstore to include the array of theories circulating in our world. This book was intended to alert you to some alternatives and choices you might not have been aware of or understood. Our presumption was that with greater choice you would have greater freedom and wisdom too.

The choice you eventually make will depend on all of the influences that overdetermine you. If your choice is empiricism or rationalism, then you will likely join the debate over the truth of neoclassical versus Marxian theory. If your choice is against empiricism or rationalism and for a nonabsolutist epistemology, then you will likely find yourself basing your choice between economic theories not on a criterion of truth but rather on the alternative consequences of the theories that exist in our world. In either case, we hope that you will be aware of how and why different people choose differently. We also hope that you will find far more awareness, tolerance, and discussion of theoretical differences than has been the tradition in the United States generally and in the discipline of economics in particular.

Solutions to long-standing economic problems often require that we try different ways of thinking about those problems. They require grappling with different theories. Marxian theory is different from the neoclassical orthodoxy that prevails in America today. It is a careful, logical, and elaborated way of thinking about capitalist economies. Its critical and revolutionary thrust makes it different in a way that is understandably troubling to many. However, just those qualities allow it to produce analyses of the U.S. economy that are not only different but arrestingly original and eye-opening. Nothing is to be gained and much will be lost if we continue to ignore Marxian theory's interpretation of the structure, dynamics, and problems of capitalist economies.

D.4. A Final Thought

Nothing written here is intended to make you throw up your hands in frustration at the choices confronting anyone who takes seriously the workings of the mind. That alternative theories of truth, economics, and indeed everything else exist is a premise of this book. That you therefore confront choices among all of these alternatives is, we believe, a condition of life rather like breathing, eating, and so forth. In our view, there can be no neutrals, no way of escaping your freedom of choice.

Making your choices, periodically reexamining them to open yourself to the possibility of making different choices—these are important, exciting, and invigorating parts of a full and self-aware lifetime. We wrote this book to aid you in realizing the existence of these choices. We also wrote it to stress the importance of the choices we all make. They matter enormously in our personal lives as well as in our societies, whose direction and future depend on those choices and their complex consequences.

We strongly believe that there is nothing admirable in pretending that choices do not exist. We understand that faced with difficult decisions, people easily become frightened. It may be tempting for them to deal with hard choices by acting as if there really were no choice to make, as if it were a simple, obvious matter. In thinking about economics, all too many people proceed as though there were one obvious way to ask and answer all questions. They think of economic theory as a single concept, not a theoretical plural. They avoid the hard theoretical choices by ignoring them, falling into line behind whatever happens to be the majority view at the time. They run from their own freedom of choice to the comfort and security of accepting other people's choices without recognizing that they too can choose, that alternatives do exist.

If you become aware that your way of thinking involves a choice from among such alternatives, you will, we hope, want to learn more about those alternatives. You will, we hope, want to struggle honestly with past choices you have made to see if they remain the choices you want to make today. We aim our words above all at those of you who think of yourselves as responsible citizens determined to use your minds to the utmost. Theoretical choices are terrible things to waste.

E. Suggested Readings

Dobb, Maurice. *Theories of Value and Distribution Since Adam Smith: Ideology and Economic Theory*. Cambridge: Cambridge University Press, 1973.

A superb critical discussion of the different approaches to economic knowledge by a famous Marxist.

Heilbroner, Robert. *The Worldly Philosophers*. New York: Simon and Schuster, 1953.

A well-liked and most readable account of famous economists and their ideas.

McCloskey, Donald. *The Rhetoric of Economics*. Madison: University of Wisconsin Press, 1985.

A fascinating discussion of the nature of economic theorizing which touches on several issues discussed in this chapter.

Resnick, Stephen A., and Wolff, Richard D. "Neoclassical Economics and Marxism." *Monthly Review* 36, no. 7 (Dec. 1984).

A concise analysis of the differences between and consequences of neoclassical and Marxian economics.

Robinson, Joan. *Economic Philosophy*. London: Penguin, 1966.

A thoughtful and provocative analysis of different forms of economic thinking.

Schumpeter, Joseph. *History of Economic Analysis*. New York: Oxford University Press, 1954.

A superb critical discussion of the different approaches to economic knowledge by a famous non-Marxist.

Index

Richard D. Wolff and Stephen A. Resnick are both professors of economics at the University of Massachusetts, Amherst. They are also coauthors of *Knowledge and Class: A Marxian Critique of Political Economy.*